Barbara Arrowsmith

FOUNDATIONS OF THE SINGER'S ART

FOUNDATIONS OF THE SINGER'S ART

Victor Alexander Fields, Ph.D.

Professor Emeritus of Voice and Diction
The City College of New York

VANTAGE PRESS
New York Washington Atlanta Hollywood

By the same author:

TRAINING THE SINGING VOICE
THE SINGER'S GLOSSARY

FIRST EDITION

*All rights reserved, including the right
of reproduction in whole or in part in any form.*

Copyright © 1977 by Victor Alexander Fields, Ph.D.

Published by Vantage Press, Inc.
516 West 34th Street, New York, New York 10001

Manufactured in the United States of America
Standard Book Number 533-02566-4

To
MARY ELIZABETH

Contents

Foreword

I.	Fundamentals of the Voice-Training Program	1
II.	How the Mind Governs the Singing Voice	11
III.	Breathing Principles and Mechanisms	32
IV.	Breathing Methods Used in Vocal Training	50
V.	Structure and Function of the Vocal Organs	74
VI.	Internal Mechanisms of the Larynx	94
VII.	External Mechanisms of the Larynx	105
VIII.	Vocal Acoustics and Resonance	126
IX.	Ear Training for the Singer	149
X.	The Singer's Musicianship	165
XI.	Vocal Intonation and Its Problems	183
XII.	Classifying the Singer's Voice	206
XIII.	The Singer's Diction	230
XIV.	Interpretation in Singing	255
XV.	The Role of the Performing Artist	268
XVI.	Song Study, Repertoire, and Recital	286
XVII.	Hints and Helps for the Artist Student	316
XVIII.	Summation of Guiding Principles	332
	Index	343

Foreword

There is certainly no lack of scientific interest in the human voice. A wealth of research information is available and many eminent scientists are now working in this field. However, most of this information emanates from the laboratory, not the studio, and for this reason it is not always readily understood by the teacher of singing. Modern vocal research frequently covers such highly technical areas as pathology, neurology, stroboscopy, spectral analysis, electrical analogs of the vocal function, acoustical theory, and the like, with little or no reference to the musical expression of the voice. It is therefore difficult for singers or teachers of singing to understand or accept the implications of experimental research in these areas.

Unlike the physician or the physicist, the voice teacher observes the singing performance as the embodiment of certain esthetic values which, in his opinion, cannot be dissociated from the vocal act. Objective experimentation and unbiased analytical procedure are therefore less appealing to him. For this reason, there are overtones of controversy and confusion in many of his writings and a situation inimical to professional progress is thus created which is further compounded by an ambiguous terminology.

Scientific information is valuable, to be sure, but adequate pedagogical implementation is also required. Unfortunately, the voice teacher does not usually make these interpretations for himself. Nor does he attempt an original adaptation of inherited methodologies that are deeply rooted in the tranquil traditions of an illustrious past. All too often he finds it easier to agree with predecessors than to venture the justification of his own ideas and we find much inherited misinformation being thus perpetuated in the pedagogical literature on singing.

Obviously, a new and beneficial approach is needed that would correlate a diversified and widely diffused scientific arena; bring to light problem areas that require further investigation; establish basic principles for the guidance of teachers and pupils; set up acceptable boundaries, procedures, and tenable explanations for a comprehensive training program; and focus attention on the real needs of the singing profession.

Such, indeed, is the general plan and purpose of this book. In it I have emphasized the formulation of those principles and procedures that will guide and govern all our teaching methods. The reader will find a reasonable balance between authority and opinion throughout, since I have endeavored to make necessary interpretations while accurately observing the facts as I find them.

To achieve this purpose, information has been distilled from many sources, artistic and scientific, that can shed light on the obscure, fragmentary, and often controversial concepts that pervade the literature on singing. A vast bibliography had to be consulted, including many professional books, periodicals, journals, published interviews, and research findings that relate to our subject. A published bibliography of 750 annotated items may be found in my earlier book *Training the Singing Voice*, and it was recently supplemented and brought up to date with 803 additional annotated bibliographical items in John Burgin's excellent published volume *Teaching Singing*.

I gratefully acknowledge the valuable contributions all these sources of information have made to my own thinking. Notable among them, also, is the published work of Dr. John Howard (1839–1904) a distinguished singer, voice teacher, and physician who presented a unique approach to singing from the combined view of physiologist, performing artist, musician, and vocal pedagogue. Negus's monumental work on the comparative anatomy and physiology of the larynx was also invaluable, and there are a host of others whose pioneering labors have opened the way to clearer thinking on many aspects of the vocal phenomenon. Four decades of diversified singing, teaching, and lecturing experience, and many years of varied activity in the administrative affairs of the National Association of Teachers of Singing have also provided me with fresh insights into the practical needs of the singing profession.

No doubt it is easier to write volumes on what vocal teaching is not than to say simply what it is. But as author of this text I have sought to maintain an affirmative frame of mind, avoiding argument or controversy in favor of positive assertion. The results are not argumentative, defensive, or authoritarian, but expository and explanatory. Interpretative conclusions have to be reached, when necessary, for without them our thinking would tend to be imitative rather than creative.

This project is, therefore, an outgrowth of many years of professional experience, vocal study, and research, supplemented by an investigation of all known areas of related information. These include such subjects as physiology, anatomy, acoustics, ear training, diction, musicology, history of singing, and voice culture, esthetics, operatic and dramatic training, musicianship, health and hygiene, song literature, educational psychology, program building, interpretation, music theory, phonetics, foreign language study, and teacher-training requirements.

I recall the comment of a noted British educator when he cried out despairingly: "What makes singing so thorny a problem to discuss nowadays is that one cannot establish anything positive without clearing away stacks of useless controversial rubbish!" I was often reminded of this situation during the preliminary work on this treatise. A path had to be cleared through the debris of conflicting ideas in order to construct a positive and pertinent platform of sound scientific principles and acceptable working procedures that would support a constructive approach in the training of artist singers and teachers of singing. A diversified but systemmatic treatment of subject matter is therefore programmed, with suitable references, under numerous captions and categories, and a cumulative understanding is thus built which, in its entirety, provides a well-rounded preparation and foundation for every teacher of singing and for every professional singer.

Victor A. Fields

FOUNDATIONS OF THE SINGER'S ART

I

Fundamentals of the Voice-Training Program

Voice is a natural endowment. Basically it is the sound that is uttered at birth through the use of lungs and larynx. At first a reflex action, a nondescript cry announces life in a newborn babe. In time, this vocal sound acquires special character that associates it with feelings and thoughts of the individual, and thus it evolves, through use, into a medium of self-expression and communication. Eventually, through learned phonetic differentiation, linguistic patterns emerge as forms of oral expression so that the vocal function remains at all times a deep-rooted psychological instrument governed by the normal mental and emotional growth of the individual.

The question arises: is singing an acquired skill? The answer is obvious. To produce nondescript musical tones by vocal means may be a natural function but the art of the professional singer requires much technical and musical training that must be carefully learned. Furthermore, in modern living, the processes of learning are strongly dependent on methods used in teaching, since the learning process is seldom self-administered. It is reasonable to assume, therefore, that the art of singing today rests on a firm foundation of pedagogical knowledge and that the successful preparation of any professional singer really depends on the adequate training of his teachers. In effect, this means that the singer of today is largely a product of instruction received in the vocal studio and classroom.

Therefore, although the vocal function itself is inherent in each person at birth, the ability to sing well is largely a product of discipline and training. In other words, singing is acquired by the exercise of the vocal function in a special way, supported by a musical aptitude which governs its intelligent use as an art form. The art of singing, as we know it today, refers to the expression of beauty through voice and emphasizes the application of esthetic principles and a high development of musical skill and taste on the part of the performer.

So many of our latent abilities are dormant until training and use bring them into expression. Sometimes the training program engages abstract mental processes, as in mathematics and logic; sometimes a particular function or sense is employed, as the eye in painting or the ear in composing music; sometimes the entire body is called into play, as in dancing or gymnastics. In the case of a pianist, digital dexterity is important, while a dancer may be more concerned with the pedal extremities of the body. The carilloneur may utilize his fists for striking the hammers of a bell-tower keyboard; the prizefighter learns the skillful use of fists for other purposes.

In each case of acquired skill, technical proficiency and artistic performance emerge only through prolonged intelligent use, in a specialized manner, of some function or faculty of mind and body. Singing is no exception, and it is well to remember that all singers are developed through obedience to this principle or law: *when a function is used it will grow.* Conversely, and equally important, what we do not use we eventually lose.

It is the law of exercise. It applies alike to the development of mind, nerve, and muscle, to the cultivation of esthetic tastes, to the control and sublimation of emotions, to habits of self-indulgence and self-restraint, to the sensitivity of eye and ear, to powers of concentration and attention, to the discipline of the intellect, to acquiring courageous attitudes toward life, to the flexibility, coordination, and control of movements of the body, and, finally, to linguistic and vocal skills and the effective and colorful interpretation and communication of musical ideas by vocal or instrumental means.

Therefore, we say that the singing voice, like any other performing skill, develops through functional growth, largely through the intelligent and constructive applications of the laws of exercise. Naturally, such exercise calls for guidance, direction, and useful practice. The teacher enters here.

The vocal function and the capacity for singing are indeed the gifts of nature, but artist singers are not *born;* they are *made.* Minimal requirements include *health, intelligence, education, musical knowledge, vocal technique, repertoire, diction and language study, keyboard mastery, a finely trained ear, sight-reading ability, dramatic training,* and *stage presence.* It takes all these and more to make a professional singer.[1]

Singing Is an Art and a Science

In its creative aspects, singing may be regarded as a fine art. Its value as such lies in the bringing forth of forms of expression with imagination and taste for the sheer pleasure of so doing. It is also a means of communication, since both singer and audience participate in, and contribute to, the final outcomes of performance. The esthetic appeal of a song may very well be considered a product of performing skill and listener response. It is a communicative process in which a masterful performance will inspire and uplift an appreciative and receptive audience, and, on the other hand, an eager and enthusiastic audience will stimulate a performer to greater artistic endeavor. This reciprocal demand for excellence spells enjoyment on both sides.

In its pedagogic aspects, however, singing may be regarded as both art and science. The teacher, therefore, uses an approach that is both creative and analytical. As an art, singing is as old as mankind: an impulsive groping of the soul for self-expression, for the release of pent-up feelings, and for the communication of deeply felt moods. But as a science it is still in its infancy, since the method of describing and analyzing the observable behavior of singing in terms of underlying causes and their effects is far from adequate and needs further exploration.

It may be stated, in general, that art is concerned with creation for its own sake and without relation to the utility of the object created, while science, on the other hand, is more descriptive and utilitarian. Science attempts an analysis of the artistic product without doing violence to its essential beauty or effect. Science is the knowledge possessed as a result of such an analysis in a field of investigation in which we are primarily concerned with observation, identification, the classification of data, and the formulation of verifiable laws governing them. In other words, basically, a science teaches us to *know* and an art teaches us to *do*.

In science, we construct a system of logical thinking whereby our diversified observations and experiences may be interpreted by correlating them with previously formulated theories and also by referring them to certain standardized norms of measurement. It is a process of making comparisons and evaluations which can be transmitted to others. Science is therefore precise, analytical, objective. Art, on the other hand, is concerned more with the finished products of expression even if they be vague, illusory, subjective, or sometimes indefinable.[2]

Naturally, in terms of the foregoing, the teacher is concerned with scientific explanations, descriptions, and analyses, and with definitions and illustrations. In the aggregate, therefore, the language of pedagogy is necessarily scientific, since it is concerned with the how and why of things, with precise applications and useful outcomes, with measurable results, with the elimination of guesswork or haphazard procedures, with the delineation of laws and principles and with student response.

In the light of such criteria, a student's performance is a product of training and discipline laid down by a teacher. A tremendous responsibility thus rests upon the singing teacher to know as much about the processes of learning and the procedures of instruction as is humanly possible, to avoid the costly methods of haphazard thinking and trial-and-error teaching.

Art Is Unique

A characteristic of all artistic expression is its essential uniqueness. This is especially true of singing. The highest type of art is individual, not stereotyped. We think and feel differently. No two human beings are identical. Indeed, it may be said that there are no two identities in all nature—no two blades of grass, leaves in the forest, snowflakes, grains of sand, crystals of rock, that have identical forms or patterns.

However similar human beings may appear at birth, their gradual physiological and psychological development also accentuates individual differences. Apparently, nature abhors a stereotype, and growing things tend constantly toward greater uniqueness, not greater sameness, as they develop. Individuals are, therefore, identifiable by their peculiar physical and mental traits, whether it be in a fingerprint, the features of the face, the processes of thinking and feeling, or in the patterns of normal daily behavior and the quality and expression of the voice.

Individual artistic growth in singing, therefore, tends toward uniqueness rather than conventionality. An artist singer will find the restrictive forms and styles of conventional behavior more and more tedious and irksome as he grows in artistic stature. In all forms of art—literary, musical, graphic, terpsichorean—there is a continual self-assertive trend, a challenge to traditional modes, a seeking for originality, not as an end in itself, but because originality spells freedom of growth and expression and such freedom brings enjoyment. On the other hand, conventionality of behavior means self-restraint. The sincere artist is caught between these two extremes and must partake of both in the course of his development.

The artist, therefore, finds no fulfillment in imitating the works of others. He may study the masters, analyze their media and experimentally emulate their creative and technical skill, but then he strikes out boldly for himself. Art is boldly imaginative, creative, original, free; and the ultimate in artistic achievement is not mere conformity to prescribed patterns of expression, but rather a release from these. In the process of artistic development there is eventually a complete surrender to the creative and imaginative impulses that originate *within* the artist himself.[3]

Imitation plays an important but subsidiary role in the development of an artist. It is a process of sampling the experience of others who have worked in the artist's own creative medium. But imitators are not artists. Hence we say that art is unique and we recognize that the art of the singer is likewise governed by principles of individual growth toward greater creativity and freedom of expression.

The Language of Pedagogy

It has long been apparent that most of our difficulties in teaching singing arise when we try to *explain* what we do. The factor of language and communication poses a serious problem, always.[4] The language of teaching is essentially the language of science. Explanations are essential in the instruction of a pupil and, since we all think and feel differently, even the simplest explanations require individual interpretations. Thus, precise communication is rather important, especially in teaching the art of singing, and a knowledge of vocal terminology is therefore indispensable.[5] The terminology used by the teacher will enhance the entire communicative process and expedite the transfer of ideas.

Principle versus Practice

Equally important in every aspect of vocal training is the recognition and application of those *principles* that govern the learning process. Both science and art are founded on principles. All codes of ethics, systems of philosophy and logic, procedures of learning and teaching are likewise founded on principles, for they are the infallible guides to action.

What are principles? The word is derived from the Latin *principium*, which means *beginning*. A principle is a place of beginning, in a sense, and therefore a foundation for further study or investigation. In other words, a principle is a fundamental truth, a comprehensive law or doctrine that has been universally established and accepted and from which other laws are derived or upon which other laws or doctrines are founded. Every explanation or scientific procedure begins with a principle. Principles are, therefore, direction-finders and governing rules of behavior established as basic or fundamental truths from which all subsequent behavior is derived.

Practices are things to be done; *principles* are the laws governing them. When principles are violated, practices and actions become aimless and fruitless. Principles, therefore, give purpose and direction to actions. Whether in navigation, brick-making, dentistry, or voice-training, the practitioner first seeks out those established principles which will guide him to a successful outcome in his particular work. Consequently, the study of basic principles of vocal expression is an essential part of the preparation of the teacher of singing.

For example, a teacher of singing must see all vocal behavior as a duality of mind and body, for it would be costly, if not futile, to correct faulty actions without dispelling the faulty ideas or attitudes that engender them. A teacher, therefore, recognizes the sovereignty of mind in controlling and coordinating the physical actions of the body. Especially is this principle applicable to all forms of vocal expression.

The Role of Intelligence

The peculiar adaptation of the mind to learning is a curious phenomenon. Mind, as contrasted with body, is the collective term used for all forms of the awareness of life, the total of an individual's mental faculties. It is the seat of the intelligence and the intellect, and, more significantly, the *thinking* part of the consciousness. And *thinking* is largely a creative process whereby we bring into concrete existence the ideas, images, impressions, and recollections we have, for the purpose of establishing belief and controlling action. In other words, through thinking we formulate, motivate, and govern our actions. The mind, or intelligence, obviously is an all-important instrument of learning.

Voice, because it is a means of expressive action, is also an instrument of the mind. However, we must be able to create mentally before we can create physically or vocally. Thought is the cause. Expression is the effect. Voice is not unique in this respect. We apply this principle of mental control in everything we do.

It is well to remember, therefore, that the student of singing is simultaneously training his mind along with the nerves and muscles of his body, whether it be through a conditioning of the larynx, the breathing apparatus, or the ear. Obviously, then, a vocal studio should be more than a gymnasium for practicing techniques and exercises. The ultimate object of vocal training is musical self-expression, a form of artistic behavior that embodies correct thinking as well as correct vocal action.

Teaching an Integration of Learning

Of course, let it be understood that we separate these two concepts of mental and physical training only for purposes of discussion. In actual experience they are interwoven into every step of the learning process and neither can function effectively without the other. Scientific specialization provides us with numerous subdivisions of learning. The study of singing, for example, might be said to encompass such departments as acoustics, phonetics, music theory, physiology, repertoire, etc.

But the ultimate role of the educator, the teacher of singing, is to correlate these separated fields of learning, for the pupil's benefit, into integrated and meaningful areas of esthetic endeavor. In this way the *wholeness* of human behavior may be better realized and the individual afforded an opportunity to express himself as a creative artist rather than as a mechanical robot.

In *summation,* singing is both science and art. Science is concerned largely with laws, rules, and techniques, with methodology, purposes, and goals. Art is concerned with finished outcomes, with perfected expression. Science may be regarded as the *means,* art the *end,* of learning.

In a *technical* sense, a singer must execute with ease and accuracy all the melodic and verbal patterns that are prescribed by the notation and text of his musical score. Technically considered, he translates symbols into sounds with the use of his vocal organs and the various expressive movements of his body mechanism.

But in an *artistic* sense, he must do more. As an artist, he must be able to *create,* out of these song patterns, living and exciting vocal images of his *innermost* thoughts and feelings; and he must be able to *communicate* the messages contained therein to an audience. His singing is not merely a correctly performed *technique.* It is also a creative and highly individualized form of *self-expression* whose impact on an audience is meaningful, purposeful, and uplifting.[6]

Finally, it is well to remember that the pupil's progress may be related as much to thinking, hearing, and feeling values as it is to physical movements or to physical sensations. Therefore, the vocal training program must include such considerations as freedom of expression, musical talent, mental health and mental discipline, emotional stability, personality development, self-confidence, the value of concentration, ear training, the use of imagination and visualization, esthetic enjoyment and interpretative effects, as well as the proper placing of tone, ease of production, good posture and physique, flexibility of the vocal muscles, good diction, and the manipulation and control of the breathing and vocal organs themselves.

In short, vocal training is both *art* and *science*. It aims at developing a flexible muscular control and a behavioral pattern that is dictated by musical conceptions, by musical *thinking*. The true artist attains this result. Thinking, hearing and feeling values must be taught and integrated in the vocal studio, side by side with the technical training program. From the very first lesson onward, the emphasis on *self-expression* continues until the finished artist emerges and is ready to appear in public.

REFERENCES AND NOTES

1. Victor A. Fields, "What Makes a Professional Singer," *Music Journal* 13 (New York, 1955): 7; "The Road Ahead for the Career-Minded Pupil," *THE NATS Bulletin* 14 (Chicago, 1957): 2.

2. Carter V. Good, Editor, *Dictionary of Education,* Second Edition (New York: McGraw-Hill Book Company, Inc., 1959), pp. 38, 485.

3. James L. Mursell, *Education for Musical Growth* (New York: Ginn and Company, 1948), Chap. 7.

4. Wilmer T. Bartholomew, "The Role of Imagery in Voice Teaching," *MTNA Proceedings for 1935* 30 (Oberlin, Ohio, 1936): 78.

5. Victor A. Fields, *The Singer's Glossary* (Boston, Mass.: Boston Music Company, 1952).

6. Robert Donington, "The Performer's Contribution," *Journal of the American Musicological Society* (Richmond, Va., 1965), p. 424.

II

How the Mind Governs the Singing Voice

The development of an artist is a refining process through countless musical experiences and the prolonged and specialized use of certain faculties of mind and body. A singer's training program is not artistically complete until all his vocal techniques have become as automatic as subconscious reflexes or until habits have been formed that are completely responsive and subservient to creative and interpretative impulses. In other words, he must mold his life into an expression of song.

To help the student achieve these aims, a teacher of singing must prepare himself with a knowledge of the philosophy and psychology of the learning process. He must also clarify his understanding of the physiology of the vocal tract, acquire skill in the diagnosis and correction of vocal faults, learn how to build good habits of tone perception and production, and perfect his own ability to demonstrate, analyze, or explain, by precept and analogy, any of the innumerable problems of performance that might arise in administering the vocal training program.

He must also remember that successful teaching is geared to demonstrable outcomes, not by a process of aimless experimentation but by a predetermined practice procedure in pursuit of predetermined goals. Much theoretical and technical information is therefore needed to equip the teacher of singing with factual knowledge, underlying principles, and a frame of reference for the many forms of instruction that are used in cultivating the singer's art.

In analyzing the pedagogy of singing, therefore, the following seven objectives must be kept in view:

1. Developing the mental faculties that control singing;

2. conditioning the vocal organs to sustained freedom of action;

3. developing strength, flexibility, and skill in tone production;

4. cultivating a sensitive ear along with musicianship and artistry in the execution of song forms;

5. acquiring linguistic skill in voice and diction;

6. improving vocal expression in declamatory, dramatic, and interpretative arts adaptable to song media; and

7. cultivating expertness in the public performance of an extensive and varied repertoire.

These seven categories will guide the discussions which follow.

Developing the Mental Faculties for Singing

The first objective concerns itself with four psychological principles that are of fundamental importance. They may be stated as: a) mental imagery controls vocal action; b) the singer's art is a product of habit formation; c) self-expression is a basic human instinct; and d) singing is essentially related to enthusiasm or joy in life. Each of these four principles will be discussed from the teacher's point of view.

The Role of Mental Imagery

Artistic singing is governed by the ideas or concepts that fill the singer's mind during his performance. A concept is the mental image we form of an action or thing and it is unlikely that we could ever perform an act of intelligible utterance without having formed such an image. Conception is therefore the power or process of forming ideas, a necessary antecedent to any act of expression. The effectiveness of all oral communication may be said to lie largely in the clarity, coherence, and completeness of the mental image that precedes or accompanies it. The formation of the sounds of the voice and their adequate projection are direct outpicturings of these underlying concepts, and vocal projection is therefore said to be governed by the singer's powers of visualization and mental imagery.[1]

Our deepest impulses find utterance in voice. A cry of anguish or of physical pain, warning of danger, anger, joyous laughter—these are manifestations of intense feelings that find outlet in spontaneous vocal expression. In each case, the output is a direct result of a strong mental or emotional stimulus. The thought engenders the action.

True, vocal performance engages many muscles and parts. But the singer is not necessarily aware of the contributory mechanisms of the act of singing. In other words, it is not merely a certain muscular activity that produces vocal tone. Rather, it is the mental concept or image of the tone, and the impulse to communicate it, that governs and produces the muscular activity concerned therewith.

As a man thinketh so is he. This ancient maxim may very well be amplified to read: as a man thinketh so does he speak and, therefore, sing. Basically it is the *mind* that sings, not the voice. You can say or sing only what you can think. Therefore, you sing only as beautiful a tone as you can think, since your voice always follows your thought.

Whether we are conscious of it or not, vocal expression is governed by this law. Hence we must learn to sing in thought, for the tone is embedded in the idea that produces it. Thinking motivates pitch, intensity, expressional nuance, and other technical factors of voice production. Lofty ideas beget expansive tones. Angry thoughts produce harsh tones. Introspective thoughts tend to inhibit, subdue, or constrict the voice. In other words, man is largely a product of his ideas, his way of thinking; and mental imagery, be it lofty or debased, is a governing influence in creating overt behavior and, therefore, vocal behavior.

We must teach the mind first, then the muscles, for understanding precedes the operation or functioning of the vocal mechanism. To reverse this process is to train muscles by the mere imitation of meaningless actions. This is slavish imitation of memorized patterns, devoid of initiative, creativity, or motivation. It is mechanistic behavior.

This point of view is important. Man is not a body containing a mind; he is a mind expressing through a body. Voice is not merely a mechanism of the body producing a tone. It is the tonal image projecting itself through physical channels into audibility. In terms of pupil instruction, then, the foregoing discussion may be translated into seven steps of mental discipline:

1. Create a tonal image or tonal pattern.
2. Visualize it in detail.
3. Discuss it and understand it.
4. Study a living model.
5. See yourself in the finished role.
6. Prepare a plan of study and action.
7. Remove all obstacles by systemmatic practice.

The results of this procedure will bring about the formation of a strong and unwavering mental image worthy of attainment, an ideal that is nourished by constant reflection and meditation until it finds adequate and fearless expression in life.

It may be difficult for older pupils to accept this explanation, at first. After a long period of struggling with the consciously controlled muscular responses of the vocal tract, it is sometimes difficult to accept the supervisory control of the mind or to surrender oneself completely to it. Many pupils have been conditioned by years of trial-and-error teaching in which physical effort was ever uppermost. By reverse thinking, they have been frustrating the expressional impulses used for artistic singing. All this must now be changed, and the changeover is not always easy. The pupil must now be taught to keep the mind steadily focused on what is tonally desired, that is, on the tonal ideal. He returns to this image again and again, patiently but persistently concentrating on it, no matter what type of vocal exercise he is practicing.

Concentration is the state of mind that focuses and sustains the attention on one point or common center to the exclusion of all other thoughts and conditions. By concentration and tonal imagery, energy is directed into prepared and receptive vocal channels with optimal efficiency and economy of effort. The pupil must learn that, in any vocal performance, it is really the mind that sings, not the muscle. And he must learn to keep it that way. We reiterate our first principle, therefore, that *mental imagery governs vocal control.*

The Role of Habit

The second guiding principle is that the singer's voice is a product of habit formation. Through habit the body becomes an obedient servant of the mind.[2] Training makes this possible. It is a remarkable phenomenon of learning that newly studied techniques can be made to function as *involuntary* actions if we repeat them often enough. How long this conditioning process takes depends upon the industry and intelligence of the individual and the complexity of the desired performance. In every case, the ultimate result in habit formation is an effortless and automatic outcome. When a learned activity is unconsciously but correctly performed, it has become an acceptable habit, but not until then.

Habits are reflex-like responses conditioned into the nervous system through intelligent training. They are patterns of behavior that become easy through practice until they can be performed without hesitancy, conscious thought, or concentration. Habits can be either mental or muscular, or both, affecting either our manner of associating ideas or our manner of performing physical skills. In any case, they are an acquired predisposition to respond in the same way to given stimuli.

Habit, therefore, buys us freedom from conscious control; and yet, learned habits are usually built through conscious discipline and conscious control. This apparent paradox applies to all kinds of technical training. A ballet dancer attains freedom and grace of movement through a regimen of rigidly applied bodily disciplines that regulate every aspect of physical behavior. A child learns the freedom of walking only by first learning to control the movements and coordination of his limbs. A typist at first consciously masters certain prescribed finger movements and is later able to translate thoughts into printed words with great freedom and fluency. The pilot learns to fly an airplane by repeatedly and endlessly practicing the manipulation of a complex but exact regulatory mechanism.

Complicated controls likewise enter into learning how to speak a language freely, how to be an actor, how to sing. It is the paradox of all artistic training, indeed of all education, that before you can *free* yourself you must first learn to *control* yourself. In other words, self-control brings freedom of action only when correct habits have been formed.

But the habit-training procedure involves certain hazards. Our zealous devotion to a fixed routine of practice can lead to a one-sided technical development that is mechanically perfect but artistically barren. Both teacher and pupil are caught between these two objectives—consciously controlled technique, on the one hand, and released expression on the other. An effective teacher must learn to reconcile these apparent opposites so that the end product will be a balanced artist rather than a sterile technician.

To a certain extent we are all products of habit formation.

Our natural behavior is largely due to the habits we have acquired. The so-called *natural* voice is also a product of habit formation. *Natural,* in this sense, means *habitual.* Any action, however complex or awkward it may seem, can become second nature through persistent repetition, or until habit takes over. Then we say it seems "natural."

We aim at naturalness in all our singing. But it is the *illusion* of naturalness that we are seeking, for anything can be made to feel natural if it has been trained until it becomes a habit. A truly artistic performer always gives this impression of naturalness or complete ease of execution. Effortless mastery is, indeed, the prime object of all voice training. To be natural in singing is to abandon yourself to your habits, provided, of course, the habits are good ones.

What can be done when previously established bad habits intervene? They may be reeducated through corrective exercises. Thus, we isolate the bad-habit problem for separate treatment. But this type of remedial drill is, at best, a part-learning procedure which will eventually contribute to, but not supplant, the whole act of expression. In other words, when the bad habit is reeducated and the correct action habitualized, the newly corrected drill pattern must merge with the total responses of the singing act at the proficiency level of the completed performance. The techniques of singing may, therefore, be a product of repetitive drill and exercise. But they are not a finished product until, through habit formation, they become effortless and serve as channels through which vocal behavior is released in response to the communicative urge from within.

Only faults impart sensations. When you sing correctly, you do not necessarily know what is happening nor how it is being done. Even the best artists cannot always tell exactly how they sing, because the vocal response is automatic and habitual, and therefore no longer subject to conscious control.

It is the teacher's function, therefore, to guide and supervise this physical and mental growth of the pupil through the application of appropriate but carefully graded practice and study routines. The result is dependable, habitualized artistic behavior under all circumstances. *Artistic singing is a product of habit formation.* That is our second guiding principle.

Self-expression Factors in Singing

The third principle is that self-expression through voice is a basic human instinct. It is primitive. It is inborn. An infant cries at birth without previous training. The primitive development of the vocal function is also closely related to survival and well-being, as in the case of cries for help, cries for food, cries of defense and offense, exclamations of joy, surprise, pain, etc. Gregarious members of any species will call and cry out to keep in touch with one another vocally.[3]

Man has evolved language from what originated as simple cries and calls. Through the use of his intelligence he has codified these sounds and, thus, the words of speech were gradually formed. Later, he developed the forms of vocal relaxation and entertainment that we call song. Whatever the mood—love, anger, joy, or hate—the voice produces corresponding effects. But basically, it may be said that all vocal utterance is founded on this primitive impulse to express and communicate.

The artistic expression of the singing voice is therefore but an outgrowth, an evolution through specialized development, of this basic function. The vocal student must capture the idea that all vocal utterance, and therefore singing, is built upon the desire to express something. Thus he preserves the innate spontaneity of the voice, even while technical virtuosity is being achieved through discipline and specialized training.

The accomplished artist, therefore, sings to communicate his ideas, not merely the tones of his song. His desire to say something influences his method and manner of voice production. This long-established principle was recognized by bel canto masters. They pronounced the dictum that there is no singing without saying, that technique and expression are inseparable, and that it is necessary to teach them together, side by side, from the start. "You must sing as you speak," they would say. "Say something as you sing, and have something to say."[4]

The primary purpose of voice teaching, therefore, is to develop a singing personality, not a routine mechanical skill. The aim is to free, not freeze, the pupil's personality, and all technical instruction subserves this end.

Artistic singing is to be regarded as a *whole* response, supported by every function and faculty of the human organism. Therefore, we must get away from the notion that a singer is a mere performer on the larynx. He is much more than that. He in engaged in an act of artistic creation in which the entire individuality is brought into play. Furthermore, he is both instrument and performer combined. Mind, heart, lungs and larynx, muscles, nerves, glands, sight, hearing—all are united into one marvelously synchronized instrument of expression.

The extent of the whole vocal instrument in man, and the harmony of all its parts in performing its true function in singing, will be discussed in depth in succeeding chapters. At this point let it suffice to consider the whole organism, not merely as the arithmetic sum of all its parts, but also as the harmonious agreement of each part with all other parts.

Therefore, we cannot readily isolate a specific element in the vocal tract for separate treatment without considering its effect on the synchronous action of the whole organism. When this principle is violated, however slightly, trouble appears. Even the minutest deviation exacts a toll in wear and tear, injury, or failure to perform its normal function.

It is this *wholeness* of individual expression that makes singing different from the performance of any man-made instrument.

We conclude, therefore, that a primary purpose of vocal training is to free the voice from self-conscious behavior. You don't have to work to sing. You *let* yourself sing as you might let yourself see or hear or breathe. Self-conscious vision is impaired vision. Self-conscious singing is stilted singing. *Don't strive—let!* is the motto for singers.

To obtain this effect, all preliminary technical disciplines must ultimately surrender to the processes of thinking, to mental controls, and, as previously stated, to correctly formed habits.

Singing thus becomes a means of self-expression. It is governed by concentration, interest, and enthusiasm, by right thinking and feeling, and the desire to communicate these thoughts and feelings to others. Therefore we accept as our third guiding principle that *self-expression through voice is a human instinct* which will condition every vocal response in singing.

The Joy of Singing

A final principle emerges in this review of mental controls. It is that singing is essentially an expression of joy in living. People sing spontaneously when they are enjoying themselves. *Joy* is defined as a sense of well-being and exhilaration of spirit that comes from the experience of being free from worry or restraint of any kind. Complete freedom of mind and body is conducive to enjoyment. Conversely, a mood of enjoyment helps to release and relax every part of the body, including the vocal organs. Joy spells freedom; freedom brings enjoyment. A person is happiest when free. In daily living, whenever we sing, we sing for sheer enjoyment and we enjoy what we sing.

The singing lesson itself, therefore, should be a joyous experience. If it is not, inhibitions, frustrations, emotional tension, and restrained behavior will be built into the vocal act.

Overcautious teaching methods, with an overdose of rules and warnings, will tend to dampen a pupil's enthusiasm for learning. It is, therefore, perhaps unwise to use such directives as: *Don't let your chest slump! Don't forget to hold your chin in! Keep your posture erect! Breathe with your diaphragm!*

Don't keep your tongue too high! Place the tone upward and forward! Don't forget your phrasing! Watch your diction! Close the vowel! Open the throat! etc.! etc.! How can a pupil be joyous under these conditions?

Critical admonitions like the foregoing are inimical to good vocal behavior, since criticism begets self-consciousness, caution, and fear. The antidote, of course, is praise and encouragement. The teacher should find something genuinely praiseworthy and use that element of commendation as a basis for instruction whenever possible.

Substituting *dos* for *don'ts* and praise for criticism will build a mood of enjoyment during the singing lesson. Why enjoyment? Because the voice functions at its best when the singer is buoyant and exhilarated, because carefree attitudes are conducive to vocal freedom.

Laughter is, therefore, an exercise that will improve freedom of vocal action. When laughter is difficult there is evidence of tension, either mental or physical, in the student's makeup. Ask him to laugh on each tone that is sounded. If he can do this readily, vocal action will tend to be free, because genuine laughter is not possible under conditions of strain, fear, or worry. Even the singing of sad or tragic music must be enjoyed to be effective.

In other words, joy is the great corrective. Joyous moods expand the breathing, relax muscles, and correct faulty coordinations. They release the voice and make for efficient operation of the vocal organs because singing *is essentially an expression of joy.* That is our fourth guiding principle.

We have thus far uncovered four fundamentals that suggest how the mind governs the singing voice. They are: 1) mental imagery governs vocal control; 2) the singer's voice is a product of habit formation; 3) self-expression through voice is a basic human instinct; and 4) singing is essentially an expression of joy in life.

Guiding principles like these translate themselves into specific objectives, which may now be restated as: 1) cultivating mental imagery; 2) building good habits; 3) developing freedom of expression; and 4) stimulating joyous attitudes. These four principles underlie all other teaching and practicing procedures.

Freeing the Voice

Our second main objective in vocal pedagogy is to condition the vocal organs to freedom of action. The singer, unlike other instrumentalists, develops his instrument while he is learning to master it. Such mastery is a product of mental and physical training, a composite of thinking, feeling, and doing. Daily behavior in life will, therefore, tend to condition a pupil's attitude toward all his endeavors and will affect his receptivity and response to learning. Habits of indolence and indifference, resentment, disappointment and fear, timidity and restraint affect the very health and tonus of the muscular tract, and vocal expression will bear the quality and characteristics of those muscles that generate the voice. That is why people sound pleasant or forbidding, warmly genial or harshly metallic, depending on the prevailing mood or disposition of their daily lives.

Obviously, implanting correct mental attitudes toward learning is extremely important in cultivating a voice. We call this *motivation*—a process of arousing, sustaining, and regulating the interests and incentives of learning for the purpose of causing a pupil to perform in a desired way.[5]

In general, three main factors enter into the freeing process. These are: 1) relaxation; 2) economy of effort; and 3) overcoming inhibitions and fears. They are considered separately in relation to the attitudes and daily behavior of the pupil and also as an approach to the specific problems of tone production which appear later on in the training program.

Importance of Relaxation

What is meant by *relaxation?* The term causes considerable perplexity among singers because concepts of relaxation are often related to those of *rigidity* and *inertia*. It might be well, therefore, to clarify the application of these three terms in the voice-training program.

Rigidity is a condition of *tightness*. It implies the absence of flexibility in a muscle and considerable resistance to change or movement. On the other hand, during *inertia* there is complete muscular inaction; the inert muscle is devoid of motivating power and a languid or lifeless condition prevails.

Relaxation is an intermediate state. In relaxation, neither rigidity nor inertia occurs, but a condition in which healthy firmness of muscle fibers (tonus) is normally present, even while muscles are at rest.

In other words, relaxation is not a looseness of the vocal organs. It is a relative condition calling for the absence of abnormal tightness, interference, or restraint of any kind. Relaxation is not limpness or inertia, nor is it rigidity. It is the balance between these two extremes. It is a state of *readiness to perform*.

In vocal instruction, it is well to apply this principle: *when the thought is removed from a muscle, it relaxes*. Singing requires the use of many muscles, but they must be allowed to work together effectively rather than hinder one another. The human body is built up of many muscle systems. They must be able to perform in proper balance and in properly coordinated movement or synergic action.

It is hazardous, therefore, to attempt the localization of any muscular control in the vocal tract. Vocal faults are frequently generated by voluntary tensions that are opposed to, or in conflict with, normal muscle response.

Economy of Effort

When correctly performed, singing is a type of spontaneous behavior in which the body automatically coordinates with the thought. As in any unstudied and well-established action pattern, like using the telephone, climbing a flight of stairs, writing a letter, or talking to your neighbor, the body outpictures the thought with effortless ease and accuracy, free from strain or fatigue. The artist singer, also, learns to manage his vocal organs with economy of effort.

The fact that the voice tires with use is an indication of incorrect singing methods, since a well-used voice is practically self-sustaining and indefatigable. Like the heartbeat, peristalsis, respiration, or other reflexes, vocal action does not tire with correct use, even after prolonged and repeated performance.

The demands of operatic repertoire are such that supreme vocal virtuosity is required, along with conversational ease of expression. But there must be no evidence of vocal strain or fatigue during such a performance. An artist's vocal capabilities must give evidence of remarkable strength, freshness, flexibility, and endurance, even after hours of intermittent singing.

To become a professional singer, therefore, a student must learn that a well-used voice does not tire, because phonation at its best is effortless. Therefore, in freeing the voice, teachers and pupils are forewarned that *if it feels like work, the method is wrong.*

As previously stated, the artist singer imagines himself the channel through which his voice flows. *Don't strive—let!* is his watchword in performance. A voice produced with maximum ease will last longer and will have better resonance and carrying power because singing, like wind-instrument playing, is strained and distorted by excessive blowing or forcing. The supreme vocal virtue, therefore, is effortless mastery or economy of effort.

Overcoming Inhibitions and Fears

What is meant by *inhibition?* It is the restraint of an impulse or function by an opposing force from within. Inhibitions in normal behavior are often contracted during early childhood and adolescence when schooling, ridicule, or threats of punishment are used as forms of censure, suppression, and correction. Fear is a common result, showing symptoms of self-consciousness and other types of restrained behavior in the presence of others. Thus, fear and inhibition are interrelated.

Fear contracts muscles and constricts throats. It may be described as a mild emotional upset which induces a desire to escape from the situation or condition that causes it. In acute cases it may cause rigidity or semiparalysis of the muscles of action and temporary aphasia. People have been known to become speechless with fright, and milder forms of speechlessness or vocal restraint are manifest whenever there is alarm or anxiety over the outcome of action or utterance. Stage fright is also a manifestation of fear. It produces similar symptoms, checks spontaneous behavior, disturbs the mind, and freezes the impulses of self-expression. The problem, then, is how to eliminate fear.

From the performer's standpoint, fear is a state of *divided attention* between what one wishes to accomplish and what one wishes to avoid. The antidote is *singlemindedness* or unwavering concentration on the *desirable* aspects of performance. Persistent worry is a mild form of fear. It grooves a channel into the mind which drains all other thoughts into it. Concentration or fixed attention can be cultivated by the exercise of willpower over the activities of the mind.

Fear may also be described as inverted faith; it is faith or belief in failure instead of faith in success. Fearless performers are those who give undivided attention to *success* in their work, without worry. *Success* may be defined as the elimination of one's toleration of error, even in trivial actions.

Any performance, however complex, can be reduced to a series of simple actions. The favorable outcome of each such action will accrue to the success of the entire performance. Thus, any larger achievement is made up of tiny atoms of success. If the knowledge of success is based upon previously proved results, the mind of the performer will learn to visualize a perfect outcome. Having already proved each step in the performance, he will find it easier to abandon himself to overall accomplishment without worry or fear. Every error that goes uncorrected plants a seed for future failure, and ultimate failure in any performance is but the accumulation of such neglected errors.

Of course, the general health of the body is not to be overlooked as a fear resistant. Rest, recreation, adequate nourishment, and balanced living, without excess, will help provide a reservoir of physical strength and nervous energy to sustain the most rigorous practice and rehearsal schedule. Good planning will allow for the proper alternation of work and recreation periods so that the anxieties caused by hurry and a sense of incompleteness will not be allowed to accumulate.

Finally, laughter may be used to capture the feeling of joyous release in singing. Some pupils may have to learn how to laugh! Laughing up and down the scale can provide good exercise for freeing the voice. It may be adapted to any vocalization. Laughing through an entire song may also be helpful, until the release of laughter comes freely and unrestrainedly. This will teach the pupil how to let go and will also serve as an antidote for fear.

The Carry-over from Speech

Through years of restraint, timidity, and self-analysis, the speech of an individual may become so limited that the entire vocal function loses its spontaneity. There is a strong carry-over of such inhibitions from speaking to singing. A teacher of voice accepts the premise that inhibitions of the singing voice are largely outgrowths of the speaking personality. He cannot ignore this relationship in planning and administering the voice-training program.

The singing personality should not be allowed to become artificial, stilted, bombastic, or grandiloquent. It is not necessary to sing like a heroic figure in grand opera. The singing personality should be gracious, sincere, and convincing, as effortless and unaffected as is the best speaking personality.

Too often, pupils regard the singing experience as a stepping out of life into a role that is artificial or unreal. This impression should be corrected as early as possible. The pupil should learn that it is just as easy for him to break into song as it is to break into speech, with simplicity and sincerity of mind and heart, without any more fuss, pomp, or preparation than it would take to declaim a similar idea or phrase in a similar speaking situation.[6]

Conclusions for Teachers and Singers

In singing, the action of the vocal cords is controlled by the *will* to make a sound. The very anticipation of tone automatically sets the glottal aperture and the mucular complex and therefore controls phonation. The tone must be imagined or mentally heard, not physically felt. In this respect, the *mind* sings, not the larynx.

Anticipation also controls pitch. Think any pitch within the vocal range and the laryngeal adjustment will be instantly made, provided hearing is normal. Conversely, an individual who is unable to preconceive a given pitch usually finds it impossible to sing on that pitch. The importance of ear training is therefore obvious.

Phonation has three stages: *thinking, attacking,* and *sustaining*. The first is a matter of anticipation of tone, an *imaginative* process. The second is a function of self-expression and the impulse to communicate, a *releasing* process. The third calls for steady concentration, mental focus, and intensified breath support, so that a continuous and unwavering tonal fabric may be produced, a *sustaining* process. In all of these, the mind and ear are primary governing factors.

More than a dozen pairs of muscles are externally attached to the voice box. The internal laryngeal structure likewise embodies seven or eight sets of intrinsic muscles. All of this complex musculature will be later described. A singer could not possibly learn to control any of these muscles individually without disturbing the coordination of all of them. Indirect procedures are therefore used as a way of unifying and coordinating the muscular response that produces satisfactory tones for singing. Three preliminary procedures are recommended:

First, remove all self-consciousness and fear regarding the vocal act. If singing is to be taught as a soul-satisfying experience, the mind must be set at ease. Harmful tensions can be generated by attempts at direct control of the larynx. Particular attention should be given to procedures that will free the voice from local tensions and the singer from self-consciousness.

Second, develop tonal imagery through ear training. This is a process of imagining a tone so vividly that the vocal effect can be "heard" mentally before it occurs physically. The value of tonal imagery resolves itself into a simple statement of principle: *the anticipation of a tone controls its production.* Phonation is governed by this law. *Anticipation,* in this sense, may be defined as a form of mental prevision or visualization of a sound in expectation of its oral expression. When the anticipation is strong, a prepatory action of the vocal organs occurs before the voice is actually produced. The student must therefore practice silent or mental singing, from time to time, as a type of tonal imagining.

Third, tone production should be properly motivated so that the vocal act is generated by a strong desire to express and communicate something, accompanied by an incentive or fruitful purpose. The combination of personal interest, purpose, intense desire, esthetic feeling, and enthusiasm helps promote free and effective vocal action. Under these conditions, vocal tones become firmer, stronger, and more meaningful, not shallow, synthetic, or expressionless.

In summation, corrective exercises can serve a helpful purpose if they are used to uproot or reeducate bad habits. Such exercises may be used to limber up inert and unused muscular mechanisms. But they should not be confused with the finished product. Exercising the voice is not singing. Therefore, for the pupil's benefit, the following rationale may be used during the vocal lesson:

To become an artist, start being one. See yourself imaginatively as the finished product. If a good model is available, learn to emulate it until you can step out on your own. Imagine yourself singing like that person and clearly visualize your ideal at all times. Naturally, under a teacher's guidance, you will be able to recognize a good vocal model and identify it clearly so that you can keep it before you during your studies, much as a painter would clearly visualize his subject before attempting to paint it.

Your own singing performance during this formative period may be modest, to be sure, circumscribed as it is by your present lack of ability. But, even as you practice with presently undeveloped vocal resources, you can continue to see yourself in the role of the finished product, for the imaginative mind knows no physical limitations. By steadfastly entertaining your ideal, with diligent practice you will gradually grow toward its realization. We are the product of our ideals.

At first you may flounder because the vocal intrument is not quite ready for such skillful execution. But with each trial in practicing you acquire more and more of the strength, endurance, tenderness, vitality, poise, dramatic expressiveness, and dignity that is possessed by the accomplished vocal artist. Thus, you grow constantly toward your ideal.

Under a teacher's watchful eye and ear, your bad habits can be nipped in the bud. Rehabilitative procedures are prescribed to correct existing faults, and good practice methods are thus implanted. But artistic stature is not acquired overnight. One does not practice exercises and songs and then suddenly "arrive." This growth is guided gradually over a period of months, and even years, like any other development. Remember that good singing evolves from correct thinking, as well as from correct doing.

So much for the pupil. On the other hand, the teacher is reminded that it is the function of vocal instruction to awaken a pupil's potentialities for expression and artistic growth. This is accomplished by directing his daily activities, vocal practice, physical behavior, and thinking. All reveal the hidden possibilities of artistic growth. Such purposes are not to be forced upon him all at once.

It is erroneous to type a pupil at the outset. Let him discover himself. Under proper guidance, he will have the opportunity to sample the experiences that quicken artistic interest and awaken latent abilities. It is a process of gradual self-realization. A pupil is not necessarily aware of this unfolding process. The teacher always is.

Let him try all kinds of music. Don't restrain him. Don't dwarf his ambitions by restricting him to a diet of innocuous song literature. The interpretative sense will develop as he sees himself reaching toward the role of the singer he wishes to be.

Practice devices must be modest, at first, as measured in terms of the pupil's comprehension, competence, and vocal range. But larger works can be discussed and listened to. Fragments of good music may be sung from time to time, and the experience and challenge of good musical literature savored through samplings and through experimental or exploratory treatment.

A teacher must be careful not to force arbitrary patterns of growth on a pupil. One can stimulate and guide only that which emerges from individuality. In other words, the pupil must be permitted to grow toward his own ideals, not those of the teacher.

In freeing the voice, the conscientious teacher will therefore carefully consider the most effective ways of achieving these seven objectives: 1) cultivating mental imagery; 2) building good habits; 3) developing freedom of expression; 4) stimulating joyous attitudes; 5) relaxation, both mental and physical; 6) economy of effort in every aspect of voice production and expressional behavior; and 7) elimination of inhibitions and fears, both in speaking and singing.

Finally, we must remember that difficulties cannot be overcome or growth stimulated if we perform only that which is easy. Difficulties present a challenge and suggest a need. We grow by surmounting obstacles. They stimulate latent abilities. Therefore, difficulties need to be overcome, not avoided. The question is, what difficulties are the pupils ready for? That is to be the teacher's decision, and good teaching judgment will pave the way with exercises and problems that promote vocal growth along desired lines. Such a program provides powerful motivation for mind and body and influences the sustained mental activity and interest that governs the growth of the singing voice.

REFERENCES AND NOTES

1. Percy C. Buck, *Psychology for Musicians* (New York: Oxford University Press, 1944).

2. James L. Mursell, *How to Make and Break Habits* (New York: J. B. Lippincott Company, 1953), Chap 8.

3. V. E. Negus, *The Mechanism of the Larynx* (London: Heinemann Medical Books, 1957), pp. 335, 480.

4. *Grove's Dictionary of Music and Musicians,* 5th edition (New York: St. Martin's Press, Inc., 1959), s.v. "Singing."

5. Carter V. Good, Editor, *Dictionary of Education,* second edition (New York: McGraw-Hill Book Company, Inc., 1959), p. 354.

6. William Vennard, *Singing: The Mechanism and the Technic,* revised edition (New York: Carl Fischer, Inc., 1967), p. 185.

III

Breathing Principles and Mechanisms

A competent singing teacher needs a general acquaintance with the subject of anatomy and physiology of the vocal tract so that methods of instruction may be developed that do not conflict with the laws of nature. The present problem, therefore, is to present a discussion of basic physiological concepts that will furnish a background for further study in this formidable subject. Both structural and functional aspects will have to be reviewed, for it is obvious that one's ideas regarding the function of the organs of vocal expression are intimately related to one's knowledge of the structure of the vocal tract. But such analyses are only procedural implements of vocal study. When their purposes have been fulfilled, they may be discarded and forgotten. In other words, technical explanations are the props of learning and not the props of performance.

In this respect, a teacher becomes an archanalyst and plans instructional procedures, lessons, and steps of learning accordingly. But his mind's eye is always fixed on outcomes and objectives, on goals and principles, the purposes of instruction being not merely mechanical perfection but esthetic creation.

Especially is this true of breathing, which is a necessary function in life, and, also, a necessary function in singing. Poor breathing is a primary cause of vocal tension and, conversely, good breathing habits quickly induce proper coordination, freedom of vocal action, and ease of performance. Here are three guiding principles.

First, singing is an overlaid function and, as such, it must not do violence to the fundamental processes of life. Breathing mechanisms are basically the same for living as for singing. Respiration supplies us with oxygen and helps the body eliminate gaseous wastes. But it also provides the motive power for phonation. Respiration also plays a part in such natural reflexes as laughing, coughing, yawning, gasping, sneezing, spewing, etc. Obviously, habits of breathing have an important bearing on the general health and efficiency of the body both for singing and daily living. But there are differences as well as similarities to consider.

In life, the normal respiration rate of an average resting adult is fourteen to seventeen breaths per minute, with nearly equal intervals between them. But singing employs the breathing function in a special way. In singing, the breath may be so regulated that a fairly large amount of air is inhaled quickly and made to escape rather slowly over a prolonged period and at a perfectly steady pressure. Breathing rhythms may thereby be reduced to as few as five to ten per minute. This means that expiration must be controlled in singing and that the *retention* of breath and its gradual release are important factors in sustaining a singing tone.[1]

Second, because singing demands special use of the breathing muscles, it may be regarded as a form of exercise. Indeed, the continual vigorous employment of breathing muscles in singing will tend to strengthen them. Therefore, breathing will improve as voice production improves, and vice versa, since the two are reciprocal or simultaneous functions of the vocal act.

Third, although correct breathing itself does not create good voice, artistic voice production is not possible without correct breathing. Bad breathing habits have destroyed many potentially good voices. Our primary concern, therefore, is to avoid or eliminate faults that are caused by an overmechanization of the breathing process and to release inherent artistry in a pupil, uncorrupted by habits of self-analysis and synthetic breath control. A good rule for the beginner is: *do not think of breathing while singing*.

Questions of pedagogical procedure enter here. Since the teacher's major interest is ultimate expression, any methodology that will contribute to artistry in the finished performance would be justifiable. But he must be watchful against overemphasizing breath control, especially at a time when the beginning student is concerned with freeing his voice.

With these safeguards in mind, the repiratory function may be considered in two phases: 1) postural development, and 2) physiology and coordination of breathing action.

Postural Development

Good posture is conducive to good breathing and is therefore a basic requirement of the singer's art.[2] Pupils who live sedentary lives acquire habits of inertia and drooping posture. In such cases, it is necessary to strengthen the supporting muscles of the body. The pupil's daily habits of standing, sitting, walking, and moving about must therefore be observed and corrected.

For the beginner, correctives may be practiced as independent exercises. Many of the chest movements can be brought under voluntary control. Respiratory muscles can be expanded, contracted, and relaxed, even while the breath is momentarily stopped. Deliberate actions of this kind may seem uncomfortable at first, but such practice movements will help make a student aware of the postural muscles he is trying to develop. Naturally, these exercises are not to be associated with voice production. They are engaged in experimentally as a body-building formula, much as the leg or arm muscles are developed by flexing them voluntarily in a gymnasium for ultimate use in running, jumping, and boxing.

A student who slumps and slouches habitually may be given this three-part corrective exercise[3]:

Step One: From a standing position, stretch the arms aloft, as if to grasp a high bar just beyond reach. Keep head and eyes level and heels on the ground.

Step Two: With arms thus raised, concentrate on the newly elevated position of your lowest ribs.

Step Three: Without lowering your ribs, gradually drop the arms limply to their former position at the sides. Note the difference in posture.

In this new posture, rotate the head and roll the shoulders slowly so as to induce relaxation in neck and shoulder muscles. Practice at frequent intervals until the new posture is recognized and retained.

Note, also, that the entire chest is not to be pushed upward from below, but, rather, pulled upward by reaching the arms aloft. Extraneous neck, shoulder, and abdominal tensions are thus avoided. The positions of the collarbone, breastbone, and shoulder blades, with their numerous rib attachments, are all affected by the elevation of the rib cage. Avoid extremes.

Posture Defined

Correct posture for singing may now be defined as a carriage of the body that allows the efficient functioning of all its parts. When posture droops, the chest cage pulls upon the neck and throat. This stretches and strains these muscles and crowds them into an area normally occupied by the larynx. Consequently, the latter is pulled away from its position against the spine, thus interfering with phonation and resonation.[4]

With chest properly elevated, the strain on neck muscles is relieved and the laryngeal musculature is freed for correct action. The adam's apple recedes into surrounding neck muscles and the larynx finds its correct position for effective use. The head is never tilted backward. It is normally balanced for free movement. The chin is also relaxed, neither tilted upward nor pulled back.

Posture for singing is not a military carriage with head rigid and shoulders thrust stiffly backward. Rather, shoulders are inclined forward ever so little, but not exaggeratedly. The spine is inclined forward slightly, and the elbows also moved slightly forward and outward, away from the ribs.

Within the format described, such a posture should be assumed and maintained with ease and grace of movement. Phonological and respiratory reasons for each of these directions will soon be made apparent.

The pupil also learns to carry his body correctly in everyday living. Gradual steps of training should be used. Avoid tormenting suggestions that might make him body-conscious or that would interfere with vocal expression. It may take months to accomplish this result, since the building of habits cannot be hurried or forced. However, when they are established there will be an obvious carry-over into the singing performance.

Psychological Influences

Good posture and deep breathing usually accompany correct attitudes in life. Chronic depressed moods tend to produce chest-fallen posture. Exalted moods induce deeper breathing and an improved posture. Joyous attitudes enrich the voice and expand breathing. Hence it is easy to sing or shout for joy. Conversely, when in a dispirited mood, the body droops, the voice loses buoyancy, and a dull, gloomy monotone results. Both speech and song become labored under these conditions.

Expression itself tends to regulate breathing action. That is to say, the thought and mood content of a song can automatically induce breathing rhythms that will express that mood. To illustrate, when you shout to warn someone of impending danger, there is an unconscious preparatory intake of breath that helps project the voice for that purpose. A person about to say "I love you," with feeling, will breathe more expansively than if he had occasion to say "I'm sorry," or "I don't care." In other words, if you can sing each phrase as you would speak or declaim it, with true intent, you will more likely capture the appropriate breathing rhythm for the effective communication of that phrase. This demonstrates the principle that *each thought takes its own breath.*

We don't usually breathe first and then sing, because, under strong motivation, breathing and singing are simultaneous actions that are governed by the same expressional impulse. Breathing action will thus tend to grow through correct *use* in the meaningful singing of songs.

In summation, correct breathing and posture may be approached indirectly by implanting lofty aspirations and ideals. Muscles that support breathing may also be strengthened as a nonsinging activity by practicing graded physical exercises. Finally, the singing performance itself should be maintained as a joyous, intensely felt, creative expression that is unmolested by conscious breathing controls.

Physiology of Breathing Action

Physiology is the study of characteristic action, in life, of the human body. Such a study encompasses all organic and muscular functions and the operation and movement of animate parts. *Anatomy* views the inert structural makeup of the body, while *physiology* describes its use in normal living. Obviously, the two subjects are interrelated and the teacher of voice should make a survey of the constituents of both, especially in relation to the art of singing. Such a study can also help prevent many of the pitfalls of mechanized breath and voice control. Here are four basic principles:

> a. It is a physiological fact that all the muscles of movement in the human body have the inherent capacity to shorten themselves by contraction. But they are not capable of self-elongation or self-expansion.
>
> b. Therefore, when a moving muscle has expended its energy in contraction, it usually requires the assistance of some other muscle to pull it back to its original position before it can be ready to contract again.
>
> c. Likewise, to maintain its stability, position, and direction of movement, a muscle is necessarily attached to other parts and sometimes to other muscles.

d. Muscular movement is therefore rarely a single action, but is usually part of a larger, coordinated pattern.[5]

For this reason, the consideration of the mechanical operation of any single body structure can offer only partial evidence of its correct functioning in the complicated whole responses of singing. *Coordination* is therefore a key word to be applied in all vocal instruction.

Many singers confuse breath intake or inspiratory movements (inhalation) with expiratory efforts (exhalation), and the muscles of inspiration are incorrectly activated at the time when expiration is taking place. Muscular conflicts thus arise. When the inspiratory effort is wrongly maintained for expiration, or vice versa, the abdominal wall becomes tensed when it should be completely relaxed. Likewise, the chest wall is often mistakenly raised during expiration when chest muscles should be held firm or allowed to subside. Such bad habits must be corrected before proper coordination of the breathing mechanism is possible.

The following rule is useful: *gradually relax all inspiratory muscles at the instant voice begins*. An artistic singing tone is the product of expiratory effort only, and is therefore governed by the compressive action of expiration. Therefore, inspiratory effort should have ceased the moment voice begins. Failure to observe this principle can cause many abnormalities of voice production.

It will, therefore, be helpful to determine just what muscles or combination of muscles are active during intake of breath for singing. The voluntary release of these same muscles during expiratory effort should also be studied so that a conflict between two sets of muscles will be avoided.

To illustrate, while maintaining a high-chest posture, take a full breath by whatever means. Then exhale suddenly, *without lowering the chest*. Now, repeat this action, but sound "ah" at the instant of expiration, much as when sighing or groaning audibly. Finally, repeat this action with a more sustained "ah" sound. Gradually prolong the "ah" with each trial. Use a comfortable pitch level throughout.

This demonstrates the *basic* type of expiratory release that is required for vocal intonation. Whatever its later refinements may be, this basic expiratory control must not be violated in singing. The simplicity of this approach is often difficult to accept; so many students want to force the action of the abdominal and chest muscles. Bad habits result. Corrective exercises should be so planned, therefore, that they will oppose, divert, or neutralize the activity of the muscles that caused the fault, thereby neutralizing their effect.

To this end, a series of general relaxation and deep-breathing drills are administered. Deep vocal sighing, yawning, moaning, and groaning are also helpful when used to capture the effect of unrestrained release of breath and voice. But such exercises should not be allowed to interfere with the maintenance of good posture and an elevated chest.

Because artistic singing often requires intensified and sustained dynamic utterance beyond the dimensions of ordinary conversation, the muscular activity of breathing for singing is nearly athletic in character at times. For this reason, special controls are often required. An artist singer must be made ready to meet exacting demands upon his physical strength, endurance, and breath capacity. Naturally, the chest and lungs are at the center of all breathing action.

The Chest Described

Briefly reviewed, there are twenty-six spinal vertebrae in an adult. From top to bottom, these are divided into five sections consisting of seven cervical, twelve thoracic, five lumbar, one sacral, and one coccygeal bone. Viewed laterally, from the left side, four curves are noted in this vertebral column. The cervical curve is convex forward with its crest at about the fifth or sixth cervical vertebra; the thoracic curve is concave, the lumbar curve is convex, and the pelvic or sacro-coccygeal curve is concave, ending in the coccyx.

The cervical and thoracic sections are especially important because they lie adjacent to and support the vocal and respiratory apparatus. It will be helpful, therefore, to study the following descriptions and to visualize their relation to the properly functioning singing voice.[6]

The average larynx is situated in front of the fifth (sometimes sixth) or foremost cervical vertebra. The thorax, or rib cage, is located in front of all twelve thoracic vertebrae. The lumbar vertebrae support the abdominal region of the body.

Each one of the twelve thoracic vertebrae of the spine is joined, on each side, to the end of a rib, thereby forming the posterior boundary of a twelve-rib cage. The upper seven pairs of ribs are connected at their front ends to the side of the sternum, or breastbone. The lower five ribs do not reach the sternum in front, but three of them are indirectly joined thereto by means of cartilagenous extensions. The lowest two pairs are called *floating* ribs because they are relatively unattached in front. However, all ribs are embedded in a complex of muscles, cartilages, and ligaments that form the basic structure of the continuous thoracic wall.

The ribs slope outward from their points of attachment at the spine, at first downward and *backward* from the spine; then they curve around downward and *forward* toward the front of the body. At the place where the curve changes from a rearward to a forward direction, an *angle* is formed on the rib itself, resembling the angle of a boomerang. Counting downward, the topmost seven pairs gradually increase in length, and the last five pairs gradually diminish in length, so that the first and twelfth pairs are the shortest ribs.

The *thorax,* or chest cavity, is the entire space enclosed between the ribs, spine, and breastbone, and between the neck and abdomen. The thorax is barrel-shaped and is wider below than above. It is also deeper backward than frontward, due to the concave or backward curvature of the thoracic spine. Its transverse diameter is larger than its front-to-back dimension.

The chest cavity contains the trachea, or windpipe, lungs,

heart, esophagus, and connecting muscles, membranes, blood vessels and nerves. The upper or smaller opening of the chest admits the trachea, esophagus, large veins, and nerves. The lower or larger boundary is covered with a muscular-tendinous sheet called the *diaphragm*.

By means of the diaphragm, the chest cavity above it is closed off from the abdominal or visceral cavity below. The thorax is, therefore, a closed box, and its interior is completely filled with respiratory and circulatory organs. There is no space, normally, between the outer surface of the lungs and the interior wall of the thorax, even when the lungs are exhausted, since the moving thoracic wall always conforms to the shape of its contents.

A horizontal clavicle, or collarbone, lies at either side, above the first rib, at the upper anterior part of the thorax. Each clavicle is supported at its inner anterior end on the sternum and first rib, and at its outer or posterior end on a shoulder blade or scapula. The clavicles are firmly bound to these parts by means of ligaments and muscles so that clavicular movements are influenced by the movements of the sternum, ribs, shoulder blades, or arms, and vice versa.

The Lungs Described

In their more general aspect, the lungs may be described as two pyramidal bodies, composed of spongy elastic (not muscular) tissue, suspended in the thorax.[7] They are attached to bronchial extensions of the lower end of the trachea. The lungs are filled with tiny air sacs, bronchi, and blood vessels used for the transfer of oxygen to the blood stream. Each lung is conical in shape and has a rounded apex which extends upward into the root of the neck. The lower surface of each lung is concave upwards and rests, in part, upon the heart and upon the two convex dome-shaped surfaces of the diaphragm, the right dome being higher than the left.

Each lung is divided, by deep fissures, into lobes. The

right lung has three such lobes and the left lung only two, the difference being caused by the position of the heart, which also fills part of the area occupied by the left lung.

The heart is enclosed in a special membrane, or pericardium, the lower surface of which is attached to the dome of the diaphragm. The heart occupies a space in the thorax about the size of a person's fist. It lies immediately behind the sternum at the level of the third to sixth ribs, and a portion of it rests upon the diaphragm, displacing the lower forward part of the two lungs.

About two-thirds of the entire heart extends to the left of the midline of the sternum, the other third toward the right. The lower front portion of the lungs thus partly encircles the heart with its complex system of connecting blood vessels and nerves. The posterior border of the lungs is, therefore, much longer than the anterior border. The lung tissue is also thicker at the back than at the front.

The volume of uninterrupted lung tissue is greater along the rear wall and in the upper region of the thorax. For this reason, to develop efficient breathing, it is important to the singer that rib action along the lateral, posterior, and upper portions of the chest wall be well developed.

Breath Capacity and Related Structural Elements

The amount of breath used in normal breathing varies with the individual. For an average adult, physiologists estimate about 500 cc. (one pint) of *tidal air,* which is the amount that actually passes in and out of the body with each normal, quiet respiratory cycle. About 1500 cc. of *complemental air* may be added to the tidal air during maximal inhalation and, during maximal exhalation, about 1500 cc. of *supplemental air* may be forcibly expelled beyond normal exhalation.

Even after the lungs are depleted in maximal expiration, there still remains about 1500 cc. of unexpelled *residual air* in the breathing organs that cannot be forced out voluntarily. All this adds up to a potential lung capacity of about 5000 cc. (about five quarts), or the sum of tidal, complemental, and residual air. About 3500 cc. of this amount represents the *vital capacity* or respiratory capacity available for the average singer's use. Thus, the vital capacity is defined as the largest volume of air (breath) that can be forced out after the deepest inhalation is taken.[8] Of course, vital capacity is related to posture, age, and size.

Obviously, there is considerable room for the additional intake of breath for extraordinary needs, as in singing. Since lung capacity varies with chest expansion, the singer's problem, here, is to be able to expand his thorax adequately so as to utilize his potential lung capacity with effective results. The posture of the body, the inclination of the spine, the flexibility of the rib cage, unimpeded by the wrong use of the diaphragm, and the position of the arms and elbows are all factors to consider in the efficient use of the respiratory organs for artistic singing.

Although the chest is wider at the base than at the top, the quantity of breath filling the base of the lungs is actually less than that filling the upper region of the lungs. This is due to the presence of the heart muscle and its arteries and the domes of the diaphragm which occupy a portion of the lower area of the thorax.

The lungs are designed to expand more extensively where their cells are more numerous. For this reason, the surrounding framework of ribs is more yielding and moveable in the upper thorax. In other words, the six upper ribs encompass more actual lung space than the six lower ribs.

The *larynx* is a pulmonary valving device that is situated at the upper entrance of the trachea or windpipe, much as a nozzle is attached at the end of a garden hose. The trachea is the tube that carries air into the lungs. It does not enter the lungs at their upper region but reaches downward to enter the lungs about one-third below their upper boundary. Thus, the air we breathe is admitted into the lungs near its middle section and not at the top.

The *trachea,* being tubular, is composed of from sixteen to twenty incomplete cartilage rings which are interjoined by a continuous fibrous membrane, thereby creating a flexible and continuous passageway from lungs to larynx. The larynx opens upward into the pharynx, which leads into the nasal and mouth cavities.

The tracheal tube is about four and one-half inches long, and extends from the larynx, through the neck, into the thorax. There are also minute muscular fibers within the walls of the tracheal tube which are capable of narrowing the tube considerably, as in coughing.

The trachea is subdivided into two main and several smaller branches or tubes, called bronchi, of similar structure. These bronchi run to the lower part of each lung, giving off numerous smaller subdivisions which extend throughout the entire lung tissue. The air we breathe is thus distributed through the bronchi and enters the lungs in all directions at once, so that inflation is not a progressive but a simultaneous action of the entire lung area. It is impossible to fill any part of the lungs first, or to direct the air intake into any local area.

The *esophagus* extends downward close behind the trachea and in front of the spinal column. It is the tube that conveys food from the mouth and pharynx to the stomach. Part of its upper end is attached to the larynx. Its lower portion pierces the diaphragm, and enters the abdomen. In the adult man, the esophagus is about nine inches long. When collapsed, the upper entrance or pharyngeal part of the esophagus provides a thin cushion between the base of the larynx (cricoid cartilage) and the fifth (or sixth) vertebra of the spine. This cushion is known as the *cricopharyngeal sphincter.* It always remains closed, in tonic contraction, except during swallowing.[9]

In swallowing (deglutition) the entrance to the esophagus is opened by a set of muscles which simultaneously close the entrance to the larynx. Some of the muscles of phonation are engaged in this service. Swallowing action is always associated with the immediate backward movement and elevation of the larynx and closure of the glottis. Likewise, the act of swallowing always inhibits the movement of the respiratory muscles. Thus, it would be impossible to breathe or phonate and swallow at the same time.

With these preliminaries in mind, we can approach the complexities of the breathing mechanisms and view their significance and practical application in vocal pedagogy. It must be reemphasized, however, that, although each part is discussed separately in terms of its service to the singing act, there is no intention of stressing the importance of any single element. Normally, all parts of the breathing function work together in a state of unity and balance that is made possible by the coordinating function of the brain.

The Vocal Function Related to Breathing

Physiologically speaking, vocal tone production involves a combination of five coordinated actions that provide *motive power, phonation, pitch control, intensity,* and *resonation* for the singing voice. These may be summed up as follows:

1. The lungs, abdominal muscles, diaphragm, and muscles of the thorax generate the motive power, which is breath pressure.

2. This energy, directed upward against the adducted vocal cords, creates a suction (Bernoulli effect) which holds them together and also forces them apart intermittently, causing them to vibrate and produce sound or phonation.

3. The ratio of breath pressure to glottal resistance or glottal tension controls the adjustment for vocal pitch.

4. Likewise, the ratio of breath pressure to glottal mass affects the adjustment for vocal intensity.

5. The sound that is thus generated is simultaneously reinforced and amplified by a chain of intrinsic and extrinsic muscles, ligaments, bones, cavities, and surfaces

which are located in the larynx, chest, throat, mouth, and nose, and elsewhere throughout the body, producing resonation which affects the quality of the singing voice.

To these five basic actions, a sixth may be added for the singer. It is *diction* (articulation) or the molding of phonetic and verbal patterns by supplementary movements of the tongue, mouth, lips, and teeth, thus providing the final output of intelligible and communicable speech and song.

All this is a coordinated action governed by, and correlated with, a mental tonal image which may be said to monitor the entire vocal output. The nervous system of the human body provides paths of neural conductivity and biofeedback between various aural stimuli, brain centers, and the appropriate muscular responses of the vocal tract that coordinate to produce the singing voice.

Phonation for artist singers, therefore, requires that the lungs hold a somewhat greater quantity of breath than is necessary for ordinary speaking (though not maximal). Breath must be firmly compressed but *economically* expelled through the glottal aperture at a carefully controlled rate and pressure. When action is correct, the emission of breath during phonation will be infinitesimal.

Thus, in a sense, the singer creates and maintains a subglottal air cushion of compressed breath that is constantly supporting his singing tone. This gives the illusion that he is *singing on the breath.*

There are indications that the thorax is more efficiently adjusted for bodily effort when the lungs are not filled to maximum capacity.[10] This would suggest that extreme breath intake is not essential except for unusual physical exertion. A singer will learn, likewise, that a maximal intake of breath is not necessarily conducive to optimal tone production. Too much breath is as bad as too little. Therefore, the proper budgeting of breath becomes an important part of a singer's technique.[11]

Laryngoscopic observation shows the vocal cords closed

during powerful arm efforts.[12] This action can be illustrated by pressing the palms of both hands together, against resistance, with considerable force. If vocal sound is attempted during this effort, a staccato grunt will be produced, resembling the so-called *coup-de-glotte,* or glottal stroke, which is a device formerly used by teachers to energize or strengthen the glottal muscles during the vocal training program.[13]

The *coup-de-glotte* is a very light, dry glottal cough that induces a sphincter-like narrowing of the entire laryngeal passageway. When this glottal stroke is alternated with a voluntary swallowing action, the muscles of the glottis can be contracted and relaxed alternately, thus providing a light muscular gymnastic for these delicate parts. It is to be practiced with caution and with frequent rests to avoid strain.

Finally, we are reminded that the larynx was not evolved in man exclusively as a sound-producing organ. Basically, it is a valve-like mechanism that excludes everything from the lungs during the act of swallowing. Its valvular action also serves to retain air in the lungs during moments of great exertion while working with the arms, as in weightlifting, pulling, reaching, hugging, rowing, pushing, and striking.[14]

This gives a clue to the peculiar structure and operation of the larynx as a vocal organ both in breathing and in phonation. When an individual uses his arms in lifting an unusually heavy object, the laryngeal valve automatically closes so that air cannot enter the lungs. The chest is thus prevented from expanding. Under these conditions the ribs will remain stationary and thus provide a fixed anchorage for chest-to-arm (pectoral) muscles, thus enabling them to contract with full force and pull on the forelimbs. This fixation of the thorax is assisted by the simultaneous contraction of the lateral chest wall and the abdominal and diaphragmatic muscles, illustrating the combined action that is also used for forceful vocal utterance.[15]

Another observation may be made at this point. The primary function of many parts of the vocal mechanism is for purposes other than sound production (e.g., coughing, swallowing, etc.). Hence, the phonatory function is largely influenced by muscles that are frequently otherwise employed in non-phonatory uses, with ramifications in many parts of the torso that operate for other than vocal purposes. In continuing this introductory discussion, however, our principal interest will be to describe the foregoing mechanisms of breathing as they relate to voice production in singing. In this frame of reference, correct posture for singing may be described as that position of the body that permits maximum rib expansion and the maximum retention and compression of breath during phonation.

REFERENCES AND NOTES

1. L. S. Judson and A. T. Weaver, *Voice Science* (New York: Appleton-Century Croft, 1965), p. 27.

2. Wilbur P. Bowen, *Applied Anatomy and Kinesiology* (Philadelphia: Lea & Febiger, 1949), Chap. 6.

3. V. A. Fields and J. F. Bender, *Voice and Diction* (New York: The Macmillan Company, 1949), p. 22.

4. John Howard, *The Physiology of Artistic Singing* (Boston: John Howard, 1886), p. 100.

5. Henry Gray, *Anatomy of the Human Body,* 27th edition (Philadelphia: Lea & Febiger, 1959), p. 411.

6. Carlo Meano, *The Human Voice in Speech and Song,* transl. A. Khoury (Springfield, Ill.: Charles C Thomas, Publ., 1967).

7. Gray, *Anatomy,* p. 1196.

8. Sir Victor Negus, *The Biology of Respiration* (Edinburgh: Livingstone, Ltd., 1965), p. 161.

9. Ibid., p. 60.

10. R. H. Stetson, "The Breathing Movements in Singing," *Archives Neerlandaises de Phonetique Experimentale* 6 (1931): 115.

11. Lilli Lehmann, *How to Sing,* 3rd rev. edition (New York: Macmillan, 1929).

12. V. E. Negus, *The Comparative Anatomy and Physiology of the Larynx,* 2nd edition (London: Wm. Heinemann Medical Books, Ltd. 1963), p. 153.

13. William Vennard and Nobuhiko Isshiki, "Coup de Glotte, a Misunderstood Expression," *NATS Bulletin* (Feb. 1964), p. 15.

14. V. E. Negus, *The Mechanism of the Larynx* (London: Heinemann Medical Books, 1957), pp. 458, 474.

15. Ibid., p. 251.

IV

Breathing Methods Used in Vocal Training

Although the singer is not necessarily aware of specific breathing controls while he performs, it is apparent that during the training period preceding the mastery of his art he needs much expert guidance. New habits have to be established so that ultimate performance may eventually become the unconscious utilization of these habits. Moreover, the approach to this achievement often demands rigorous training or retraining of muscles and movements that are used in quiet breathing or in everyday speech behavior.

In normal quiet respiration, a constant renewal of air in the lungs is made possible by movements of the diaphragm and walls of the chest cavity or thorax. The part played by the lungs is entirely passive, in response to differences in thoracic air pressure created by the expansion and contraction of the chest wall.

For *inspiration,* the thorax is enlarged, thereby creating a pulmonary vacuum. The lungs instantly swell to fill the increased space thus provided, thereby drawing air in through the nose, mouth, and trachea.

For *expiration,* the thorax contracts, thereby diminishing its capacity and air is consequently expelled from the lungs through the trachea, mouth, and nose.

Chest expansion in *quiet* breathing is possible in three directions: 1) frontal or *sternoclavicular;* 2) lateral or *intercostal;* and 3) ventral (downward) or *diaphragmatic abdominal*. Any or all of these three methods may be used.[1]

Since the boundaries of the thorax consist largely of the rib cage, spinal column, and diaphragmatic-abdominal wall, these areas will be considered as they relate both to normal quiet breathing and to voice production for singing. The following physiological elements should first be studied and visualized.[2]

Interrelated Actions of Ribs, Diaphragm and Abdominal Wall

1. The ribs have a natural downward slant. They curve obliquely *backward,* then frontward, from the spine. Except for the lowest five, including the floating ribs, they curve slightly *frontward,* then backward from the breastbone.

2. Whenever the breastbone or sternum is pulled frontward, as in quiet breathing, the front end of each rib is raised where it is attached to the breastbone, while its rear extremity remains stationary where it is attached to the spine. This movement causes a lateral (outward) rotation of the ribs.

3. As the sternum is thus lifted and the thorax enlarged, there is also some stretching of the rib cartilages and tendons which promotes an elastic return of the rib cage in expiration.

4. During maximal inhalation, the ribs can be raised still farther by a straightening of the vertebral column due to contraction of the sacrospinalis muscle. This produces a slight backward straightening of the lumbar spine. When the ribs are raised and their spinal angles thereby increased, the transverse diameter of the thorax is enlarged. Boosting up the collarbone or clavicle, without allowing for a forward movement of the sternum, will have little inspiratory effect, since the ribs cannot rotate outward to their fullest extent unless the clavicles and

sternum also move slightly forward and upward.

6. Clavicular-sternal expansion is therefore one in which the highest degree of sidewise rib expansion is possible. It is the breathing movement used in deep yawning and in panting after extreme exertion, as in running.

7. All upward and outward movements of the ribs are *inspiratory* movements. All downward and inward rib movements are *expiratory*. A combination of inspiratory and expiratory muscles acting in graded sequence can produce a restraining effect on either or both of these movements.

8. Diaphragmatic-abdominal movements are coordinated with rib action. The *diaphragm* is a large fibro-muscular partition between the cavities of the thorax and abdomen. It has a double dome, and it is arched upward toward the thorax. It consists of a sheet-like central tendon and a peripheral muscular margin, the circumferance of which is attached posteriorly to the upper four lumbar vertebrae, laterally to the lower six ribs and their cartilages, and anteriorly to the lowest segment of the sternum (xiphoid process).

9. The diaphragm is therefore part tendon, part muscle. A large portion, nearly half, of its entire dome-shaped area is tendonous. The possible extent of the contraction of the diaphragm is thereby much reduced, being limited largely to its muscular periphery.

10. In the cavity below the larger dome of the diaphragm, on the right side, lies the liver, while the smaller dome on the left side is occupied by the stomach and spleen. Below these lie the intestines and other visceral organs. Normally, the viscera are pressed upward against the under surface of the diaphragm by the elasticity of the front abdominal walls. As a result, when the diaphragm contracts in quiet breathing, it pulls its domes downward, pressing downward on the contents of the abdominal cavity so that the front abdominal wall swells outward passively with each inspiratory movement.

11. Conversely, the convex abdominal muscles, upon contraction, exert inward pressure against the abdominal vis-

cera, and this pressure is transmitted upward against the diaphragm. These opposing factions can be controlled to bring about a fixation of the diaphragmatic-abdominal mechanism and can thus provide a sensitive regulatory action for breath compression in singing.[3]

12. The diaphragm, in rising, does not free itself from the ribs, but is bound to their inner surfaces by means of a serrated peripheral band of adhesion that is approximately four inches wide in the average male adult and about three and a half inches wide in a female.

13. There are three main openings through the diaphragm to accomodate the positions of: a) the aorta, or main artery, which carries blood from the heart; b) the vena cava, a large vein which carries blood back to the heart; and c) the esophagus, through which food passes to the stomach. Several smaller apertures allow the passage of nerves, arteries, etc., into the abdominal region.

14. The vena cava passes through the central tendon of the diaphragm. It is adherent to the latter and can be stretched downward and narrowed somewhat by the tendon's descent, a possible cause of dizziness during improper breathing.

15. Finally, there are four principal layers of powerful muscles fronting the abdomen. The outer two are oblique, the middle layer is transverse, the inner one perpendicular. These four layers constitute most of the convex wall of the abdomen. All of them cooperate in preventing extensive outward movement of the abdominal wall. All have attachments to the lower rib cage and to the bones and spine on either side.

Respiratory Factors in Singing

Glottal action in sustained phonation for singing may be compared to the kissing action of the closed facial lips when a person indraws air between them. This action is also similar to the compression of a trumpeter's lips as he forces a thin but steady stream of compressed breath between them in order to produce tone. It is important, therefore, to visualize the act of phonation for singing in three stages:

1. The vocal ledges or glottal lips are brought together by the action of intrinsic laryngeal muscles in a preparatory closure called *adduction*.
2. An expiring breath stream simultaneously creates continuous upward suction (Bernoulli force) between the glottal lips and thus maintains their closure while;
3. Continuing expiratory breath pressure overcomes glottal closure and causes an *intermittent* upward displacement of the elastic glottal ledges, thereby forcing them into vibration and producing tone.

In other words, adduction of the vocal cords is only a preparatory action. The expiring breath stream maintains the glottic closure by means of suction and also helps to activate and energize the continuous vibratory action of the vocal cords.

Muscular elasticity and the inherent firmness of the closed glottal lips increases this vibratory response. Under the unconscious guidance of the singer's ear, glottal resistance will vary with expiratory breath pressure so that the firmer the vocal tone desired, the firmer the glottal resistance.

A sustained but controlled expiratory breath pressure is therefore all-important in singing. That is to say, the singer imposes a combined regulatory contraction of the diaphragm, thorax, and the abdominal wall so that the issuing glottal tone may be augmented or diminished, sustained or repeated, varied in pitch or cut off at will, to suit the needs of song. With this basic action in mind, respiratory requirements for singing may now be considered in greater detail.

To begin with, the high-chest posture, which is mandatory in artistic singing,[4] will help prevent neck and throat tensions that might interfere with laryngeal action. Furthermore, when the sternum is considerably elevated in the established high-chest posture, inspiration permits enlargement of the thorax in only two dimensions, lateral and ventral, instead of three. Respiratory controls in singing thus become more localized and, as a consequence, intercostal and abdominal-diaphragmatic movements are synchronized to support a singing tone.[5] How is this accomplished?

Through their points of attachment, the abdominal muscles can exert a powerful rib-pulling action, and they can, therefore, perform an important expiratory service in singing. For this reason, expiration that governs the singing voice involves a controlled rather than a passive return of the abdominal wall during a very gradual, simultaneous compression of the chest boundaries.

Indeed, inward movement of the abdomen, coordinated with inward lateral pressure of the ribs, must last as long as the singing tone is maintained. This is not a fitful pushing action but a sensitively regulated and restrained compression of the thorax to prevent explosive release of breath during phonation. The combination of intercostal and abdominal action therefore provides the mechanism needed to regulate expiratory breath pressure, or *breath support*. In many instances, abdominal compression alone, against a nearly stationary thorax, will provide the singer with a sensitive breath support during sustained and legato intonation.

In principle, therefore, the three-way expansion of the thorax first described above is available for extreme needs, especially during strenuous singing passages. However, the singer mainly employs only the intercostal and abdominal controls for sustaining his voice. (The rib cage forms approximately four-fifths of the chest boundary.)

What about the diaphragm? With the chest properly elevated in a singer's posture, the ribs are automatically raised and the thorax is considerably expanded thereby. Because this posture expands and widens the rib cage, the diaphragm becomes somewhat flattened. Consequently, when its muscles contract, the diaphragm invariably pulls *inward* upon its peripheral attachments at the ribs. When the periphery of the diaphragm pulls inward, it causes a contraction of the rib cage and the volume of the chest is reduced. This is an *expiratory* and not an inspiratory movement. The diaphragm is therefore considered an *expiratory* agent in singing.[6]

Although contraction of the diaphragm itself is not usually subject to conscious control, contraction of the abdominal muscles can be regulated by the singer. The abdominal muscles, through their peripheral attachments, will draw the rib cage inward and thereby assist expiratory breath support. A sensitive balance is thus developed by regulating the voluntary compressive action of the abdominal wall and the inflating-deflating effort of appropriate rib muscles. Mastery of this sensitive combination of intercostal-abdominal breathing will achieve the necessary basic breath support.

In summation, expiratory action is important because it is used to regulate the pressure of outflowing breath. With the glottis closed for phonation, it is this expiratory breath support that provides a constant subglottic air cushion that makes phonation possible. The high-chest posture assists in this development.

It is important to note, therefore, that phonation is always accompanied by an *expiratory* action and that the abdominal wall moves *inward* and *upward,* not outward, during the sustained vocal act. The front of the abdomen should not be tight or rigid, however, but fairly flaccid to the touch, even when the abdominal wall is receding inward for expiratory effort. It is well to bear in mind, also, that the restraint of abdominal and intercostal pressure is equally important, so that a checking or retarding action as well as a compressive action may be used in breathing.[7]

The foregoing are physiological coordinates in the singing process. They should be studied until they can be visualized as factors in the efficient functioning of the breathing apparatus.

Breath Economy

Breathing for singing, at all dynamics, resolves itself into a continuous pressure of subglottic air which forces a minute intermittent displacement of the adducted but resilient vocal lips. This calls for constancy of chest compression, delicately regulated by breathing and glottal muscles according to the pitch and power of the tone desired. A crescendo or change of vocal pitch would call for progressive readjustment of the balance between cord tension and breath pressure so as to maintain an unwavering quality of voice. The singer's ear supervises this control through the use of inherent neural feedback mechanisms which are unconsciously responsive to auditory perception. *Feedback* is the constant cyclic interplay or interchange between ear and muscle by means of nerve stimuli that activate both.

No doubt the concept of "singing on the breath" which the Italian masters taught arose from the need for this constant regulatory support of the breath during the emission of a singing tone.[8] But voice is not breath. Rather, it is the transformation of breath pressure into acoustical energy. In phonation, therefore, a fast-moving air stream is not to be released by the vocal cords. Quite the contrary, breath emission must be reduced to an absolute minimum. Indeed, when the voice is being properly used, the flame of a candle, held within a few inches of the singer's mouth, will not flicker at all during tone production. This is true, regardless of pitch or intensity, because very little breath actually issues from the glottis during phonation.

From a singer's standpoint, therefore, the chest stroke initiates the tone and good intonation spells efficiency in converting breath pressure into voice. This means that the quantity of intake at a given moment is exactly commensurate with the needs of the phrase to be sung. Effortless singing is built upon the habit of quick, but *unforced* inhalation, followed by economical, sustained exhalation. In other words, one never fills the lungs to utmost capacity for an ordinary phrase and it takes very little air to sustain a relatively long phrase.[9] To promote these results, the following two exercises for breath economy may be practiced:

1. Prolong the vowel *ah* on an even, medium pitch level,

at a fixed volume. Time the duration for ten to fifteen seconds. Repeat several times. Now, sustain the tone longer and longer with each trial, until a maximum duration is gradually achieved. After several days of repeated trials one should be able to prolong any tone for as long as forty, fifty, or even sixty seconds. Eventually, this exercise may be repeated at different pitches and with changing dynamics.

A double purpose is thus achieved. *First,* steady, prolonged control of the expiratory muscles is developed. *Second,* this drill will gradually reduce breath emission and thus improve breath economy in phonation. It will be noticed also that voice quality improves with breath restraint during the prolongation of any single tone. The drill may eventually be varied with gradual crescendos and diminuendos (messa di voce) on any pitch, using a single sustained vowel. Test for breath economy with the candle flame, from time to time.

2. Now, try prolonging hummed tones in the same way, with similar results. Time each utterance until maximum prolongation is attained without forcing.

The classic *messa di voce* or swell tone is described as the gradual crescendo of a single tone from pianissimo to maximum power, followed by a slow diminuendo to its starting point. It was always believed that a singer cannot attain mastery of his art until he can control his breath steadily through a thousand degrees of gradual swelling and diminishing, without the slightest variation of pitch, quality, or technique of phonation.[10]

Breath Renewal

An accomplished singer must also be able to take in breath with lightning speed. The air he breathes must pass through a channel which bends at the nose, again at the pharynx, and again on entering the larynx. A fast runner will thrust out his head in an effort to straighten this airway for ease in breathing. But the vocalist may not thrust out his chin since, in doing so, he will lose the ability to maintain a stable laryngeal position with firm closure of the glottis. A singer must, therefore, learn to renew the breath without tossing the head.

To do this effectively and imperceptibly, he learns to breath noiselessly, in an instant, through either mouth or nose, or a combination of both, when necessary.[11] At times, he may have to insert a minute pause, or *half-breath,* on the ending note of any phrase so that it will not disturb the rhythm of the next entering phrase. This is helpful when there is not enough rest time for a full breath. Depletion of the lungs must be prevented at all costs, so as not to interrupt the phrase and to avoid gasping.

In singing, breath renewal serves a dual purpose. It sustains vocal sound and also provides oxygen supply. The need for oxygen is increased by the fact that the inspiratory act is short, while the expiratory act is prolonged. It is, therefore, sometimes necessary to renew the breath during sustained passages by taking short inspiratory gulps at convenient pause points without disturbing the flowing pattern of the music. Such intake should, of course, be appropriate to the interpretational effect desired. The ability to accomplish breath renewal silently and unobtrusively is essential for all legato singing.

Breath Retention and Breath Support

It is also imperative to be able to retain or conserve breath until it can be renewed. The artist learns to hold back, not at the throat, but at the source of breathing action. Correct voice production always involves skillful restraints in breathing, since singing is not merely pushing breath against a throaty constriction, but rather a gradation of expiratory controls that will afford minimal exhalation under all tonal conditions.

Breath support, therefore, means budgeting the breath and supplying just the right amount of compressive expiratory energy against the glottis. Excessive breath pressure produces harsh, off-pitch intonation. Breath insufficiency results in devitalized, tremulous, off-pitch singing.

The control of breath pressure is, therefore, equally important for loud or soft tones, since firm adduction of the glottal edges and the amplitude of their vibratory swing depend, in large measure, on the sustained pressure of breath that is applied to them.

Summary of Respiratory Demands for Singing

In summing up the foregoing, the following conclusions are arrived at:

1. Respiration is carried on by alternating the activity of inspiratory and expiratory muscles. Since they are antagonistic actions, these muscles cannot be expected to perform both inspiratory and expiratory functions.

2. For phonation, a very slight lateral-dorsal compression of the thorax is maintained, accompanied by a slight inward-upward pressure of the abdominal muscles.

3. For unusual breathing demands, the chest space may have to be enlarged to a maximum degree, a condition made possible only when the ribs have been raised and everted until they are nearly at right angles with the spine.

4. A very slight *forward* inclination of the spine reduces the necessary elevation of the chest cavity and thereby improves the efficiency of inhalation.

5. When expiratory efforts become forceful for sustaining or intensifying tone, the abdominal muscles contract inward past their neutral positions and gradually travel upward against the viscera, thus reversing inspiratory actions.

6. If maximum chest expansion is called for, it is accomplished largely through additional rib movement, not diaphragmatic movement. With chest high, the diaphragm becomes somewhat stretched out and flattened and can therefore provide only a small portion of the breath intake that is required.

7. Certain accessory back, spine, and neck muscles assist in maintaining body posture and contribute to efficient chest compression. It is evident, therefore, that general physical culture will strengthen the functioning of this complex breathing musculature.

The advice to beginners would be: start with good posture. Then, for inhalation, expand the chest laterally. Do not push forward the abdomen. Rather, allow it to flatten itself passively as the chest dilates. The breastbone need not move appreciably because it is already thrust forward due to postural elevation of the chest. The rib curvatures, near the spine, rise and push *backward*. This entire process is reversed for expiration. Bear in mind, also, that the elasticity of stretched muscles and cartilages encourages their return from an expanded position and, thus, to a certain extent, assists expiratory action. If extreme expiratory pressure is needed, as in sustaining higher notes at full volume, the costal ribs are moved *inward* and the abdominal muscles are simultaneously lifted *inward* beyond their flattened position, without allowing any stiffening action therein.

A word of caution is appropriate at this point. Sensations in singing are often misleading because an effort often excites a sensation not where it is made but where it causes the movement of distant parts. Therefore, an indirect approach may be safer than specific directions which require conscious control of each part of the breathing apparatus.[12] Thus, laughing, yawning, coughing, gasping, and even outright vigorous, unrestrained, and joyfelt singing can often provide suitable stimulation of unused breathing muscles and can help the student capture the fullness and freedom of correct respiratory action needed for artistic singing. Swelling the chest is not a separate preparatory breathing action. Each thought or phrase should take its own breath according to context and intensity of mood. In short, we may use gymnastics to strengthen the vocal instrument but we do not sing with these gymnastics.

It is also desirable that we describe respiratory controls in terms of abdominal and thoracic movements, rather than by diaphragmatic action alone, since such terminologies are less confusing to the student singer. For example, the following explanation of *breath support* may be used:

a. Inhalation for singing differs from quiet or passive inhalation in that the former may demand a more extensive expansion of the lungs than the latter.

b. The chest posture is always high for singing and the ribs expanded to a greater degree, thereby stretching out the diaphragm and flattening it so that it cannot, by itself, add much to the capacity of the thorax.

c. During inhalation for singing, the convex abdominal muscles are relaxed and allowed to travel inward to a more flattened position while the ribs are being laterally distended.

d. Quiet or passive exhalation differs from exhalation for singing in that the former requires a relaxed return of all muscles used in inspiration, while the latter requires a *controlled* exhalation. That is to say, the return of the chest wall would be sudden and convulsive were it not for the restraining action of certain inspiratory intercostal muscles which hold back the collapse of the ribs and control a gradual subsidence of the lateral chest wall during all degrees of sustained intonation. Thus, a balanced interplay between expiratory and inspiratory muscles, acting in graded sequence according to need, makes possible the gradual return of the lateral chest wall while the vocalist is sustaining a singing tone. The proper control of this sensitive interaction is called *breath support*. The gradual inward compressive force of the chest walls is also accompanied by *inward* movement of the abdominal wall. This combination of costo-abdominal compression is needed to maintain firm and constant air pressures against the glottis during the emission of tone. In some instances, abdominal pressures alone will suffice to provide sensitive breath support, while the rib cage remains expanded but stationary. In any event, this entire action must be controlled to suit expressive needs. It is never a spasmodic action.

e. In quiet or passive expiration, the chest wall and abdominal walls subside, thereby gently forcing air out of the lungs. In exhalation for singing, however, the diaphragm, being already stretched to a maximum degree because of an elevated chest posture, will, on contraction, pull inward on the ribs. The diaphragm thus becomes an expiratory muscle, and its expiratory power is increased by the preliminary expansion of the ribs. Therefore, expansive and contractive rib actions are considered all-important for singing.

f. In sustained forte singing, the inward-moving abdominal muscles oppose the downward-flattening expiratory action of the stretched diaphragm. In this action the viscera become an unyielding mass upon which both abdominal and diaphragmatic muscles come to rest. They will thus pull upon the ribs with additional expiratory lung-compressive effect.

g. The combined compressive action of chest and abdominal muscles can therefore provide a sensitive, continuous breath pressure for phonation. *Breath support* is thus created for firm intonation.

BREATHING CORRECTIVES

The following exercises provide typical working models that may be modified to suit particular needs. They should be administered at regular intervals during the period of postural growth:

1. Practice yawning to capture the natural feeling of full breathing. Frequent yawning exercise will activate the entire respiratory musculature and promote deep-breathing sensations for later use in the voice-building program.

2a. Blow out candles (real or imaginary) placed at varying distances. This develops the muscles that apply force to expiration. A deep, quick intake preparatory to exhalation is also stimulated, thus building firmness in the inspiratory muscles for later use in singing.

b. Read a song text in a very loud *whisper*, without voice. Loud whispering strengthens auxiliary muscles of breathing and phonation without tiring the voice.

3. Rowing and swimming are excellent breath builders. They stimulate the use of muscles that control the breathing apparatus. Through mild exertion they also develop and strengthen the muscles that support a firm approximation of the vocal cords during phonation.

4. Laughing is also a breath corrective. The muscles of laughter include those that expel and compress air during voice production. Laughing action also creates resiliency of breath support. Try laughing your way buoyantly through an entire song as a type of vocalizing-and-breathing exercise.

5. Deep sighing, both silent and audible, will exercise and strengthen chest muscles in all directions with resultant breath-control benefits for singing.

6. Panting requires a rapid, short spasmodic breath sequence and will strengthen the controls needed for quick inspiration and vocal attack.

7a. Gasping, like panting, enforces the quick inhalation needed for singing. In gasping, intake is much deeper and retention prolonged, thereby promoting the use of chest muscles that control deeper breathing. Try gasping quickly, as though you were about to shout "Look out!" to warn someone of impending danger.

b. Now gasp before singing each note in a scale passage or phrase of a song. Note the quick intake required for each tone that is uttered. Singing will require this type of breathing at times, and it is a breath control that should be mastered and made easily available for future use.

8a. Sigh deeply and groan audibly in a glissando *downward* sliding pitch. Try this on every note of the scale.

b. Later, attack each pitch accurately and use distinguishable vowels and even syllables as you slide downward in a legato, diatonically accurate groan or audible sigh. Even the highest pitches in the vocal range respond readily to this type of attack. Breath control, not pitch control, is to be uppermost while practicing this exercise. The improvement in breath control will become apparent as the exercise is mastered.

9a. *First,* laugh staccato on a single tone at a comfortable pitch level; *next,* repeat the tone with a longer duration. *Finally,* attack and sustain each tone with the same force of expulsion of breath that is needed to laugh on it.

   b. Now try laughing in duplets, on a single pitch, then on a different pitches.

   c. Try this also on triplets and quadruplets, at different speeds and on different pitches, always starting with a series of repeated tones on the same pitch.

   d. Now, try laughing staccato on arpeggios, broken cords, and disjunct intervals. Ultimately, you should be able to laugh your way through fragments of scale passages, in any direction, without perceptible variations of vocal quality.

10. Finally, try the prolongation of a single vowel on a monotone. Gradually increase its duration. Then use different pitches and different dynamics until you can prolong a single tone for thirty or forty seconds, on one breath, without wavering or diminishing. Try the same maximal prolongation exercise in a gradual crescendo and decrescendo *(messa di voce)* featuring steadiness and firmness of tone throughout. Maintain good posture.

Inhalation Tests and Exercises

Respiratory action can be tested from time to time by applying the following procedures. The student may administer these under a teacher's guidance *after* correct posture has been established:

11. To activate back rib and shoulder muscles, lie on a hard floor and roll over on your stomach. Now, yawn deeply and feel the back ribs expand. Capture this action for upright breathing. Resume a standing posture but continue the same back-rib expansion as an exercise.

12. With chest high and ribs fully expanded, place the hand upon the front abdominal wall. Now inhale slowly and deeply. If the abdomen remains stationary or expands and pushes against the hand, the action is correct. Repeat several times.

13. With the chest held high and the ribs collapsed, clasp your sides with both hands. Inhale deeply, but restrain all rib movement while the abdomen only is protruded. Note that little air will be inhaled in this manner, compared with the additional amount that results when the ribs are released and allowed to expand with each inhalation. Repeat several times.

14. In a sitting position, lean comfortably, not heavily, against the straight back of a chair. Place the hand flat upon the upper part of the chest, just below the collarbone. Now, inhale slowly and deeply. If the hand is stationary or if it rises nearly straight upward, the action is *not* correct. If, however, the chest bears the hand more decisively forward than upward, the action is correct and the muscles that expand and lift the rib cage are properly at work. Repeat often.

15a. In the same sitting position, place the hands against the sides, as far back as the thumbs can reach and as high as possible. Inhale slowly and deeply. If the back ribs are felt to rise decisively and move rearward where they are being clasped, the action is correct; otherwise, the muscles that govern this upward and rearward expansion are not functioning.

   b. As a corrective exercise, assume a sitting position, lean forward, and rest your chin on both fists with elbows on your knees. Now, yawn deeply. Note that the lower ribs expand backward and sidewards. This is correct action. Now, sit upright and continue this rib action. Repeat often.

16. Having inhaled a full breath, suddenly relax all the inspiratory muscles. Note whether the upper chest recoils more backward than downward. If it does, the action is correct. If not, practice until correct action is induced.

17. Repeat test sixteen but note whether the ribs in the back recoil downward. If they do, the action is correct. It should be apparent that the outward movement of the ribs is

more extensive in the back than it is in the front of the thorax. This rearward expansion of the rib cage is favored by two postural conditions: a) a slight forward tilting of the entire spine (or torso) above the waistline, and b) holding the elbows forward and away from the sides by a distance of four or five inches. This posture is conducive to correct action, but avoid rigidity. Practice often.

18. Inhale a maximum breath with the shoulders and arms hanging loosely downward. Then raise the shoulders and add more breath. Now, raise the arms overhead and add still more breath. Notice how the positions of arms, chest, and shoulders influence the quantity or depth of breath that is taken. Now, inhale to a maximum degree with the spine held in a vertical position. Then, bend the upper spine forward slightly and note that an additional intake of air is now possible and with less strain or effort. Practice accordingly.

19a. Assume a standing position with the spine inclined slightly forward. Now, allow the arms and shoulders to droop downward loosely. Then inhale with the fullest possible breath. You will experience a helpless feeling of restricted effort and realize that your breath supply is small.

b. Now, while still holding the breath intake, raise the shoulders slightly and separate the upper arms from the body, moving the elbows sidewise. The restricted sensation vanishes and much more breath will be admitted, illustrating the correct posture for maximal inhalation. Practice accordingly.

20. When the upper arms are held firm and fixed in the sidewise position that is advised in No. 19b, the arm-to-ribs muscles can act with strong inspiratory effort to expand the upper ribs. To prove this, inhale with the fullest possible breath while your arms remain close to the sides. Then move the arms away from the body laterally for several inches and note that a large amount of additional breath will be admitted. Practice accordingly.

Observations drawn from the above inhalation correctives may be applied to actual singing practice as soon as chest action has been strengthened. The techniques derived therefrom are embodied in the breathing habits of a singer. The pupil must be cautioned to take breath silently at all times and to learn to inhale swiftly, as needed. Breath renewal should always take place just as soon as the last word of a phrase is stopped. There can be no breath gaps in legato singing.

Exhalation Tests and Exercises

21. Grasp the sides of the body about halfway from hips to armpits, with the thumbs pointing backward and inward toward the spine. Inhale slowly and deeply, as before, with correct expansion of the chest and back. Be certain that the upper chest wall and collarbone are traveling in a forward and upward direction. Then sing "ah" on any pitch. As the vowel is being prolonged, note whether the thumb and five fingers of each hand are gradually traveling toward each other. This inward movement of the fingers should begin at the very starting of the voice. If so, the breathing action is correct. If not, or if the action is delayed, the expiratory muscles are not functioning properly, or else the inspiratory muscles interfere and have not relaxed as they should at the instant of phonation. Repeat until mastered.

22. Reach the back of one hand upward as high as possible upon the back. Place the other hand upon your upper front chest. Then inhale slowly and deeply. Now sing a prolonged "ah." If both your front chest and your back sink downward and gradually come together at the very inception of tone, the breathing action is correct. Otherwise, it is faulty. Practice accordingly, as needed.

23. At about the level of the lowest ribs, grasp the *front* of the chest between the widely spread thumb and forefinger of the right hand. Now, inhale slowly and deeply. Sing a prolonged "ah," as before. Notice whether the parts touched by the thumb and forefinger gradually come nearer together. If they do, the action is correct. If not, the action is faulty. Practice as needed.

24. Place a hand upon the front abdominal wall. Inhale slowly and deeply, and, while doing so, note the correct *outward* movement of the abdomen. Now, sing a loud, firm "ah," and note that at the inception of tone there is a very slight inward bounce of the abdominal wall, followed immediately by a continuing *inward* movement of the latter, as the tone is sustained. This action is correct. If the posture is correct, the abdomen is never distended. Its neutral position is nearly flat, and it moves inward and outward from this position. Practice accordingly.

25. Repeat test No. 24, but this time sing and prolong a loud tone. Observe that when you stop, the sudden ending of a prolonged note or energetic phrase produces the same slight inward bounce of the abdominal wall. This is caused by the outward recoil of the indrawn ribs and is a correct reaction.

Needless to say, specific directions like these represent the ultimate in acquiring correct breathing habits. They may be applied as part of a preliminary training program, the purpose of which is to build automatic breathing responses into the singing act.

During the early training period, simple songs, graded to the pupil's vocal abilities and embodying various problems of breathing, may be used as teaching and practice materials. The singer's chest carriage should be fairly high at all times, and all breathing exercises are to be based on this posture.

A REVIEW OF BREATHING MUSCLES

The most active respiratory muscles are listed here. Detailed descriptions and the technical functions of these muscles may be reviewed in a good physiology text.[13] The present purpose is to provide a summation of essential singing components inasmuch as medical books are not likely to describe the specific functioning of the vocal apparatus used for singing.

The teacher will note that the complexity of the respiratory system precludes the conscious manipulation of any one of its parts during the vocal act. Anatomical surveys may be helpful in visualizing the functioning of the entire system and in applying suitable remedial exercises, but at no time should the synergy of these parts be disturbed during the vocal act itself. The pupil must be taught that artistic singing eventually becomes an integrated response. It is never to be molested by conscious controls. Basically, the artist-singer's ear governs the entire vocal output after correct habits have been formed.

Note, also, that the primary activators of the chest wall are dependent upon a supporting action of accessory postural muscles. The former can not act effectively unless the latter first provide a fixation of adjacent body members.

For example, muscles that support the head and shoulders coordinate instantly with the intercostals and other breathing muscles in order to fix the position of the head, shoulder blades, and arms, and thus provide a stationary fulcrum for the effective movement of the rib-raising muscles. Likewise, the latissimus dorsi and serratus anterior muscles could not pull upon the ribs unless the upper arms were first held in a stationary position by the combined action of the deltoid, levator scapuli, rhomboid, and trapezius muscles.

If the singer's posture is poor, the shoulders tend to hang limply with the result that maximal inhalation will be restricted and the breath supply will be small. On the other hand, when the chest and shoulders are properly postured and the upper arms slightly abducted, the restricted feeling vanishes and more breath will be admitted.

It follows, therefore, that whenever unusual breathing demands are made in singing, a firm, stationary position of the entire body and the upper arms is mandatory. In other words, maximal expansion of the chest requires the aid of accessory postural muscles.

Inspiratory Muscles

1. scalini (anterior, medius, and posterior)
2. subclavius

3. pectoralis major and pectoralis minor
4. serratus anterior (serratus magnus)
5. serratus posterior superior
6. latissimus dorsi (if arm and shoulders are fixed)
7. external intercostals
8. iliocostalis cervicis
9. levatores costorum

Expiratory Muscles

1. subcostales
2. longissimus dorsi
3. internal intercostals
4. serratus posterior inferior
5. quadratus lumborum
6. iliocostalis lumborum
7. iliocostales dorsi
8. transversus thoracic
9. abdominal (oblique external, oblique internal, transverse and rectus)
10. diaphragm (triangularis sterni, transverse thoracic) In the high-chest position used for singing the diaphragm becomes expiratory, since it draws inward upon the peripheral ribs.

Accessory Muscles

These are the principal postural muscles that help maintain the erect position of the head, spine, and body members against the downward pull of the rib muscles. There are others relating to the general posture of the body that are not listed here:

1. deltoid (with arms in abducted position)
2. trapezius
3. rhomboid major and rhomboid minor

4. levator scapulae
5. sternocleidomastoid
6. sacrospinalis (erector spinae)

In conclusion, having attained a better comprehension of the respiratory system and its complex musculature, we may now proceed to a study of the structure and function of the vocal organs themselves. Both internal and external phonatory mechanisms are to be reviewed. This will complete our survey of vocal physiology and will help clarify and explain many teaching methods and procedures that are needed for improving intonation in singing.

It should be apparent that a fragmentary knowledge of the complex vocal mechanisms will only limit a teacher's understanding of these training procedures. However, a complete review of vocal physiology can reveal the relevancy of each technique that is used to the total behavior pattern of singing, and this knowledge will enable a teacher to avoid those procedures that may inhibit or impair the synergy of interrelated parts.

REFERENCES AND NOTES

1. Henry Gray, *Anatomy of the Human Body,* 27th edition (Philadelphia: Lea & Febiger, 1959), p. 451.

2. Wilbur P. Bowen, *Applied Anatomy and Kinesiology* (Philadelphia: Lea & Febiger, 1949), pp. 223–225.

3. D. Ralph Appelman, *The Science of Vocal Pedagogy* (Bloomington, Ind.: Indiana University Press, 1967), p. 12.

4. Van A. Christy, *Expressive Singing* (Dubuque, Iowa: Wm. C. Brown, Co., 1961), p. 21.

5. Viktor Fuchs, *The Art of Singing and Voice Technique* (New York: London House and Maxwell, 1964), p. 75.

6. John Howard, *The Physiology of Artistic Singing* (Boston: John Howard, 1886), p. 133.

7. Fuchs, *The Art of Singing*.

8. Giovanni Battista Mancini, *Practical Reflections on the Figurative Art of Singing*, trans. Buzzi (Boston: The Gorham Press, 1912), p. 53.

9. Edgar F. Herbert-Caesari, *The Alchemy of Voice* (London: Robert Hale, 1965), p. 19.

10. Pietro Francesco Tosi, *Observations on the Florid Song*, transl. Galliard (London: 1743).

11. John Burgin, *Teaching Singing* (Metuchen, N.J.: The Scarecrow Press, Inc., 1973), p. 53.

12. Wilmer T. Bartholomew, *Acoustics of Music* (New York: Prentice Hall, Inc., 1942), p. 140.

13. For example, see Gray, *Anatomy*.

V

Structure and Function of the Vocal Organs

The larynx, or voice box, is a most misunderstood part of vocal anatomy. It is the focal point of sound production in the body and, as such, subject to the closest scrutiny as a possible source of vocal competence. But although *phonation,* the inception of tone, is believed to be centered in the larynx, the product known as the *singing voice* is a resultant of many cooperating parts which extend beyond the larynx. None of these parts functions independently.

The tonal generator, therefore, is an extensive apparatus of coordinating muscles, ligaments, cartilages, and bones, all of which are directly affected by the vibratory activity initiated within the voice box. Most printed illustrations showing cadaveric dissections present the vocal organ in isolation, as though it were an independently functioning unit. Nothing is further from the truth.

The external muscles that surround and support the position of the larynx in the throat are, in fact, just as important as the interior portions of the voice box, since neither could function without the other. Even the bony skeleton of the body plays a role in tone production. It will bear repetition, therefore, that vocal sound, although it originates in the larynx, is a network production.[1]

One might say that, basically, voice functions as part of a

general behavior pattern, that the whole body reacts in vocal expression. This response involves the central nervous system, with its many extensions. It also engages muscles that compose the entire vocal tract: muscles of respiration, laryngeal, neck, and throat muscles; mouth, tongue, jaw, pharynx, palate, postural muscles, and the muscles of facial expression, gesture, and body movement. The auditory mechanism is also part of this complex.

The quality of the singing voice is especially related to the health and conditioning of the singer's body. When general health is good, nerve responses are optimal, muscular tonus is good, and vocal timbre improves. When vitality is low, the muscular system is enervated or flabby and the voice becomes dull, weak, and unresponsive. In a physiological sense, therefore, whatever affects the health of the body affects the voice.

Acoustical airways and the vibratory transmission route of the complex structure and musculature of the entire vocal tract are therefore conditioning elements in voice production for singing. For this reason, both internal and external mechanisms of the vocal apparatus deserve careful consideration by the teacher of singing.

The following discussion of the vocal mechanism is presented in two main parts. One approach reviews inert structural components with respect to vocal function. The second part presents a closer view of the vocal act itself, involving those elements previously described. Unrelated anatomical and functional details of the human organism are purposely omitted (e.g., origin, course, and insertion of muscles) since they may be reviewed, when needed, in any physiology text.

The terminology used is likewise simplified, avoiding inaccuracies, so that it will not be necessary to wade through a complex descriptive technical vocabulary to construct a visual image of the working mechanisms of the voice. Names of muscles are accurately stated, however, and they agree with authoritative medical sources. The pedagogy of singing is uppermost in all these discussions.

Properties of Muscles Reviewed

First of all, to dispel some common misconceptions regarding vocal action, the following basic physiological facts regarding muscles and muscle action in the human body should be reviewed[2]:

1. A muscle is an organ whose special function is the positioning, adjustment, and movement of various parts of the body. Each muscle is composed of bundles of individual fibers which contract when stimulated.
2. Nearly all the voluntary and skeletal muscles of the body occur in pairs that are bilaterally placed. This is also true of muscles in the vocal tract.
3. Any individual muscle fiber will not contract in parts, nor will it only partially contract. Each contraction is therefore a maximal contraction, all or none. The gradation of muscular power is therefore achieved by varying the number of fibers or muscle spindles that are brought into play in a given muscle and also by introducing the restraining action of opposing or antagonistic muscles. Such action is observable in the larynx, breathing mechanism, and in other parts of the vocal tract.
4. The names of voluntary muscles are derived from:

    a. their position (e.g., *pectoralis*)
    b. their direction (e.g., *obliquus*)
    c. their action (e.g., *flexors*)
    d. their shape (e.g., *deltoid*)
    e. number of divisions (e.g., *bicepts*)
    f. points of attachment (e.g., *sternothyroid*)

The longer compound names are usually spelled in a single word (e.g., *sternothyroid, cricoarytenoid,* etc.).

5. Practically every muscle acting upon a joint is matched by another muscle which has an opposite action. Each muscle is therefore the *antagonist* of the other.
6. Muscles fall into three classifications: a) prime movers;

b) fixation muscles; and c) synergistic or cooperating groups.

7. A muscle's working power is always increased if one of its points of attachment is held stationary while it is being contracted.

8. A muscle's contraction always consists in an effort to shorten itself. It can never lengthen itself.

9. If its extremities are pulled apart by extraneous forces which prevent a muscle from shortening itself, the muscle, upon contraction, will not thicken but will actually become thinner, no matter how much it contracts. This is true of the glottal muscles.

10. A muscle is weakened by being either shortened or lengthened beyond its normal length and it then proportionately loses power. In other words, it retains maximal strength only when it *maintains* its original length. Therefore, when it is elongated by external means during contraction, a muscle tends to increase its contracting effort to offset the weakening effect of lengthening. This is also true of glottal muscles.

11. As a muscle contracts, it stiffens. Pulling on its extremities causes it to resist by contracting and stiffening. That is why the glottal muscles become more elastic under longitudinal tension and therefore vibrate more rapidly during phonation at various pitch levels.

12. The diameter or thickness of a muscle, not its length, determines its power of contraction. Therefore, the longer muscles of the body are not necessarily the stronger ones.

13. A muscle will contract much more powerfully to maintain a part of the body in a stationary position than it would to move that part of the body to a new position.

14. Muscles that are arched, bowed, or curved in their original shape tend to straighten themselves upon contraction. Certain palatal, throat, and abdominal muscles are arc-shaped, as are many of the intrinsic laryngeal muscles. Such muscles contract by straightening themselves inward, and when they lie adjacent to each other they approximate under contraction in a sphincteric action that *narrows* the aperture or cavity which they enclose.

15. When a muscle stimulus is repeated rapidly enough, the individual stimuli accumulate in a sustained overall increase of contraction which results in an increased peak of performance. Each stimulus that a muscle receives makes that muscle more and more ready to respond. Therefore, the stimuli producing muscle action become more and more effective with each repetition, and it is easier to sustain or repeat a given action than to initiate it.

16. All muscles receive their stimulation by means of *intermittent* nerve impulses. Each impulse is therefore followed by a minute refractory or rest period, during which the nerve or muscle does not immediately respond to excitation.

17. When a stimulus is prolonged in the excitation of any muscle, an infinitesimal interruption or intermittent rest interval, called a *chronaxie,* occurs which may always be measured within that stimulus. A chronaxie is, therefore, the index of excitability of a muscle fiber expressed in time constants. Vocal pitch frequencies are believed to be determined, partly, by chronaxic responses of the fibers embedded within the vocalis muscles (vocal cords).[3]

18. The frequency of intermittent nerve stimuli may vary with different parts of the body. Certain muscles of phonation are said to be stimulated, normally, with an estimated frequency of five to eight per second. This intermittent response of muscle fibers in respiratory, cricothyroid, and other larynx-connected muscles causes a quivering tonal effect during sustained phonation that is called *vocal vibrato*. It is also believed that the functioning synergism of opposing glottal muscles is responsible for the vibrato.[4] The vibrato is, therefore, a characteristic of any well-developed singing voice.

19. The tendency of a muscle to return to its original size or shape after having been stretched, compressed, or deformed in any way is termed *myoelasticity*. Myoelastic responses of the glottal muscles help determine the frequency and intensity of the tone emitted by the voice.[5]

20. In normal bodily health, a state of partial contraction

of all muscle fibers always exists, even while they are at rest. This sustained, residual contraction or *tonus* (tonicity) is not associated with an increased expenditure of energy. Therefore, no signs of fatigue are evident as a result of the normal tonus of muscles in a state of relaxation, poise, or readiness to perform. On the other hand, abnormal or excessive tension is a cause of fatigue even when muscles are inactive or in a neutral position and apparently resting.

With the foregoing principles in mind, the physiology of the vocal organs can be better understood and interpreted in its applications to the training of the singing voice.

Structural Aspects of the Vocal Organs

In essence, the internal or *intrinsic* structure of the larynx must provide the necessary framework and mechanism for initiating, strengthening, and sustaining the fundamental vocal tone. The external or *extrinsic* mechanisms simultaneously support these initiatory functions and also provide the means of reinforcing, amplifying, resonating, and beautifying the tone, as well as articulating the intelligible sounds of language needed for a singer's diction.

Mechanically speaking, the larynx is a transformer of energy. Its valve-like action at the glottis converts thoracic breath pressure into acoustical energy which is then amplified and propagated into the surrounding atmosphere as vocal tone.

The larynx itself consists of a rigid framework and numerous muscular parts. The framework is held in position by intrinsic and extrinsic muscles and has the function of keeping the air passage open. It also provides mobility for all the valving parts and a place of attachment for its many muscles. The *intrinsic* musculature can approximate (adduct) and separate (abduct) the vocal folds. Its muscles and ligaments can also bind cartilages together and allow them to move on each other. The *extrinsic* muscles support the larynx as a whole and serve to stabilize its position during the activities of phonation.[6]

The Laryngeal Framework

From a singer's standpoint, therefore, the laryngeal framework consists of seven structural features:

1. a ring-shaped *cricoid cartilage* which forms the base of the larynx;
2. a pair of pyramid-like *arytenoid cartilages* which surmount the posterior portion of the cricoid ring;
3. a pair of *corniculate cartilages* which form tiny apical extensions of the arytenoids;
4. a V-shaped *thyroid cartilage* which surmounts the anterior and lateral portions of the cricoid ring;
5. a U-shaped *hyoid bone* which lies horizontally above the thyroid cartilage;
6. the *epiglottis,* which forms a cartilagenous flap at the base of the tongue; and
7. two tiny *cuneiform cartilages* which are embedded in the upper walls of the larynx.

All these parts are bound together by ligaments, muscles, and membranes so that a unity of function is achieved and a continuity of surface provided, both internally and externally. It will be helpful to memorize these interrelated structural components, since they will be referred to in the discussions which follow.

1. Cricoid Cartilage. The cricoid lies immediately above the uppermost ring of the trachea and is firmly connected with the latter. Its position in front of the fifth (or sixth) cervical vertebra of the spine provides an anchorage for the entire laryngeal mechanism. Thus, the cricoid cartilage is a relatively stationary base for the more mobile thyroid and arytenoid cartilages that rest upon it.[7]

The cricoid cartilage is shaped somewhat like a signet ring

with the narrow band of the ring anteriorly placed and its broad flattened *plate* nearest the spine. To the back of the cricoid ring is attached the cricopharyngeus muscle, which is the sphincter-like portion of the inferior constrictor forming the entrance to the esophagus.

The esophageal entrance which lies behind the cricoid plate is closed and in tonic contraction during the act of phonation. It is attached anteriorly to parts of the cricoid, thyroid, and corniculate cartilages. Therefore, the entrance of the esophagus provides a thin, flat, muscular cushion between the cricoid plate and the spine.[8]

On either external side of the cricoid ring, toward the rear, are two smooth articular surfaces which provide contact with the lower horns of the thyroid cartilage. The upper posterior border of the cricoid plate is somewhat elevated and provides two smooth surfaces upon which rest the twin arytenoid cartilages.

2. Arytenoid Cartilages. Each of these two tiny pyramidal bodies rests on an independent convex base on the superior boundaries of the cricoid plate. Each arytenoid narrows upward and is curved sharply backward at its apex by an elongation called the corniculate cartilage (cartilage of Santorini).

At the base of each arytenoid there is a rigid horizontal forward projection called the *vocal process* to which is attached the posterior portion of the *vocalis muscle* or vocal cord. Thus, a firm posterior anchorage is provided for each muscular ledge of the glottis. The rigid vocal process forms only about two-fifths of the entire glottal rim.

By means of at least four sets of muscles, later to be described, the arytenoids can be rotated toward each other or separated from each other on a vertical axis. These movements can either approximate or separate the vocal processes and thereby either close (adduct) or open (abduct) the glottis for such functions as swallowing, coughing, phonation, or quiet respiration. Associated with such rotation is a lateral gliding movement of the arytenoids, and they can also be braced backward by these muscles so as to produce or maintain longitudinal tension of the vocal cords.

3. Corniculate Cartilages. During swallowing actions of the throat and larynx, these two tiny, hook-like extensions of the arytenoids are tilted forward and upward toward the epiglottis, thereby assisting in the opening of the mouth of the esophagus, or inferior constrictor, to which they are attached. At the same time, they help close the entrance to the larynx and trachea.[9]

The corniculate cartilages are also believed to assist in closing the small triangular space left between the two arytenoid cartilages when the vocal ledges are brought together. By means of muscular attachments, the corniculates, which are firmly pressed together during phonation, close this interarytenoid gap against the unnecessary escape of air from the lungs while voice is being produced, thereby sealing off the posterior rim of the glottis during phonation.[10]

4. Thyroid Cartilage. The *thyroid*, largest cartilage of the larynx, lies above the cricoid cartilage. It consists of two large surfaces, lamina or wings, vertically placed, which converge and are fused in front to form the thyroid angle or prominent notched bulge known as the adam's apple. These wings are widely separated as they extend backward like the partially opened covers of a book. Their posterior borders extend upward and downward in horn-like projections.

The superior horns curve upward and meet the posterior ends of the hyoid bone above. The inferior horns curve downward and embrace the posterior sides of the cricoid ring, forming a pivotal joint with the latter. This makes possible a slight off-center, up-and-down rocking movement of the thyroid upon the cricoid (and vice versa).

The paired vocal lips, folds, or ledges are the *thyroarytenoid muscles,* the medial or *inner* margins of which are known as the *vocalis muscles*. They extend backward from a common point of attachment at the thyroid angle to separate attachments at each arytenoid cartilage. Since they are separable only at their posterior ends, these muscular ledges form a V-shaped aperture when the arytenoids are moved apart, as in abduction of the vocal folds for respiration.

Several important *extrinsic* muscles of the larynx have points of attachment on the outer surfaces of the thyroid cartilage. These will be later described. It is interesting to note, also, that the angle between the thyroid wings of a child's larynx is very wide, the angle being smaller in the adult female and much smaller in the adult male. In proportion to size, the male larynx is therefore much narrower than the female larynx. This could account for the greater prominence of a man's adam's apple. It might also partly explain why the vibrating vocal margins of the male glottis, being closer to each other, are more thickly approximated during phonation, resulting in a lower range. They are more thinly attenuated in the female glottis, since the vocal margins of the latter have to reach over a wider distance in being closed for phonation. The relative thinness of the vibrating margins in the female glottis produces a higher pitch range than in the male.

5. *Hyoid Bone.* Although it is not so classified anatomically, from the singer's standpoint the *hyoid bone* is a functioning part of the laryngeal framework. It is shaped like a horseshoe, with its closed curve in front and its open ends projecting backward. It lies in the upper part of the neck, directly above the thyroid cartilage. The hyoid bone holds open the upper entrance of the larynx. It also provides an anchorage for the epiglottis and many important *extrinsic* laryngeal muscles. The hyoid bone is thus directly connected, muscularly, with the chin, jaw, tongue, cranium, and pharynx above, and with the breastbone, shoulder blades, and thyroid cartilage below.[11]

Through its muscular and ligamentous attachments, to be described later, the hyoid bone can be made to move as a unit with the thyroid cartilage during phonation. Thus, hyoid movements are imparted to the thyroid cartilage, and vice versa.[12] Tiny *hyothyroid ligaments* also connect the knob-like posterior ends of the hyoid bone with the upper horns of the thyroid cartilage.

6. Epiglottis. The *epiglottis* is a flap-like cartilagenous body bound to the base of the tongue. As it narrows downward, it passes just inside of the anterior curve of the hyoid bone and is also bound to the latter by an elastic band, the *hyoepiglottic ligament.* Its lower extremity or stem is attached to the inner angle of the thyroid cartilage by an elastic cord or *thyroepiglottic ligament.* It is also attached to the walls of the larynx by membranous tissue and extrinsic ligaments. Thus, the epiglottis provides a connecting link between the larynx and the tongue. Since much of the epiglottis lies within the larynx, from the singer's standpoint it may be considered a structural part of the latter.

7. Cuneiform Cartilages. These are a pair of tiny cartilaginous rods or nodules (cartilages of Wrisberg) that are embedded in the upper membranous walls of the larynx, just above the arytenoid cartilages and anterior to the corniculates. They appear to act as props or supports in the muscular lining that connects the larynx with the pharynx in much the same manner as a strip of whalebone is used to support a shirt collar. Although they add firmness to the inner surface of the laryngeal passage, they are apparently inactive in phonation. They are pressed together in swallowing, while the arytenoids are drawn forward toward the epiglottis.[13]

The Interior Laryngeal Surface

Despite the foregoing part-by-part descriptions, the laryngeal passage should be visualized as a continuous extension of the trachea, narrowing itself upwards into the pharynx, where it connects with the mouth cavity. The inner and outer surfaces of the larynx are provided with a fairly smooth covering of integumentary muscles, ligaments, and membranes. These connecting surfaces serve to prevent displacement and to secure a quick return of the parts to their original positions after they have been moved for other than vocal functions (e.g., swallowing).

Although these ligaments and membranes are elastic, they are always firmly bound together, and all intrinsic and extrinsic muscles are maintained in a state of relative fixity by the tonic contractions of their internal fibers and by the constant equilibrium of all their functioning parts.

In its simplest aspects, therefore, the interior of the larynx itself may be viewed as a continuous surface beginning at the upper laryngeal entrance and extending downward until it blends with the lining of the tracheal tube. This interior surface is divided into two main parts by the medial projection of the vocal folds. Above the folds is the *laryngeal vestibule*. Below the folds is the *conus elasticus,* so called because the laryngeal lining emerging upward from the trachea forms a continuous elastic conical tube. This tube is wide at its juncture with the trachea and it narrows gradually toward the top where it blends into the overhanging glottal ledges or V-shaped aperture between the vocal cords.[14]

Three features are to be noted in the overall interior shape of the larynx. *First, the subglottal area is eliptical, from front to rear, except where it joins the circular trachea. Second,* its surface tapers inward as it rises from the trachea to the glottal closure. *Third,* its walls are sharply indented laterally above the glottis so as to form two deep horizontal fissures or *ventricles,* one on either side, just above the vocal folds.

The ventricles are bounded by an upper and lower pair of overhanging margins which are called *false vocal cords* and *true vocal cords,* respectively. The more prominent *lower* margins form the *glottis*. The space between the cords is the *glottal chink*. The indented area above the glottis is the *laryngeal vestibule*. The glottis is the focal point of vocal tone production.

A common cause of confusion in many texts on singing is a loosely used terminology. The vocal cords are variously described as vocal bands, margins, lips, cushions, edges, ledges, ligaments, shelves, or vocal muscles. But basically they consist of a pair of muscular folds that project into the cavity of the larynx at the level of the arytenoid cartilages and in such a manner as to intercept the outflowing breath stream when they are properly adducted or closed.

No attempt is made to standardize this terminology, but it should be understood that, in its functional aspects, the vibrating edges of the vocal folds, or vocal cords, consist of flat borders of elastic tissue. These may be viewed as the calloused rims of the *thyroarytenoid muscles*. These calloused edges are also called *vocal ligaments* and the terms *vocalis muscle, vocal ligament, rima glottidis, glottis,* and *vocal cord* are often interchangeably used. They really refer to specific portions or subdivisions of the larger *thyroarytenoid muscles* which form the *entire* ledge that vibrates during phonation to produce vocal tone.

The upper, and less prominent boundaries of the ventricles are the so-called *false vocal cords,* also known as *ventricular folds*. They are fibrous bands, thickly covered with mucous membrane. The few muscle fibers they contain are capable of reinforcing the approximation of the true vocal cords, as in coughing or extreme exertion. However, laryngoscopic observation shows that they are not so employed for phonation and therefore have no direct influence on voice production.[15] In other words, they do not normally vibrate during phonation.

In the act of coughing, both upper and lower muscular bands engage in a sphincter-like constriction of the entire laryngeal cavity so as to close off the tracheal tube. This closure provides the increase of pulmonary air pressure needed to eject foreign particles. Fixation of the thorax under extreme physical exertion of the body also engages the sphincteric closure of the ventricular bands and exercises these muscles. It is also probable that, for high pitches, the firming action of the ventricular folds indirectly contributes to the support of the glottis during phonation.

Functional Aspects of the Vocal Organs

Phonation for singing requires a *stationary* vibrating medium and a *constant* subglottal breath pressure. The relative fixity of the vibrator and constancy of breath pressure assure *stability* of the tone produced. Two opposing forces are at work here: 1) internal contraction of the adducted thyroarytenoid (vocalis) muscles, which tends to shorten them; and 2) a balancing longitudinal pull at their extremities, which tends to lengthen them. These opposing forces must be *equalized* to maintain a *stationary* vibrator and an even, steady intonation pattern.

During phonation for singing, therefore, the vocalis muscles remain *stationary* while the glottal ledges are stiffening and thinning out in varying degrees. This combined action regulates vibratory frequencies, and also influences intensity and quality factors of the singing voice.

In correct vocal action no appreciable movement of any of these parts should occur. It is unlikely that the vocal cords need to be stretched beyond their normal length during phonation, since their terminal attachments are held stationary by the balancing actions of antagonistic muscles. The *elasticity* of the vibrator thus varies without the appreciable movement of any of its parts.[16]

Furthermore, during intonation, sensitive and delicate neuromuscular controls are constantly being dictated by the hearing concepts of the singer. A kinesthetic sense thus enables him to produce a desired tone without external prompting. His highly developed nervous system is constantly receiving local impulses and instantly relaying instructions to the vocal tract through processes of neuromuscular auditory feedback.[17]

Thus, the tiny muscle fibers in the glottis instantly assume the proper degree of tension for each tone, with simultaneous appropriate gradations of the respiratory mechanism needed to support each tone.[18] Other muscles serve, largely, to hold the arytenoid and thyroid cartilages in a fixed and suitable position for phonation.

The maintenance of firm glottic closure against steady air pressure is, therefore, an indispensable factor in phonation for singing. This capability in the vocal cords themselves determines the firmness of vocal attack, the strength of breath support, pitch accuracy, gradations of quality and volume, and the evenness of legato singing. During phonation, all internal muscular parts of the larynx seem to support this function of maintaining rigidity and elasticity of the approximated vocal margins, supplemented, of course, by the steady positioning control of the extrinsic muscular complex.[19]

The glottal closure thus vibrates as though it were composed of a pair of heavy membranous reeds. This action may be demonstrated by laying two fingers of the hand horizontally across the mouth and then pressing them lightly against the lips. By blowing steadily between the fingers where they are joined to the hand, a sound of definite pitch can be produced, illustrating the basic vibratory response of the glottis.

Governing Principles Discussed

Three interesting theories have evolved regarding glottal action. These have been tested out separately by their proponents, but there is strong probability that a combination of all of them will explain the vocal act for the teacher. In terms of these three theories, phonation for singing may be called a *neurochronaxic–myoelastic–aerodynamic phenomenon*. It will be helpful to visualize this triple relationship of timed nerve impulses, muscular elasticity, and subglottic breath pressure in the following summary:

1. The neurochronaxic theory holds that the frequency of

vibration of the vocal cords at any given pitch level is a direct result of a corresponding number of impulses transmitted along the recurrent nerve. This nerve supplies the numerous minute fibers of the vocalis muscle. Because these fibers terminate at the glottal ledge, the latter is caused to contract and relax rhythmically during phonation.

However, it is characteristic of nerve fibers to require a minute rest period (chronaxie) between successive stimuli. Therefore, the higher frequencies in the vocal compass are produced and maintained by the alternate innervation, in relays, of adjacent sets of these tiny muscle fibers that range along the glottal ledge like the teeth of a comb. The timing of these nervous discharges is activated by cortical brain centers and the frequency of the vibratory action is therefore determined by the frequency of these nerve impulses.[20]

Cortical stimulation of the glottis is initially patterned after the tonal concept present in the centers of audition so that we must "hear" a pitch mentally to be able to sing it and, in a sense, what we phonate is merely an imitation of what we hear. The singer does not make the tone in his throat with conscious muscular effort. Instead, the glottal adjustment, actuated by breath, is innervated and controlled by the mental image and it is just as easy to think a high tone as a low one.

2. *The myoelastic theory* declares that intermittent rapid pulsation of the glottal margins is induced and maintained by continuous air pressure exerted against the underside of the closed glottis. The vocal folds are thus momentarily forced apart with each pulsation and there is a resultant minute loss of air pressure which allows them to close again because of their inherent *elasticity*. This repetitive action continues as long as tone lasts.[21]

This sensitive combination of glottal elasticity and breath control will vary with the tonal concept that governs it. The amplitude of vibratory swing and the speed of glottal rebound are thereby affected. Variations of internal contraction and longitudinal tension determine the varying density and tautness of the vibrator, thereby producing both frequency and intensity values of a singing tone.

3. Finally, *the aerodynamic theory* likewise stresses the interplay between air pressure in the trachea and the resistance of the vocal folds.[22] Glottic response is described in the following three aspects: a) the thyroarytenoid muscles are adducted in a preparatory action; b) they are then adjusted to a given tension, mass, and shape; while c) exhaled air causes a suction that draws the vocal lips more firmly together in what is called the *Bernoulli effect*.[23] A continuous upward air pressure thus maintains the glottic closure through *suction* and also induces vibratory action by forcing an intermittent release of breath between the vocal ledges.

It is possible to demonstrate the Bernoulli principle by blowing a stream of breath between two small parallel sheets of paper. They are held about one-half inch apart, in front of the lips. The sheets will be drawn together (suction) by the stream of breath flowing continuously between them until they cleave to each other and then continue to vibrate and flutter, producing a sound. Applying the same principle, the experiment may now be repeated with two index cards held in the same manner and with similar results. A reedy tone may be produced by using two strips of rubber or bamboo, with analogous effect. Indrawing air between the closed facial lips in a light kissing action is another illustration of the Bernoulli principle. Forcing a thin stream of breath outward between the compressed lips of the face also produces a continuous sound which may be varied by increasing the pressure of expiring air, or by varying the thickness and compression (myoelasticity) of the vibrating edges of the lips.

To conclude this triple functional hypothesis, phonation in singing may now be described as a combined *neurochronaxic-myoelastic-aerodynamic* phenomenon. In this triple action, timed nerved impulses, muscular tensions, and breath pressure combine to provide correct glottal adjustments for singing. The ear plays an important role in inducing this synergic response of mind, muscle, and breath.

Summary of Structure and Function

In summation, the following seven factors of *phonation* should be remembered: 1) the true vocal cords (vocalis muscles) form the medial margins of the thyroarytenoid muscles; 2) the latter are broad muscular bands, embedded in the walls of the larynx; 3) they are adducted by the action of tiny muscles that control the movement of the arytenoid cartilages to which they are attached; 4) a continuing longitudinal pull on the glottal ledges is induced by muscles that control the fixity of both glottal extremities at their terminal attachments; 5) this longitudinal pull is resisted by *internal* contraction of the vocalis muscles themselves in a reciprocal action that tenses, thins, and stiffens them for phonation without lengthening them; 6) the force of subglottic breath provides a pressure constant that not only cushions the vocal ledges during intonation but helps maintain their suction-like closure while they vibrate to produce tone; and 7) the combination of adductor, longitudinal, and internal glottal tension is governed by an auditory concept, which initiates and monitors the pitch, volume, and quality characteristics of the singing tone.

In conclusion, this preliminary survey of structure and function is necessarily simplified for pedagogical reasons. However, to complete the action picture, it will be necessary to consider all related intrinsic and extrinsic muscles that coordinate with the glottal response. Although modern research provides acceptable clues in some areas, there is still much conjecture within the scope of this analysis. It will nevertheless be helpful to focus the attention on relevant specific parts of the vocal tract. To this end, both internal and extrinsic mechanisms will be considered in greater detail in the descriptive analyses which follow. Although the authentic muscular nomenclature is used, functional discussions necessarily conform to pedagogical needs for the benefit of teachers of singing.

REFERENCES AND NOTES

1. Richard Luchsinger and Godfrey Arnold, *Voice—Speech—Language*, transl. Arnold and Finkbeiner (Belmont, Calif.: Wadsworth Publ. Co., 1965), p. 458.

2. Henry Gray, *Anatomy of the Human Body*, 27th edition (Philadelphia: Lea & Febiger, 1959), p. 411.

3. Raoul Husson, "Multiphase Conduction of the Recurrent Laryngeal Nerve During Phonation," *NATS Bulletin* (Dec. 1956).

4. R. Mason and W. Zemlin, "The Phenomenon of Vocal Vibrato," *NATS Bulletin* (Feb 1966); *J. Acoust. Soc. Am.* 49: 136.

5. G. Portman, "The Physiology of Phonation," *J. Laryng. & Otol.* 71 (1957): 1–15.

6. *Encyclopedia Brittanica* (1966), s.v. "Voice."

7. V. E. Negus, *The Mechanism of the Larynx* (London: Heinemann Medical Books, 1957), p. 445.

8. Gray, *Anatomy*, p. 1251.

9. Negus, *Larynx*, p. 454; Gray, *Anatomy*, p. 1179.

10. John Howard, *The Physiology of Artistic Singing* (Boston: John Howard, 1886), p. 172.

11. *Morris Human Anatomy*, 12th edition. (New York: Blakiston Div. of McGraw-Hill Book Company, 1966), p. 452.

12. Howard, *Artistic Singing*, pp. 68, 77, 91.

13. Negus, *Larynx*, p. 462.

14. Gray, *Anatomy*, p. 1181.

15. J. van den Berg, "On the Role of the Laryngeal Ventricle in Voice Production," *Folia Phoniat.* 7 (1955): 57–69.

16. K. Faaberg-Andersen, "Electromyographic Investigations of Intrinsic Laryngeal Muscles in Humans," *Acta Physiol. Scand.* 41, Suppl. 140 (Copenhagen, 1957): 21.

17. Werner F. Konig and Hans von Leden, "The Peripheral Nervous System of the Human Larynx," *Arch. Otolaryng.* 73 (1961): 1–14.

18. Ibid. 74 (No. 2, Aug. 1961): 162.

19. Aato A. Sonninen, "The Role of the External Laryngeal Muscles in Length-adjustment of the Vocal Cords in Singing," *Acta Oto-Laryngol.*, Suppl. 130 (1956): 1–102.

20. Husson, "Multiphase Conduction."

21. Luchsinger and Arnold, *Voice—Speech—Language,* p. 25; Hans von Leden, "The Mechanism of Phonation," *Arch. Oto-Laryngol.* 74 (No. 6, Dec. 1961): 660.

22. J. L. Flanagan, "Estimation of Interglottal Pressure during Phonation," *J. Speech & Hearing Res.* 2 (1959): 168–172; J. Van den Berg, "On the Myoelastic-aerodynamic Theory of Voice Production," *NATS Bulletin* (May 1958): 6–12.

23. Svend Smith, "Remarks on the Physiology of the Vibrations of the Vocal Cords," *Folia Phoniat.* 6 (1954): 166–178; J. van den Berg, J. T. Zantema, and P. Doornenbal, Jr., "On the Air Resistance and the Bernoulli Effect of the Human Larynx," *J. Acoust. Soc. Am.* (May 1959): 626; J. J. Pressman, "Physiology of the Vocal Cords in Phonation and Respiration," *Arch. Oto-Laryngol.* 35 (1942): 355–398.

VI

Internal Mechanisms of the Larynx

In normal health, there is constant equilibrium between the different functioning elements of the entire human organism. This is also true of the vocal tract. Its internal and external mechanisms support a synergy of muscular action that is never to be violated by the singing artist. Although its complexity defies analytical inspection during performance, it may be examined functionally to determine its components and their relevance to vocal action. An empirical observation of these isolated structural facts rises to more useful knowledge when their correlation with effective singing technique is observed in actual performance. To this end, all the internal mechanisms of the larynx are now to be reexamined in terms of foregoing descriptions so as to provide an improved image of their function for esthetic voice production.

Fixation of the Glottis for Singing

To produce a singing voice, it is first necessary to *stabilize* or immobilize the acoustical vibrator so that the source of sound may be under control. To achieve this result, all local interferences must be removed and the laryngeal mechanism restored to balanced operation that is responsive to the ear of the singer and compatible with the laws of nature.

Fixation of the glottal vibrator is achieved by means of a multiple positioning adjustment of the extrinsic musculature. Thus, the larynx is held in a stationary position in the throat where it can withstand variations of subglottic breath pressure during phonation without undue motion.

Within the larynx itself, four types of muscular action operate during the processes of tone production. They are called *adductor tension, longitudinal tension, glottal contraction,* and *abductor tension.* The coordination and balanced control of all these adjustments makes a singing tone possible.

The Cricoid Position

For singing purposes, the cricoid cartilage, which forms the base of the larynx, should be visualized as being cushioned against the smooth surface of the fifth (or sixth) cervical vertebra. It is drawn back into this position by certain external supports, later to be described. Weakness of these external supports causes instability of the entire larynx so that it wavers during phonation, much as the unsupported nozzle of a garden hose will be caused to wobble fitfully by the pressure of an escaping stream of water.

Action of the Arytenoids

The glottal aperture is opened, narrowed, or closed through the action of two posteriorly attached arytenoid cartilages. These twin arytenoids are interjoined by four sets of controlling muscles. They are the *transverse arytenoid* (interarytenoid), *oblique arytenoid, lateral arytenoid,* and *posterior arytenoid* muscles. They rotate the arytenoid cartilages outward on a vertical axis and control side-to-side movements, thereby separating the vocal processes and opening the glottis for normal inspiration or quick breath intake. They can also rotate the cartilages inward to close the glottis for phonation, and they also provide a backward longitudinal pull on the vocal cords during phonation.

Muscles controlling these parts are therefore facile enough to bring about rapid respiratory and phonatory adjustments. The arytenoid cartilages are the center of many operations in swallowing, breathing, and tone production, which gives evidence of their mobility in controlling the valving action of the larynx.

Thyroarytenoid Muscles

When adducted, the arc-shaped thyroarytenoid muscles or vocal ledges contract and thereby straighten themselves and close the glottis. In so doing, they brace themselves in such a way that the glottal margins swell slightly and thereby create a firmer contact of the vibrating edges.

However, as the pitch of the phonated tone ascends the scale, each glottal edge becomes progressively thinner due to an increasing longitudinal pull against the increasing contraction of its internal fibers.[1] The higher the pitch, the sharper the edge, until falsetto is reached. Ideally, throughout these adjustments the length of the vocal margins does not change.

The glottal margin itself thus increases or decreases its firmness, thickness, and width (not length) proportionately with the varying effort of phonation. As the intensity of the voice increases, more and more of the glottal margin oscillates to produce tone. For maximal vocal effort, the entire width of the thyroarytenoid muscle is brought into vibration.

Thyroid Cartilage

The thyroid cartilage is the largest part of the larynx. As previously described, its flat sides or wings are joined in front at a notched angle forming the adam's apple, and its widened posterior extremities are curved upward and downward in horn-like extensions. The upper horns reach to the posterior ends of the hyoid bone. The lower horns clasp the rear outer sides of the cricoid ring. The thyroid wings thus acquire a slight up-and-down eccentric rocking action upon pivots formed where their lower horns articulate with the rear outer sides of the cricoid base.

Attached to the exterior bilateral surfaces of the thyroid cartilage are a pair of *cricothyroid muscles* which originate in the front and lateral parts of the cricoid ring and extend obliquely backward and upward to the lower borders of the thyroid wings. These muscles, if unrestrained, could draw the thyroid cartilage forward (or tilt the cricoid ring backward) and thus increase the distance between the thyroid notch and the arytenoid cartilages. This would lengthen the vocal cords, if that were possible.

However, since any anterior downward pull on the thyroid cartilage would be opposed by the contraction of the thyroarytenoid muscles and by the muscularly controlled, resisting immobility of the arytenoid cartilages, the vocal ledges will maintain a *fixed* length during phonation. One group of muscles opposes the other and thereby provides elasticity and firmness in the contracting margins of the glottis without lengthening them. It is also apparent that the vocal shelves cannot be appreciably shortened in phonation, for they would then press together too tightly to allow musical vibrations to occur and a harsh grating sound would result.[2]

Furthermore, all these muscular interactions *within* the larynx are reinforced by *extrinsic* muscles later to be considered. A *crycothyroid ligament* also provides such reinforcement. This ligament is not a muscle, but a short, strong band connecting the cricoid and thyroid cartilages at their *anterior* ends.

The *cricothyroid ligament* is always in a state of springy tension, pulling downward upon the thyroid angle in order to balance the equally tense ligamentous sheaths of the vocal cords which pull the thyroid angle backward at a higher point. Here again, a balance between opposing tensions prevails, with a resultant stationary equilibrium of all parts. Obviously, this constant state of tension and mutual balance between the cricothyroid and vocal ligaments relieves the vocal muscles themselves of much work during phonation.

A pair of *lateral* cricothyroid ligaments also binds the posterior sides of the cricoid ring to the lower horns of the thyroid wings. Thus, the thyroid cartilage is firmly attached to the cricoid cartilage by two pairs of muscles and two sets of ligaments.

Hyoid Bone Connections

We come now to the horizontal U-shaped *hyoid bone* to which are attached many of the tongue muscles and other extrinsic muscles surrounding the larynx. The open ends of the hyoid bone extend rearward more widely than the spread of the thyroid wings below it.

A pair of *thyrohyoid muscles* connects each side of the thyroid cartilage with the front of the hyoid bone. Although they perform other functions for swallowing, these muscles are maintained in tonic contraction during tone production. In conjunction with other upward-pulling extrinsic muscles, they thus hold the thyroid and hyoid parts together during phonation.[3] Thus, the thyroid cartilage is firmly held against the under side of the hyoid bone while the singing tone is being produced. Therefore, whatever pulls on the hyoid bone will, in effect, pull on the thyroid cartilage, and vice versa.[4]

This bond is increased by the presence of a smooth connective *hyothyroid membrane* that fills the entire space between the upper edges of the thyroid wings and the upper inner edges of the hyoid bone. Another pair of elastic *thyrohyoid ligaments* connects the upper posterior horns of the thyroid cartilage with the posterior ends of the hyoid bone. The hyoid bone also has many extrinsic muscular attachments that help maintain its stability during tone production and thus indirectly affect the stability of the thyroid cartilage to which it is attached.

Therefore, to a certain extent, these extrinsic muscles affect the stability of the entire vocal vibrator. The directive "drop the jaw" often brings relief from the sensation of vocal strain because a dropped jaw apparently helps prevent the hyoid bone, and therefore the larynx, from being pulled forward in the neck and away from the spine. The dropped jaw, however, is a temporary palliative and not a natural device.

The Epiglottis

The epiglottis is also related to the laryngeal framework, since it connects the latter to the tongue. It is composed of elastic cartilage and lies just within the anterior curve of the hyoid bone to which it is attached. The upper third connects with the base of the tongue and the lower end is attached to the inside angle of the thyroid cartilage by means of the *thyroepiglottic ligament*. Thus, a bond is created between these parts. Since it is a cartilage, the epiglottis may also create a possible path of conductivity for the acoustical transmission of tonal vibration into the tongue muscles and head regions of the vocal tract. More of this later.

The upper part of the epiglottis is pressed backward against the base of the tongue during the act of swallowing. In the evolution of man, the epiglottis and uvula are considered vestiges of a former olfactory function in keen-scented animals. But these parts have no known present use.[5]

The *aryepiglottic folds* are membranous bands of muscle and ligament that extend backward and downward from the sides of the epiglottis around the tops of the arytenoid cartilages, thereby embracing a large section of the upper vestibule of the larynx. A considerable number of thyroarytenoid (vocalis) muscle fibers are prolonged into the aryepiglottic folds and some of them are continued to the margins of the epiglottis.

The area thus encircled by the aryepiglottic folds is narrowed more and more as vocal pitch ascends, due to contraction of these muscle fibers, thereby reinforcing the glottal closures needed for the upper range of the singing voice. This firming action is indispensable in the vigorous production of high tones, especially when they are to be sustained.

Vocally speaking, then, the tongue and the larynx are closely related, since the larynx is more firmly attached to the tongue than to any other muscle or organ. This concept of lingua-laryngeal unity is strengthened by a consideration of the extrinsic factors of resonation to be discussed later.

Finally, the larynx is lined with a layer of epithelium which closely adheres to all its underlying structures and is continuous over the surface of the true vocal cords. Numerous mucous glands are imbedded in this membranous lining, and especially in the epiglottis, thus providing a lubricant for the entire laryngeal surface.[6]

Breathing and Phonation

In order to correlate breathing controls with the foregoing analysis, the singer's breath is now to be considered a factor in tone production. Breath provides an air supply at the glottis that will satisfy at least three requirements. *First,* it must be sufficient in quantity to sustain a reasonably long tone or singing passage. *Second,* it must be under sufficient pressure to support any desired intensity of tone. *Third,* it must be applied at constant pressure to maintain evenness of tone. In other words, lung capacity must be adequate and the respiratory and abdominal muscles so strengthened and coordinated that a volume of air can be supplied at the glottis over a prolonged period and at a steady pressure.[7]

It should be repeated that breath pressure is not vocal substance. It is merely the mechanical agency used to activate the vocal vibrator. This force is directed to the glottal closure and gradually expended during phonation. But the actual issuance of breath from the glottis is in negligible quantity. Maximum sonancy always involves a *minimum* expenditure of breath, since the breathy tone is bad for singing.

Summarizing Conclusions

In summarizing this discussion of intrinsic mechanisms it is well to reiterate the following facts:

1. The so-called vocal cords are really the ligamentous and calloused sheaths and edges of the *vocalis muscles* which, in turn, form the medial vibrating margins of the larger *thyroarytenoid muscles*.
2. During quiet respiration, these muscles are retracted or *abducted* from each other and they assume a concave position of rest. While contracting for phonation, their edges are straightened out and approximated, or *adducted*.
3. They can be tensed, thickened, or thinned out by the contractility of their *internal* fibers, associated with the relative *fixity* of their points of attachment.
4. Coincidently with this tensing action, the vocal margins of the glottis are brought in contact with each other by the rotation, sliding, and tilting action of the twin arytenoid cartilages to which they are posteriorly attached.
5. This adduction is then assisted by the suction effect of subglottic air pressure and by the supporting contraction of adjacent and underlying muscles and ligaments.

Adductor muscles are those that help close the glottis. *Abductor muscles* have the function of opening the glottis. The *adductor* group are attached to the *thyroid, cricoid,* and *arytenoid* cartilages. They comprise:

    a. The *lateral cricoarytenoid muscles* (paired) which rotate the arytenoid extensions or vocal processes inward toward the midline and thus approximate the glottal edges for phonation.
    b. The *transverse interarytenoid* and *oblique in-*

terarytenoid muscles which slide the arytenoid cartilages toward each other to close the glottis for phonation.

c. The *thyroarytenoid (vocalis) muscles* which are bilaterally placed to form the vocal margins themselves. They extend from a common point of attachment at the thyroid cartilage, near the line of junction at the adam's apple, to the vocal processes of the twin arytenoid cartilages. They can be separated only at their posterior ends, by movements of the twin arytenoid pyramids to which they are attached.

As the degree of internal glottal contraction rises, the resistance of both end supports of the glottis increases proportionately. Thus, as the glottal margins stiffen, their elasticity will be increased. It will be recalled that when the extremities of a muscle are being pulled by extraneous forces which prevent it from shortening itself, the muscle, on contraction, will not thicken but actually becomes thinner, no matter how much it contracts. No doubt this principle influences the variation of vocal pitch during phonation.

The *posterior cricoarytenoid muscles* serve the function of *abduction* by opening the glottis. They rotate the arytenoid cartilages on a vertical axis, thus separating the vocal processes and, therefore, the vocal shelves, for quiet respiration.

It is important to remember, also, that the vocal act involves a fixation or holding of muscular positions, rather than a moving adjustment of parts. Much energy may, therefore, be expended during phonation, even though there is little or no actual movement within the entire vocal tract. In other words, the larynx remains relatively stationary in maintaining its position in the throat.

Furthermore, although its musculature is constantly varying in firmness and elasticity, there is no perceptible increase in the length of the glottis during phonation.

The thyroarytenoid and other muscles of the vocal tract are constantly in a state of mild, steady contraction (tonus). Therefore, they possess elasticity or resiliency at all times.

This inherent elasticity enables them to resist external pressures and return to their original shape.

Of course, a certain amount of free play, however slight, exists in all these adjustments of the vocal muscles. Flexibility and elasticity are always called for in vocal action, rather than rigidity and absolute immobility. A rigid muscle produces a hard metallic tone. A resilient or elastic (but not inert) muscle produces a warm, sonorous tone that is vibrant and endowed with proper vibrato characteristics. Rigidity dampens vibrato and destroys expressive quality of the voice. Therefore, the positions described above, although relatively stationary, allow for the natural resiliency of all functioning parts.

The dimensions of all these phonating parts are extremely small (e.g., the rima glottidis measures about four-fifths of an inch in the male adult; about three-fifths of an inch in the female). Therefore, they will not allow for prolonged, violent, or vigorous treatment with exercise material, and, of course, frequent periods of rest are mandatory, especially for the beginning singer.

Finally, the *intrinsic* laryngeal mechanism provides for the inception of vocal tone in its fundamental pitches only. A suitable system of amplifying and enhancing tonal quality must be provided by the vocal tract itself. These *extrinsic* parts, next to be considered, are directly related to phonation, and they also take part in reinforcing, augmenting, and beautifying the tones of the singing voice.

REFERENCES AND NOTES

1. Harry Holien, "A Laminagraphic Study of Vocal Pitch," *J. Speech and Hearing Res.* 3 (1960): 361–371.

2. John Howard, *The Physiology of Artistic Singing* (Boston: John Howard, 1886), p. 62.

3. *Morris' Human Anatomy*, 12th edition (New York: Blakiston Division, McGraw-Hill Book Company, 1966), pp. 227, 331, 1417.

4. Howard, *Artistic Singing*, p. 91.

5. V. E. Negus, *The Mechanism of the Larynx* (London: Heinemann Medical Books, 1957), p. 449.

6. Henry Gray, *Anatomy of the Human Body*, 27th edition (Philadelphia: Lea & Febiger, 1959), p. 1187.

7. Negus, *Larynx*, p. 436; "Photographing the Vocal Cords," *Science* 91 (No. 2374, Supp. 8, June 28, 1940).

VII

External Mechanisms of the Larynx

We have learned thus far that the larynx is an important and sensitive, though complicated organ. Its complexity results from the necessity of coordinating many functions, like swallowing, coughing, sneezing, gasping, yawning, and other reflexes within a small area of the body. But the larynx could not work efficiently without a system of *external* supports that hold it at a position in the throat most suited to effective action and, at the same time, reinforce its internal functions.[1]

To fulfill these requirements, an intricate network of external or extrinsic muscular attachments is provided. Each of them is fastened at one end to some rigid element of the larynx and at the other end to some extraneous point of the vocal tract. These external attachments are indispensable to phonation.[2] When they are severed or paralyzed, as in disease or injury, singing is virtually impossible.[3]

This external muscular network is more complex than the internal structure of the larynx, and its analysis therefore requires considerable care. Each structural element, in conjunction with its extrinsic attachments, plays an equal part in the act of tone production. No single muscle can be moved or affected locally without displacing and influencing the adjustment of some other muscle. Nor can any single cartilage or bone in the entire vocal tract be moved without influencing the contraction of its supporting muscles.

It is also probable that the extrinsic musculature can perform an acoustical service by enlarging the area of tonal vibration. That is to say, the vibrations of sounds generated by the glottis can be transmitted directly to outlying portions of the body by bone and muscle conduction, and thus reinforced to satisfy the acoustical requirements of artistic singing.[4] This service will be discussed later as a factor in vocal acoustics and resonation.

From a singer's standpoint, therefore, the *extrinsic* vocal muscles may serve a triple function: a) to support the laryngeal framework in a position favorable to tone production; b) to assist in maintaining stability of the vibrator under the constant pressure of subglottic air; and c) to increase the vibratory area of phonation. These three areas of interest motivate the discussions that follow.

Laryngeal Action Related to External Supports

In its simplest aspects, the larynx consists of a ring-shaped base upon which three upright, hinged hitching posts are resting (one anterior and two posterior). Between these uprights, the paired vocal cords or glottal muscles are stretched. During phonation, the internal fibers of the glottal muscles contract and pull on their extremities, while a simultaneous leaning-*outward* of the end supports produces a longitudinal pull. This action is brought about by tiny muscles that control the uprights to which the glottal extremities are attached.

However, the intrinsic laryngeal musculature can achieve glottal adjustment by its own contractile strength only when it is assisted by the stabilizing and positioning power of external laryngeal attachments.[5] Fixity of the laryngeal base (cricoid cartilage) is first established so that intrinsic moving parts may have a relatively stationary platform upon which to operate. The larynx is also *retracted* against the cervical spine by the normal backward slant of certain suspensory muscles.

Anatomical and physiological conditions of the vocal tract

favor a motionless larynx for singing. It will be observed, for example, that the broad back of the cricoid cartilage, cushioned posteriorly against the collapsed esophageal entrance, accommodates itself to the smooth front surface of the fifth and sixth cervical vertebrae. The spinal area at this point is especially free from muscles and therefore provides a contact surface for the posterior cricoid plate. Furthermore, the curvature of the cervical spine brings the vertebral column more nearly forward at this point, where it will contact the larynx. It will also be noted that the spine curves backwards and recedes slightly from the larynx both above and below the fifth or sixth cervical vertebra.[6]

It also follows that if the larynx were to be drawn either upward or downward, the extrinsic muscles would be either lengthened or shortened beyond their normal length and thereby proportionately weakened. The importance of maintaining a stationary position of the larynx is therefore apparent. This factor should be kept in mind while studying the following descriptive summaries.

EXTRINSIC MUSCLES REVIEWED

Some twenty-five muscles are discussed in four groupings as *retractors, projectors, depressors,* and *elevators* of the larynx. All are directly or indirectly attached to the larynx. All but the uvula (musculus uvulae) and the mylohyoid occur in bilateral pairs. This is not a complete anatomical survey, since only those parts and functions that are directly related to the processes of phonation and resonation are considered.

Laryngeal Retractors

The entire larynx is retracted by downward and backward inclinations of the *omohyoid* (shoulder blade to hyoid bone) muscles, counterbalanced above by the upward and backward inclinations of the *stylohyoid* (cranium to hyoid bone) muscles. The cricoid cartilage is positioned against the spine by this retraction, and this position is reinforced by connections to the *inferior* and *middle constrictors*. The muscular entrance to the esophagus has attachments at the cricoid and thyroid cartilages and at the hyoid bone. It remains in tonic contraction during phonation and relaxes only during swallowing.[7]

The larynx will, therefore, tend to seek its position against the spine as a *point d'apui* for maintaining the balanced coordination of all its extrinsic supports.

Laryngeal Projectors

Three layers of paired *forward*-pulling hyoidal muscles lie at the floor of the mouth. All are unfriendly to phonation. All have their anterior ends attached to some part of the lower jaw. All are attached to the hyoid bone and therefore can affect the position of the larynx. Part of their function, normally, is to assist in opening the mouth by pulling the jaw downward. In this, they operate as antagonists to other jaw-closing muscles. These hyoidal muscles also assist in swallowing actions by pulling the larynx forward to open the mouth of the esophagus. If used during phonation, however, these hyoidal muscles can cause a forward displacement of the hyoid bone, thereby dragging the larynx away from the spine. They could also restrain the downward-tilting action of the hyoid bone and thyroid cartilage and thus impair the cord-stretching functions of the latter.

a. The bottom layer is the *digastric* (cranium to hyoid bone to chin), so called because it has two bellies (really two muscles) joined together near the hyoid bone by a tendon that is attached to the latter. The posterior or longer belly starts from the cranium, near the styloid process, and extends downward and forward to its hyoidal connection. Here it changes its direction as its anterior belly turns boldly forward and slightly upward to fasten itself upon the inner side of the chin. The forward belly of the digastric should remain immobilized during phonation, with no tension or contraction felt under the chin. The posterior belly may have the effect of counterbalancing the downward-pulling sternohyoid muscle.

b. The *mylohyoid* (lower jaw to hyoid bone) muscle constitutes most of the floor of the mouth, being attached to the inner periphery of the lower jaw. Some of its fibers extend backward and downward from near the back teeth and fasten themselves to the hyoid bone. They can also pull the latter forward with harmful vocal results similar to those caused by the anterior belly of the digastric muscle. The mylohyoid muscle should therefore be inactive and flaccid during tone production.

c. The *geniohyoid* (chin to hyoid bone) muscle lies above the mylohyoid and below the tongue. It, too, having similar connections, will draw the hyoid bone forward with detrimental vocal effect. It should therefore be completely relaxed for singing.

The under-chin area may be tested, from time to time, to determine whether tensions are present during voice production. In general, the jaw muscles are relaxed when singing, and the jaw dropped (not forced) open inertly.

Laryngeal Depressors

Five infrahyoidal or infralaryngeal attachments are to be considered for their possible effects on the larynx during the producion of a singing tone. They all connect with *lower* parts of the body and, in a sense, can counterbalance the upward-pulling extrinsic muscles of the larynx.

a. A pair of *omohyoid* muscles provide *downward*-pulling connections between the larynx and the shoulder blades. These muscles arise from the upper border of each scapula. They pass across the lower part of the neck, change their direction through a clavicular attachment, and travel more vertically upward to be inserted in the anterior curve of the hyoid bone.

Consequently, because of their direction, they exert a *downward* and *backward* pull on the hyoid bone. They can also reinforce the downward-tilting action of the thyroid cartilage and thus become a supporting element of the pitch-raising mechanism of the larynx. Poor posture of the singer's body with stooping, rounded shoulders can unduly stretch and weaken the omohyoid muscles and impair their usefulness, especially in the higher range of the voice.

b. A pair of *sternothyroid* muscles extend from the top of the sternum to both sides of the thyroid cartilage. They pull *downward* upon the larynx in an almost vertical direction. Their insertion is just above the cricothyroid pivot joint. Therefore, they have no direct influence on pitch adjustment because they could not tilt the thyroid cartilage. However, their main function would be to help maintain stability of the laryngeal position and to counterbalance the upward pull of suprahyoidal muscles.

c. A pair of *sternohyoid* muscles reach from the sternum and the clavicles, at one end, to the anterior curve of the hyoid bone, at the other.[8] Since hyoid bone and thyroid cartilage function as a unit for singing, downward pull on the anterior hyoid bone would supplement any downward-pulling action of the cricothyroid muscles. This combination would, therefore, materially assist in the maintenance of a firm glottal closure.

The flat-chest posture is detrimental in singing because it depresses the breastbone and thereby unduly stretches both sternohyoid and sternothyroid muscles which impairs their usefulness in phonation and pitch control. All down-pulling attachments are adversely affected by poor posture.

d. As heretofore mentioned, the circular entrance to the esophagus is part of the lower constrictor. It is known as the *cricopharyngeal sphincter*. Here there are esophageal attachments to the cricoid plate and to the apical tips of the arytenoid (corniculate cartilages). Hence, tonic contraction of the *cricopharyngeus muscle* could have a gentle retracting and depressing influence on the larynx.[9]

e. The *lower* esophagus can also be firmly held by the

sphincteric closure of diaphragmatic muscles that surround it in what is known as the esophageal hiatus. When the esophagus is thus held and its longitudinal fibers contracted, it becomes a possible laryngeal depressor. It is also possible that the cricopharyngeus muscle may reinforce fixation of the arytenoid cartilages during phonation, especially in the production of high tones when the pull on the arytenoids is maximal.

The *trachea* is a freely extensible tube and may therefore be ignored as a downward-pulling influence. Since the larynx sits upon the entrance to the trachea as a pulmonary valving device, any attempt to elevate the larynx will have the effect of lengthening the trachea during phonation and might therefore decrease thoracic air pressure. Such variations of breath pressure can cause off-pitch singing.

Laryngeal Elevators

The upward-pulling external attachments of the larynx comprise some fourteen sets of muscles, all of which reach into the mouth and head and find attachment at three different levels: *lingual, palatal,* and *cranial*. Because of the complexity of their combined actions, they will be discussed in two categories, i.e., in relation to the *tongue*, on the one hand, and to the *palate and cranium* on the other. Possible laryngeal influences will also be considered.

It should be noted, also, that some of these laryngeal elevators form an interconnected chain that extends from larynx to cranium by means of flexible junctures at the tongue and palate. Thus, larynx to tongue to palate to cranium may be described as a *continuous* system of muscles from which the larynx is suspended in the throat. Four intrinsic tongue muscles may also be included in this interconnected system, although they are not directly involved as elevators of the larynx.

Furthermore, the *stylohyoid* muscle, already mentioned above as a laryngeal retractor, may also serve as an elevator, since its course is backward and *upward* from the anterior portion of the hyoid bone to the cranium (styloid process). Its action can therefore counterbalance the downward-pulling action of the infrahyoid muscles (e.g., *sternohyoid* and *omohyoid*).

Lingual Muscles

The tongue is a powerful organ of great size and mobility. Its shape can be changed at will and to a marked degree. It is extensible and retractable. It can be pressed upward and forward. It can be held in flattened, arched, and hollowed positions, and can be grooved either transversely or longitudinally. It can be thickened or thinned, stretched outward or bunched into the back of the mouth and pharynx. Obviously, its great flexibility of movement is the resultant of many different musuclar components, acting either singly or in various combinations. The tongue is also bound to the chin, the floor of the mouth, the pharynx, the epiglottis, the palate, and the cranium by means of muscular strands and extensions of the membranous surfaces that cover its entire body.

The lingual body is composed of eight bilateral pairs of interlaced muscles, four *intrinsic* and four *extrinsic*. The intrinsic muscles are contained wholly *within* the tongue and are known as *superior longitudinal, inferior longitudinal, vertical,* and *transverse*. They are active in the articulation of speech sounds and in the handling of food, but are not directly involved in normal processes of phonation. Therefore, it is possible to articulate most speech sounds without disturbing phonation. The intrinsic lingual muscles can change the length, width, and thickness of the tongue in its longitudinal, vertical, and transverse dimensions. They can also contract alternately on one side only and cause a side-to-side wagging of the front of the tongue.

The extrinsic tongue muscles, on the other hand, form part of the chain of laryngeal *elevators*. As such, they are important to the singer. They can influence the position and stability of the larynx and affect the control of pitch. They are inserted into the tongue body bilaterally, four on each side, and interlaced with its intrinsic muscles. The four paired *ex-*

trinsic lingual muscles are named *hyoglossus, styloglossus, palatoglossus,* and *genioglossus,* respectively. Each will be briefly discussed in terms of vocal function:

a. The *hyoglossi* extend from rear portions and horns of the hyoid bone into and along the sides of the tongue. Here they are joined by *upward*-pulling *styloglossi* that connect the tongue with the cranium. Their combined action draws the rear portion of the tongue *backward* and slightly *upward,* thereby forming a strong bond between the cranium and the horns of the hyoid bone.

When the posterior horns of the hyoid bone are thus pulled upward, the front part of the larynx will be tilted downward. This can reinforce the cord-stretching action of the thyroid cartilage. The hyoglossus muscles may therefore have an important function in phonation in that they reinforce the cord-stretching action of the pitch-adjusting mechanisms of the larynx, provided, of course, the cricoid base retains its stationary position against the spine.

b. The *styloglossi* are a bilateral pair extending from the cranium downward and decidedly forward into and along the sides of the tongue, nearly reaching to its tip. Each muscle is fastened at its upper end to a pen-like bony projection, or *stylus,* at the base of the skull, just above and in front of the ear. Some of its fibers blend with those of the hyoglossi at their point of juncture.

These styloglossi serve to draw the tongue *backward* as well as *upward.* Combined with hyoglossi and genioglossi muscles they form a connecting bond between cranium and hyoid bone.

It is interesting to observe that a well-trained singer will produce a slight hump-like elevation in the *posterior* lingual surface during sustained dynamic intonation, at any pitch level. This posterior muscular mound becomes increasingly firm as pitch ascends. It is produced by contractions at the lingual juncture, where the styloglossi curve upward and the hyoglossi curve downward.

The student will therefore note that, if the rear surface of the tongue becomes grooved or depressed during phonation, there is evidence of malfunctioning of these two essential tongue muscles. Under such conditions, artistic tone delivery becomes impossible. There are other acoustical reasons for maintaining this arched or elevated *back-tongue* position, later to be explained. [The *palatoglossi* (glossopalatini) will be described later under the heading of *palatal* muscles.]

    c. The *genioglossi* form the greater part of the tongue. They mushroom outward and backward from the chin, and most of their fibers curve upward and terminate in the tongue itself. A few fibers at the bottom extend straight back and are attached to the hyoid bone.[10]

Most of this tongue muscle can perform useful vocal services. But the few strands that attach to the hyoid bone can draw the latter forward in the same manner as the geniohyoid muscles and with the same harmful effects. The area under the chin must, therefore, be kept completely inert for singing, even when the tongue is actively at work.

Those fibers of the genioglossi which extend into the body of the tongue can provide a fulcrum for upward- and backward-pulling styloglossi. The former oppose the latter and this opposition is reflected in sympathetic contraction of the forward-extending fibers of the tongue, with a resultant upturning of the tongue tip, especially in sustained dynamic singing and in high-range passages of the voice. The student will note that the upturning of the tongue tip is not a voluntary action, but merely the index of correct lingua-laryngeal coordination when singing in full voice.

Palatal and Cranial Muscles

    The soft palate is composed of a rather soft muscular surface which separates the mouth from the nasal cavity. It is attached to the posterior edges of the hard palate and is made up of interlacing fibers of four pairs of muscles that converge into this roof-like surface. Two pairs of muscles stretch downward equilibrium is again maintained and the level of the soft palate remains unchanged. Narrowing of the anterior and posterior palatine arches and the drawing together of the faucial walls and pillars would normally result from the proper contraction of these palatal muscles. This is a correct mechanism for singing. The notion of an *open throat* for voice production is fallacious because it advises relaxing the very efforts needed to adjust the vibrating parts of the larynx for adequate vocal performance.

   f. The *levator veli palatini* are attached to the temporal bones of the skull at points above and behind the palate. From here they extend in a downward, forward, and slightly inward curve to either side of the soft palate into which they are inserted. Their fibers spread out and meet internally from opposite sides of the palate. Some fibers also fasten upon the posterior edges of the hard palate. With such firm upward supports, the soft palate can resist considerable downward pull of all other extrinsic laryngeal muscles. Therefore, both levator-palatal and pharyngo-palatal actions indirectly contribute a firm support to the larynx during phonation.

   These two pairs of muscles also unite to close the posterior entrance into the nasal passages by pulling the soft palate (and uvula) backward against the rear wall of the pharynx (Passavant's cushion). Thus, closure of the nasal pharynx can be effected without raising the soft palate. These two pairs of muscles oppose each other in a state of equilibrium and allow neither upward nor downward movement of the soft palate during phonation. Ideally, all contracting muscles remain at their natural length, where they are strongest.

   The passage from mouth to nasal cavity (through the posterior nares) is normally closed during phonation,[11] except in the production of nasal consonants and nasal tones (e.g., French vowels), and in nose breathing.

   g. The *tensor veli palatini* are a pair of muscles fastened above to the cartilaginous walls of the Eustachian tubes and adjacent parts of the skull. They descend almost perpendicularly and then change their direction around a tiny bony projection and two upward. The downward-reaching muscles are the *palatoglossi* and *pharyngopalatini*. The upward-reaching pairs have attachments in different parts of the cranium and are named *levator veli palatini* and *tensor veli palatini*. There is a fifth single muscle, the *musculus uvulae* (azygos uvulae) commonly called the *uvula*. Since most of these muscles occur in pairs, they will be described in plural rather than singular terms:

    d. The *palatoglossi,* also known as *glossopalatini,* form the anterior pillars of the *fauces,* which forms the narrow passageway from mouth to pharynx. As their name indicates, these muscles extend from soft palate to tongue. As they descend, they diverge outward and then inward in an arc-like curve. Hence, upon contraction, they will straighten themselves, thereby causing a slight *narrowing* of the anterior pillars of the fauces, which is a correct mechanism for singing. Some of their fibers are laterally inserted into the tongue. Others extend along the sides of the tongue, blending with styloglossi fibers already described.

    Any attempt to keep the rear mouth cavity open as wide as possible while singing would, of course, defeat the narrowing action of the faucial muscles, thereby weakening the entire chain of external laryngeal supports. Tonal support would also suffer. The so-called open-throat effort can therefore cause a harmful interference to good phonation.

    e. The *pharyngopalatine* muscles extend from the soft palate directly to the larynx. They are attached to the rear borders of the thyroid cartilage. Since the soft palate lies forward of this point, this muscle can exert a strong leverage to tilt the thyroid cartilage forward upon its cricothyroid joint, thus supporting the longitudinal cord-stretching effort that is needed in pitch adjustment.

    The pharyngopalatini also exert considerable downward pull on the soft palate during phonation. This action, therefore, is opposed by an equivalent contraction of upward-pulling palatal muscles, next to be described. Thus, a *stationary* just behind the upper jaw, passing horizontally into the soft palate and extending into its ligamentous connection with the hard palate. These muscles can be contracted with considerable force and, in phonation, they act to prevent the soft palate from being displaced by the downward-pulling glossopalatini and pharyngopalatini.

h. The *musculus uvulae*, a cranial-palatal muscle, forms the greater part of the pendant fleshy lobe or *uvula* in the middle of the rear border of the soft palate. It extends vertically downward from the posterior nasal septum bone into the uvular lobe itself. Upon contraction, it draws the whole uvula upward into the palate. This creates a firmer *upward* support during phonation, thus enabling the soft palate to withstand the *down-pulling* action of tongue and laryngeal muscles. Its normal contraction during phonation is merely an indication of gradually increasing resistance to downward-pulling palatal muscles. The uvula may all but disappear into the soft palate during the singing of an ascending scale. This is a correct mechanism and should not be molested by conscious controls.

i. The *stylopharyngeus* (cranium to larynx) muscles extend from their origin in the cranium, near the ears, directly downward to the rear horns of the thyroid cartilage. At their lower ends these paired muscles are united with the pharyngopalatini, adding to the upward-pulling force of the latter and having the same effects as the latter upon the tilting and pitch-adjusting action of the thyroid cartilage. It should be restated that the membranous and muscular interconnections between the hyoid bone and the thyroid cartilage insure a unified action of these two parts of the larynx for singing purposes.

j. Finally, the *stylohyoids,* already discussed as *retractor* muscles, complete this series of laryngeal *elevators*. Their dual function as retractors and elevators is obvious, since their direction is *backward* and *upward* from the anterior curved horns on the hyoid bone to the cranium (styloid processes). The suspensory function of these muscles also contributes a partial counterbalancing of downward-pulling infrahyoid muscles (sternohyoid and omohyoid).

The Pharynx and Mouth

To complete this anatomical survey of the vocal tract, it is necessary to include reference to the pharynx and mouth, since these areas lie adjacent to the phonating mechanisms of the larynx. These cavities and their vibrating surfaces can contribute materially to the sonority and resonance of the singer's voice, and also provide continuity and connection to other essential parts of the phonating mechanism.

The *pharynx* is a conical tube located behind the nasal cavity, mouth, and larynx. It is considered part of the digestive tract and carries food from the mouth to the esophagus. The pharynx extends from the under surface of the skull downward to the level of the cricoid cartilage; and its tube-like surface, which narrows with descent, is in direct communication with seven other cavities, namely, two nasal cavities, two middle-ear cavities, the mouth, the larynx, and the esophagus. It is identified at three different levels as: 1) nasal pharynx; 2) oral pharynx; and 3) laryngeal pharynx. In an average adult, the entire pharynx is about five inches long, being almost equal in size to the mouth or oral cavity.[12]

The six sets of muscles that form the surface of the pharynx are the superior, middle, and inferior constrictors, and the paired stylopharyngeus, salpingopharyngeus, and pharyngopalatinus muscles. Of these, the previously mentioned *inferior constrictor, stylopharyngeus,* and *pharyngopalatinus* are directly connected with parts of the thyroid and cricoid cartilages, and are therefore in the laryngeal chain of external supporting muscles.

The overlapping middle and superior constrictors are active in mechanisms of swallowing. The *middle constrictor* has part of its origin along the horns of the hyoid bone although it is not otherwise directly connected to the larynx. The salpingopharyngeus likewise does not directly connect with the larynx. However, some of its fibers blend with the pharyngopalatinus muscle, whose lower extremities are inserted into the posterior border of the thyroid cartilage.

The mouth, oral or *buccal cavity,* is bounded by many muscles and parts: anteriorly by lips, gums, and teeth, and laterally by the cheeks. Its roof is formed by the hard and soft palates, and its floor by the tongue and membranous extensions thereof. Muscles of the lips and face are listed elsewhere, for reference only, since they do not function directly in the external musculature or phonatory mechanisms.

Finally, the *fauces* form the narrow passageway from mouth to pharynx. The arched soft palate is its upper boundary. The back of the tongue is its floor, and on either side are two vertical muscular curves that form the anterior and posterior pillars of the fauces. The tonsils are located in a recess between these two faucial pillars. As previously described, the faucial muscles contract during phonation for singing and are thereby correctly straightened inward with resultant narrowing of the faucial passageway.

Conclusions for Singing

In summation, the foregoing descriptions of the complex tonal generator indicate that both intrinsic and external muscular systems combine to support the four basic actions (not movements) essential for artistic singing:

    1. holding the cricoid cartilage (and larynx) backward and stationary against the spine;
    2. tilting the hyoid bone and thyroid cartilage in a forward and downward direction;
    3. tilting the arytenoid cartilages in a backward direction;
    4. adducting and tensing the vocal cords.

The teacher should visualize this coordinated action as a balanced muscular response, a synergic action that is mentally controlled and dictated by hearing concepts, a vocal output that is coordinated with the breathing controls previously described.

It is now apparent that *equilibrium* is an essential feature in the functioning of the entire apparatus. This is evidenced by the construction of the vocal tract itself. Any backward movement that could be imparted to the larynx by its external muscles is checked by its pressure against the *spine*. Its upward movement is checked by several sets of *downward*-pulling muscles. Its downward movement is prevented by a network of *upward*-pulling muscles. Its forward movement is likewise restrained by divergent *backward*-slanting muscular attachments. The resultant of all these counteractions is a state of equilibrium in which the larynx is held in a relatively low position and in which nothing moves appreciably.[13] The vocal instrument is the center of this intricate network of positioning and suspensory muscles and ligaments, whose primary function is to connect the larynx, like guy wires, to more stable portions of the body.

The singer's development is based on a gradual cultivation of vocal resources, at all levels of pitch and dynamics, without doing violence to these muscular controls that normally operate in the vocal tract. Any dislodgement of parts or changes in the balanced interplay of positioning muscles is not to be tolerated at any time. Such faults as register breaks, tremulous quality, forced intonation, and pitch strain inevitably appear when an imbalance occurs. For this reason, the teacher should work to establish balance and coordination as a permanent habit of artistic performance.

Neurological Aspects Considered[14]

There is a constant interplay between functioning elements of the vocal tract and the singer's mind. The results of voice production are perceived mentally, from moment to moment, by the singer himself, and the singer's ear and brain direct his own control of vocal action. These controls depend, in large measure, on conditioned reflexes that are essential in the learning process and in the formation of habits.

Obviously, neurological factors in singing are too intricate for detailed analysis in this treatise. Nevertheless, certain highlights of the nervous system are mentioned for guidance in further study, and to remind the teacher that there is a complex nervous apparatus that regulates and governs the learning process.

Basically, all the responses of a singer are but the products of acquired habits, reflexes, and the learned association of ideas acquired through repetitive training and practice. The intelligence of the individual, his attention, perception, and level of consciousness and the type of training he receives will, in the long run, determine the effectiveness of all these responses, and vice versa. Thus, education, study, learning, and drill leave an imprint on the nervous system that preconditions all phases of thinking and feeling, and all types of vocal expression.

The main nerve supply to the laryngeal muscles is through branches of the fifth, seventh, tenth, and twelfth cranial nerves. Other speech and respiratory muscles are innervated, wholly or in part, by cervical and thoracic spinal nerves.

The tenth cranial or *vagus nerve* is especially important. It separates into a *superior branch* and an *inferior* or *recurrent* branch. The superior branch supplies the cricothyroid muscle of the larynx and the inferior constrictor (cricopharyngeus muscle). The inferior or recurrent branch innervates all the intrinsic muscles of the larynx except the cricothyroid muscle. The vagus nerve is also one of the main conveyors of nervous energy to the vocal organs, pharynx, lungs, esophagus, alimentary canal, and heart. Hence, psychosomatic reactions of all these organs are sometimes related to the vocal function (e.g., stage fright).

The eighth cranial nerve is related to the hearing function. The principal speech-song articulation and comprehension centers are believed to be located in a lateral portion of the frontal lobe of the cerebrum (Broca's area) and in the posterior parietal-temporal zone (Wernicke's area).

A *reflex action* is an involuntary response to a sensory

stimulus. It is caused when a direct neural pathway exists between the sensory area and the responding mechanism, without the intervention of consciousness. Reflexes are often inborn and are also the basis of emotional response and conditioned behavior in man.

A *conditioned reflex* is an action or response that is acquired through often-repeated association of a particular stimulus with a specific result. This type of neural conditioning is the basis of habit formation and learning.

There are also great association areas embedded in the cerebral hemispheres of the brain, which provide regulatory centers for the coordination and integration of the entire vocal mechanism as it is used to express the ideas and feelings associated with singing and speaking. These centers also control the frequency and intensity of the nervous impulses that activate the muscles of expression.

Since artistic singing depends on the coordination of a hundred or more muscles of the body, it is apparent that both mental and physical health are paramount. In other words, the rapid transmission of nervous impulses, their proper interpretation and coordination in the brain, and the requisite stimulation of all muscles that are essential to the vocal act demand optimal health and efficiency of the entire nervous system. Hence, any form of intemperance, abuse, excess, or anything that is deleterious to mental or emotional stability or physical health may seriously disturb the vocal reflexes of the singer.

Finally, since we have little or no conscious control over the vocal cords or any detailed part of the larynx during phonation, a knowledge of the parts thereof is not considered necessary in order to be able to sing. On the other hand, it is almost mandatory that the teacher of singing be made aware of those fundamental parts and principles that apply to the operation and control of the mechanisms of phonation and ear training. Occasionally, it may be advantageous for the pupil to know some of them also, but only as a means of achieving better understanding of the learning process, never as an end in itself.

Resumé of Muscles
Related to Vocal Expression in Singing[15]

The seventy-seven sets of muscles here listed (most of them paired) are arranged in twelve categories for study and review.

Category	Items	Names of Muscles
lips and facial	11	zygomaticus major; zygomaticus minor; buccinator; caninus; mentalis; orbicularis oris; platysma; quadratus labii inferioris; quadratus labii superioris; risorius; triangularis
mandibular (jaw)	4	external pterygoid; internal pterygoid; masseter; temporalis
pharyngeal	6	superior constrictor; middle constrictor; inferior constrictor; cricopharyngeus; salpingopharyngeus; stylopharyngeus
palatal	5	musculus uvulae; pharyngopalatinus; glossopalatinus; tensor veli palatini; levator veli palatini
lingual	8	genioglossus; hyoglossus; glossopalatinus; styloglossus; longitudinalis superior; longitudinalis inferior; transversus; verticalis
suprahyoidal	6	digastric anterior; digastric posterior; genioglossus; hyoglossus; mylohyoid; stylohyoid
infrahyoidal	4	omohyoid; sternohyoid; sternothyroid; thyrohyoid
intrinsic laryngeal	5	thyroarytenoid (vocalis, thyroepiglottic, ventricularis segments); arytenoid (transverse, oblique, aryepiglottic segments); posterior cricoarytenoid; lateral cricoarytenoid; cricothyroid
respiratory (thoracic)	12	diaphragm; subclavius; subcostales; intercostalis externi; intercostalis interni; levatores costarum; pectoralis major; pectoralis minor; serratus anterior; transversus thoracis; serratus posterior inferior; serratus posterior superior

Category	Items	Names of Muscles
respiratory (abdominal)	4	obliquus externus; obliquus internus; transversus abdominis; rectus abdominis
respiratory (neck)	5	scalenus anterior; scalenus medius; scalenus posterior; sternoceidomastoid; levator scapulae
respiratory (back)	7	trapezius; latissimus dorsi; sacrospinalis; rhomboideus major; rhomboideus minor; quadratus lumborum; deltoid (if the arm is abducted)

REFERENCES AND NOTES

1. V. E. Negus, *The Mechanism of the Larynx* (London: Heinemann Medical Books, 1957), pp. 382, 447, 466.

2. Aatto Sonninen, "The Role of the External Laryngeal Muscles in Length-adjustment of the Vocal Cords," *Acta-Otolaryngologica,* Suppl. 130 (Stockholm, 1956): 96.

3. R. R. Sokolowsky, "Effect of the Extrinsic Laryngeal Muscles on Voice Production," *Arch. Otolaryngol.* 38 (1943): 355.

4. John Howard, *The Physiology of Artistic Singing* (Boston: John Howard, 1886), pp. 91, 98, 114, 251.

5. E. L. Kenyon, "Significance of the Extrinsic Musculature of the Larynx," *J. Amer. Med. Assn.* 79 (1922): 428–430.

6. K. Faaborg-Andersen and A. Sonninen, "The Function of the Extrinsic Laryngeal Muscles at Different Pitch Levels," *Acta-Otolaryngol.* (Stockholm, 1960): 51, 89.

7. Sir Victor Negus, *Biology of Respiration* (Edinburgh: E. & S. Livingstone Ltd., 1965), p. 60.

8. Henry Gray, *Anatomy of the Human Body,* 27th edition (Philadelphia: Lea & Febiger, 1959), pp. 185, 434.

9. Negus, *Respiration,* p. 380; Gray, *Anatomy,* pp. 1185, 1249.

10. Gray, *Anatomy,* p. 1235.

11. Negus, *Respiration,* p. 440.

12. Gray, *Anatomy*, p. 1241, 1247.

13. Raoul Husson, "Special Physiology in Singing with Power," *The NATS Bulletin* (Oct. 1957): 14.

14. Joseph G. Chusid and Joseph J. McDonald, *Correlative Neuroanatomy and Functional Neurology*, 11th edition (Los Altos, Calif.: Lange Medical Publications, 1962).

15. *Morris' Human Anatomy*, 12th edition (New York: Blakiston Division, McGraw-Hill Book Company, 1966), passim.

VIII

Vocal Acoustics and Resonance

The act of singing has its beginnings in the desire to express oneself vocally in accordance with a fixed musical purpose. This impulse is governed by the ear and produces a reaction of vibratory energy in the glottis that is known as phonation. Obviously, the perception of sound, a mental phenomenon, plays an important role in the functioning of the vocal apparatus. Psychological, physiological, perceptual, and acoustical aspects of tone production, therefore, become important parameters of investigation in the field of vocal pedagogy.

A teacher of singing will find it profitable to review the elements of acoustics as applied to the singing voice and, to this end, the following synoptic overview is presented, with special reference to such vocal factors as pitch, intensity, quality, and resonance.

Sound is defined as the interpretation by the brain of a succession of vibratory disturbances in the atmosphere that are generated by a tremulous or elastic body and capable of being heard.[1] The tremulous body may be the string of a violin, the reed of a clarinet, the taut fleshy muscles in the lips of a bugler, or the vibrating edges of the human glottis. In each case, the pulsations of an acoustical generator induce a rapid succession of tiny compressions and rarefactions in the atmosphere which travel away from their source as fast as they are generated until they reach the ear of a listener. The human ear translates these atmospheric pulsations or pressure waves into sound.

It is energy, not matter or mass, that is thus propagated. However, friction in the transmission route will cause a decrease in the total energy delivered to the ears of the listener. This friction produces damped oscillations and thus lessens the rate of propagation. On the other hand, acoustical reinforcement may result from reflecting sufaces, resonators, and other physical conditions that favor and reinforce the transmitted sound wave. The listener's ear is influenced by the *end product* of this chain reaction and thus receives a hearing sensation which is transmitted to the inner ear and delivered to the brain.

Therefore, the three basic acoustical requirements for sound production are: 1) a vibrating generator or source; 2) an elastic transmission medium of air, liquid, or solid which is in contact with the vibrating source; and 3) a receiving agent capable of perceiving and interpreting the vibratory energy received, i.e., its intensity, frequency, wave form, etc.[2]

It takes one cycle of compression and rarefaction in the atmosphere to complete one pulsation or sound wave. If the pulsations are rapid enough and periodic, that is, recurring at regularly spaced intervals of time, the sound is musical. If irregular pulsations are generated, the resultant sound is noise. Musical sound, therefore, involves periodic oscillations of elastic energy between a musical instrument and a listener.

When musical sound has definite pitch and individual character it is called a *tone*. Each tone may be *simple,* as from a tuning fork, or *complex,* as from a musical instrument like the violin, trombone, or human voice.

A *simple* sound wave possesses physical properties of *frequency* and *intensity*. *Frequency* is defined as the number of oscillations, pulsations, or cycles which occur in one unit of time. The magnitude or amplitude of each vibratory swing of a generator determines the *intensity* of sound.

Variations of frequency basically determine the pitch of

the sound that is heard, while the sensation of loudness is largely dependent upon intensity. In other words, *pitch* is the subjective or perceptual measurement of vibratory frequency, while *loudness* is the subjective or perceptual measurement of vibratory intensity. The former is measured in cycles per second or Hertzian units (Hz). The latter is measured in decibels (db), a symbol that relates sound pressure to energy output.

The audible pitch range lies approximately between 20 and 20,000 Hz. Beyond this limit sounds become shrill, piercing, and even painful to hear. The range of intensity from *ppp* to *fff* is about from 40 to 100 db.[3]

The conventional musical scale is a graduated series of pitch frequencies. When a given frequency is doubled, the octave above it is sounded and the seven standardized diatonic intervals of the musical scale are embodied within the octave.

A *complex* sound wave produces the perceptual impression known as *quality* or *timbre*. That is to say, when two simple sound waves of differing frequency and intensity combine, a new summary wave is formed which embodies the characteristics of its components. Such a complex wave is therefore made up of simple waves of lesser frequency and intensity.[4]

However, the lowest natural frequency of a sound wave is the only pitch that is consciously heard. It is called the *fundamental tone* and all the other frequencies embodied within the complex sound wave, that are masked by the fundamental pitch, are called *upper partials, harmonics,* or *overtones.* Quality perception may therefore be influenced by the frequency, intensity, and overtone structure of the sound, as heard.[5]

In terms of the foregoing, *quality* (or timbre) is the property of a tone that distinguishes it from other tones of the same pitch and loudness. The number, frequency, and prominence of its constituent overtones in different combinations produce changes in quality that may be subjectively described as *soft, piercing, hollow, rich, dull, bright, white, thin,* etc.

Quality can be influenced by such factors as the substance of which a musical instrument is made, the pitch level of the tone produced within the range of the instrument, and the firmness, composition, size, and shape of the channel of escape. Basically, quality depends on the spectrum of frequency and intensity variations that are contained *within* the issuing wave form of each sound that is perceived.[6]

The beauty or quality of a vocal tone therefore depends, largely, on a selective limitation of its overtones. A well-trained singing voice may contain from seven to twenty partials, or more, depending on such factors as muscular firmness or tonicity, sex, maturity, health, emotional response, hearing acuity, range, etc.

The fundamental pitch of a vocal sound is determined, largely, by the tension of the vibrating glottal muscles in the larynx. But the distribution of frequency and intensity components or partials that determine quality may be influenced by complex resonance factors inherent in the structure of the entire vocal tract.

Tones produced by standardized mechanical instruments have fixed and predictable characteristics. However, because the vocal instrument varies slightly with each individual, vocal tones are never standardized and their variations may be described as minute deviations from an acoustical norm for each tonality. Such individual deviations impart life and human properties to vocal tone without which a mechanical sameness would result.

The art of singing, therefore, consists, largely, in controlling the fluency, duration, and movement of sounds in the three dimensions of *pitch, intensity* (loudness), and *quality* in such a manner that they appear to be a living expression of the ideas and feelings of the composer and the performer. The construction of a musical melody is based primarily on a variation of tonal stability and motion in these three dimensions of pitch, intensity, and quality.

The continuation and alternation of silence and sound also create a time-value continuum as a framework for all musical expression. *Duration* and *pause,* therefore, also become acoustical factors in musical expression and in singing.[7]

The Propagation of Sound

Normally, if the field is free, unreflected sound travels in all directions simultaneously, emanating from its source in the form of expanding concentric shells or spheres. Each sound wave thus travels expansively through the atmosphere at about 1165 feet per second (at sea level in 68° Farenheit), the rate of propagation varying with temperature and climatic conditions. Sound waves are conducted best through dense media and will not pass through a vacuum. In other words, the speed of propagation varies with the density and elastic properties of the transmission medium. The more compressed an air chamber is, for example, the better it will conduct sound. The rate of transmission is five to fifteen times faster through a liquid or solid medium than through the air.[8] Thus, a given sound will take about five seconds to travel a mile in the open air, one second in water and one-third of a second in solid steel, and a compressed air medium will provide a better transmission route than the open or rarefied atmosphere.

For this reason, vibratory energy generated by the larynx is transmitted through bone and muscle tissue of the human body faster than it would travel through air passages or cavities of the vocal tract. Likewise, a firmly compacted breath chamber is a more favorable vibratory conductor than one that is expanded, limp, or flaccid.

Most of the vocal tract, from facial lips to glottis, and including all subglottic air spaces, is compressible. Therefore, by literally squeezing, firming, or compacting the air contained therein, one could probably improve the conductivity of all these air spaces.[9] By the same token, the firmer the muscle, the better its conductivity. No doubt the acoustical efficiency of phonation also increases as loudness increases, for there is then less damping of vocal sound due to laxness or depletion of tonicity in the muscles of the vocal tract.

Compression of the chest boundaries may, therefore, be an acoustical factor in singing. Likewise, when the health of the body is excellent, the firmer muscle tonus resulting therefrom would provide for the improved transmission of sound. All these are possible contributing factors in producing and sustaining a singing tone and in determining optimal vocal quality.

The distance between the crests or peaks of two successive vibratory cycles is called a *wavelength*. Wavelengths, therefore, vary with frequency or pitch: the higher the pitch, the shorter the wavelength. The wavelengths within the pitch range of the human voice will vary from a few inches to several feet. The wavelength of middle C in air, for example, is about four feet.[10]

The length of a sound wave must be small compared with a reflecting surface if the latter is to have any appreciable effect in diverting or newly directing the oncoming sound.[11] It is doubtful, therefore, whether most vocal sounds could be reflected from any of the diminutive surfaces within the mouth or pharyngeal cavities. For this reason, vocal focus in singing is, in all probability, a sensory illusion rather than an acoustical fact.

A sound wave is not like a current of air that represents a continuous stream of onward-moving air particles. Its propagation is more analogous to the wave that passes over a field of wheat when the wind is blowing. Each stalk of wheat sways a bit but then returns to rest. Similarly, each particle of air in a sound wave swings to and fro on a fixed axis. As it oscillates thus, it imparts its energy to adjacent particles which, in turn, transmit their energy similarly, in all directions at once. Thus, a kind of expansive shivering or throbbing pulsation of the atmosphere results, emanating from the vibratory source.[12]

Resonance Factors

The oscillations producing sound are of two types, *initial* and *forced*. The former proceed directly from the tonal generator, the latter from auxiliary bodies, surfaces, or systems that respond sympathetically to the frequency of the initial excitation that impinges upon them. An effect known as *resonance* is thus produced by supplemental or forced vibrations which, under favorable conditions, have the result of intensifying, reinforcing, and enriching the initial tone generated.[13]

Broadly considered, therefore, a *resonator* is an acoustic surface, enclosure, or other medium that will respond to excitations imposed from an outside source so that it vibrates synchronously with that source. In a musical instrument, the effect of the resonator is to intensify and enhance a musical tone by adding supplementary vibrations or overtones to it. The phenomenon of *resonance* in the singing voice is, broadly considered, the resultant of many such types of acoustical reinforcement that contribute, in one way or another, to the intensity and quality of the phonated tone.

Air that is enclosed in a cavity possesses elasticity, and when its molecules are disturbed by vibratory energy it pulsates in and out of the aperture that connects it with the outside air, thereby producing a resonance effect. The rate of escape depends on the size and shape of the cavity and the size of its outer orifice. The larger the cavity, the slower the rate of release and, therefore, the lower the pitch emitted.

The vocal tract includes a series of cavities of varying size and shape, with five interjoining sphincters that create irregular apertures between them. These sphincters are named by their location as: 1) glottal; 2) ary-epiglottic; 3) velo-palatal; 4) lingua-palatal; and 5) labial. Combinations of these elements of size, shape, and aperture are therefore possible contributing factors in determining the quality characteristics of the human voice.[14]

Some resonators have a *natural* or *tuned frequency* that will respond only to selective sounds of definite pitch. Others are *adjustable* and have no inherent natural pitch. They respond to many frequencies. The vocal tract is a combination of both types and will therefore reproduce many gradations of expressive quality for any pitch level in the singer's range.

When the pitch frequency of originating pulsations equals the natural frequency of a resonator, the amplitude of enforced vibrations issuing therefrom becomes great in comparison with the strength of the originating excitation. Therefore, the synchronous vibratory response of contiguous surfaces and areas may augment the initial vibratory disturbance. Thus, however, feeble the originating tone may be, its resultant reinforcement by adjacent bodies, surfaces, and resonators may add considerable power to it.

The effect of synchronous vibrations and resonance upon the originating tone is illustrated in an instrument like the violin. Initial pulsations are produced by the bow's rubbing against a string. These are conducted directly into and spread out over the entire body of the violin, thereby inducing forced oscillations in the latter. The area of the responding surface is thus considerably enlarged, creating a greater vibratory disturbance in the atmosphere, and thus augmenting the original tone. The air cavity in the body of the violin also contributes a resonance effect to the instrument.

It is worth repeating that, since the walls of a resonator also vibrate, the condition of its walls affects the efficiency of the resonator. Rigid walls are more responsive to sounds than soft, spongy walls. Therefore, the firmness and composition of the materials that compose the boundaries of all parts of the vocal tract may play an important role in promoting vocal quality and resonance. The quality of wood in a rare violin, the difference between wood or metal in the structure of any musical instrument, and, in the vocal organs, the firmness and texture of muscle and bone tissue that lines the vocal passageway can all contribute to the final tonal product.

In a so-called relaxed or flabby state, the muscle surfaces of the vocal transmission route merely absorb vibratory energy and have a damping effect on the tone produced. On the other hand, when firm, these surfaces can respond acoustically and add energy, resonance, and optimal quality factors to the phonated tone.

The action of the resonator, then, which is distinguished from that of the generator, is to reinforce and amplify certain frequencies produced by the generator while damping out or absorbing other frequencies. The effect of *resonance* in the vocal tract is to increase the intensity of the initial phonated glottal tone or to change its quality, or both, and it is not necessary for a resonator to be placed in the direct path of the current of sound to be effective. The singing voice may utilize any or all of these acoustical factors.

The structure of the larynx with all its extrinsic attachments favors the transmission of vibratory energy into adjacent parts of the human body. This would spread sympathetic oscillations throughout the vocal tract which could also reinforce volume and influence the timbre of the phonated tone. Thus, in a sense, the entire body may function as a complex resonator.[15]

ACOUSTICAL COMPONENTS OF THE VOCAL INSTRUMENT

Because of its unique and variable structure, the vocal instrument may embody acoustical features of other musical devices without being exactly comparable with any of them. The string and wind families are most often used in making comparisons by analogy.

For purposes of this discussion, therefore, it may be said that the vocal organ is in some respects analogous to an open-tube wind instrument, the essential parts being:

> 1. a tonal *generator* consisting of a cup-shaped mouthpiece (larynx) against which the closed lips (glottal ledges) of the performer are pressed, leaving a small slit (glottis) between them. The form, width, tension, density, and thickness of the vibrating vocal lips can be altered with great rapidity, thus producing many variations of tone.[16]
>
> 2. a *resonator* constructed of an acoustically responsive outlying structure which consists of bone, cartilage, and muscle elements, surfaces, and cavities, including a

convoluted open tube, all of which are capable of amplifying, resonating, and enhancing the initial laryngeal tone.

The mechanisms of the vocal tract must possess a flexible means of controlling all acoustical components in varying combinations to be effective as a musical instrument. Each tonal factor will therefore be considered separately in relation to voice.

Pitch-Controlling Factors

The combined pitch-changing capabilities of the vocal instrument in man range from about 64 Hz (cycles per second) for low C in a bass voice to about 1500 Hz for the highest f^3 of a coloratura soprano. A total *combined* range of four and one-half octaves is thus encompassed. However, the individual singer's voice, male or female, rarely covers more than about two or three octaves.

The fundamental pitch of the singing voice is determined largely by the glottal vibrator itself. Conditions that affect the elasticity of the glottal margins influence pitch control. Although the actual length of the glottal margins does not change appreciably throughout the entire range of the singing voice, a closer analysis reveals the following:

1. Density or weight of the glottal margins is controlled by contraction of the internal fibers of the thyroarytenoid and vocalis muscles, thereby creating variations of firmness or looseness in the vibrating medium. The denser and heavier the glottal margin is, the lower the pitch, and vice versa.

2. Thickness and width of the glottal margin varies with the quantity of muscular flesh that is brought together for phonation. This change may be effected by drawing more or less of the surrounding ventricular wall into the overhanging ledge of muscular tissue of the glottal margin or by drawing aside

more or less of the soft surface tissue underneath the glottal ledge. By this latter means, the edges of the vocal cords are rendered sharper and the weight of the vibrating ledge is lessened. Thinning the vibrating margin therefore raises the pitch; thickening lowers it.[17]

3. The tenseness or firmness of the glottal lips may be varied by the overall pull on its anterior-posterior extremities. A longitudinal tension is thus induced by the opposite outward-tilting actions of its terminal attachments, which are the twin arytenoid cartilages (posterior) and the thyroid cartilage (anterior). However, the glottal ledges also contract *internally* to resist this longitudinal pull and by this combined action their elasticity is increased, even though there is no increase in length. Thus, tensing raises pitch; slackening lowers it.

4. If glottal resistance remains constant and the larynx stationary, a rise in tracheal air pressure will also raise pitch. Conversely, when longitudinal tension increases while tracheal air pressure remains constant, vocal pitch will also rise. Interdependence of vibrator and resonator might also affect vocal pitch.

All these pitch variables are possible in phonation. However, from the singer's standpoint, certain controls are more efficient than others. A rise in subglottal air pressure, for example, not only raises pitch but also increases the amplitude of pulsations of the glottis. Furthermore, if breath pressure only were used, the highest pitches would require as much as six times the air pressure needed for the lower tones. Obviously, an air-pressure method of raising pitch is wasteful of breath and energy. Since the same pitch rise can be attained by increasing the elasticity of the glottal margins while air pressure remains constant, it is assumed that the latter method would be more efficient for the singer.

A comparison with strings may also be helpful. A vibrating string requires four times its normal tension to double its frequency output or raise its pitch one octave. Sixteen times its normal tension is required for an elevation of two octaves.[18] In the violin and similar instruments, where several strings are used, each string is reduced in density, weight, and thickness to compensate for the added tension required in higher octaves. Furthermore, in violin playing, the length of each string is varied by a finger stop for each note within its pitch range.

However, no such change of length is required in the functioning of the glottal vibrator. A built-in mechanism combines a proportionate reduction of *thickness* and *density* of the glottal ledges with the increase of *longitudinal tension* required for every tone in the scale. Thus, a frequency range of two to three octaves can be achieved with considerably less tension than would be necessary for comparable pitch changes in strings. Consequently, in the glottal complex there is considerably less wear and tear on the singing voice throughout the pitch range than would be true if longitudinal tension alone were used.

As previously described, stability of the vibrator during phonation is maintained by the extrinsic mechanisms of the larynx. The effort of all *intrinsic* cord-stretching muscles is thus supplemented by the proportionate pulling, positioning, and restraining power of the entire *extrinsic* muscular complex. Especially is this true during ascent of vocal pitch and in dynamic singing passages.[19]

Another point is also worth noting. The ratio of the length of a vibrator to the size of the resonance cavity adjoining it determines the ability to sound the fundamental tones in a wind instrument. This could also be true of the voice. For example, a French horn player uses harmonics or overtones exclusively because, with his relatively small mouthpiece, he cannot play the fundamental tones of his instrument.

Similarly, the female singer probably employs harmonic overtones almost exclusively and rarely, if ever, sings on fundamental tones. On the other hand, the longer vocal cords of the male adult are, in relation to the size of the larynx and its surrounding structures, more capable of producing fundamental vocal tones than are those of a female adult or child.

However, practically any adult male (e.g., countertenor) can learn to sing soprano if he will devote the same amount of time to the harmonic overtones of his voice that a woman gives them. Some coloratura sopranos can sing to the top of their range with greater ease than others. This may be explained by the fact that their vocal cords are so proportioned in relation to the size of the resonance cavities and adjoining structures that they are able to produce higher harmonics than most sopranos.

The sudden growth of a boy's larynx during the age of puberty accounts for a temporary imbalance between cord length and the size of adjoining spaces and structures. At an early age, the relative shortness of his vocal cords makes it impossible for him to produce the fundamental tones of his vocal instrument and he therefore speaks and sings on harmonic notes like a child.

While the larynx is gradually changing its size during adolescence, the unconscious domination of previously learned aural images causes the growing boy to persist in using treble pitches for a time. As a result, the voice may wobble uncertainly between treble and bass. A period of pitch-fluttering ensues during this change-of-voice period, and this condition is likely to continue until the new growth of the larynx is set and his ear learns to monitor the new adult pitch range.

Because of its acoustical construction, therefore, the male adult voice is pitched lower than the female, the difference being any interval up to two octaves.

In summation, the following conclusions regarding vocal *pitch* are drawn:

1. Vocal pitch is primarily a resultant of two forces: breath pressure and glottal resistance. The density, thickness, width, internal contraction, and a resisting longitudinal tension of the glottal margins are primary factors in bringing about the control of pitch. The peculiar muscular systems of the larynx support this conclusion.

2. In artistic singing, pitch changes are effected by vary-

ing glottal tension, while subglottic breath pressure remains nearly constant for the entire frequency range at any given intensity level. This enables the singer to economize breath energy and maintain a uniform tonal texture throughout his pitch range. Stronger glottal tension with a weaker air blast makes for better tone quality. Weaker glottal tension with a stronger air blast produces harsh, blatant, and breathy quality.

3. The needless raising of the larynx in singing lengthens the tracheal tube and thereby lessens subglottic air pressure when it is most needed, thus disturbing the adjustment for pitch. Off-pitch intonation results. A lowered but stationary larynx is therefore to be desired during the entire pitch range of the singing voice.

4. High pitches actually sound to the human ear of greater intensity than low ones.[20] Therefore, the well-trained singer purposely decreases the intensity of his higher notes, even while apparently maintaining the same loudness of tone, thereby conserving breath and energy as he ascends the scale.

5. Conversely, in a crescendo on a fixed pitch, the increasing intensity of tone must be accompanied by increasing firmness of the vocal cords to withstand the increased energy of subglottic breath pressure. Failure to make this compensation causes the vocalist to sing sharp.

6. Under certain conditions, when subglottic breath pressure is increased against the attenuated glottal ledges, tonal changes that lie within the overtone series of the fundamental vocal pitch may be induced, as in yodeling. Especially is this true in the male voice. Since these overtones or harmonics are lighter in quality than fundamental tones, they are mistakenly called "falsetto" tones. These harmonically sounded light tones are not to be confused with the lightly sung regular tones of the upper vocal range. With correct breath support and a stable larynx, the regular tones can be swelled gradually into full, loud tones without a pitch break.

7. Finally, it is reasonable to conclude that, for singing purposes, any or all of the pitch controls described above may occur in any combination. Needless to say, in the well-trained

voice, the singer's ear subtly and delicately governs all these pitch changes, for there are no direct glottal sensations perceptible to the vocalist at any time.

Intensity-Controlling Factors

In an average salon recital, the fully developed singing voice will express a range of some fifty to sixty decibels (db) without straining, and can readily double that volume in powerful singing.[21] By way of comparison, the upper dynamic limit of an average-size symphony orchestra reaches approximately 75–110 db. How is this control of vocal intensity accomplished?

First, vocal intensity may be augmented by increasing the compression (not the flow) of subglottic breath. Simultaneously, as more and more energy is applied to the adducted vocal ledges, the latter will increase their resistance to breath pressure and the amplitude of each vibratory swing will be thereby increased.[22] This adds volume to the tone, much as the player of a brass wind instrument augments volume by increasing breath pressure against his closed lips as they rest firmly against the mouthpiece of his instrument.

Second, vocal intensity may be augmented by increasing the adjacent surface area or expanse of the vibrating medium that is affected by each glottal swing. To illustrate by analogy, any string or membrane can be set into vibration by the forced oscillation of its point of support, much as a whip is cracked by the movement of its handle. Conversely, a stationary point of support may be set into vibration by the forced oscillation of the string or membrane to which it is attached, as in the violin and also in vocal tone production. If the point of support is imbedded in a tremulous or rigid surface, the pulsation of the string or membrane will be imparted to its supporting structures through these points of attachment and the entire adjacent surface area will thus be set into synchronous vibration. This is the sounding-board principle used in the violin, piano, harp, and, also, to a varying degree, in the human vocal tract.

Therefore, by this principle, the vibratory energy initiated at the glottis is propagated into contiguous muscles, cartilages, and bones of the larynx. From there it is spread throughout a considerable portion of the singer's body, being transmitted directly into the chain of connecting extrinsic laryngeal muscles and thence, by actual contact, into the muscles of the throat, tongue, palate, mouth, and pharynx and, also, into the cranium, spinal column, sternum, rib cage, shoulder blades, and even, possibly, through the singer's legs and heels into the floor boards upon which he is standing.

The total area of the vibrating medium is thus considerably enlarged, thereby augmenting the initial glottal tone. The sounding board of a piano or violin radiates practically all the vibrational energy of its strings in this manner. In the case of the human larynx, it is estimated that about eighty percent of glottal energy is radiated as synchronous vibrations into adjacent structures, while approximately twenty percent is absorbed at the glottis.[23]

Naturally, the sound energy thus radiated bears a definite relation to the total energy or subglottic air pressure available at the vibratory source, and also to the varying rigidity, density, and temperature of the solids composing the transmission route. The latter are determined by such factors as posture and muscle tonus of the singer's body which, in turn, may be governed by motivational and hearing controls that affect the purposes of vocal expression.

In summary, therefore, the following observations regarding vocal intensity may be made:

1. The volume or intensity of vocal sound is determined initially by the strength of breath pressure exerted against the under surface of the adducted vocal shelves.

2. The glottal muscles must be strong, firm, and healthy to support a firm glottal closure, when needed. The greater the available breath pressure, the greater the range of volume that can be used for singing purposes.

3. Experiments show that breath pressure demanded by full volume of voice may amount to as much as thirty times the pressure of ordinary respiration.[24] The expiratory effort of everyday breathing must therefore be augmented considerably to provide adequate breath support for artistic singing. This also relates to firm glottal closure and good compression of all the chest boundaries.

4. As vocal intensity increases at any given pitch level, there is a gradual compensatory thickening of the vocal shelves to prevent an increase in the frequency thereof. By this means, off-pitch singing is prevented. To assure uniform quality and unwavering pitch, therefore, a fairly strong breath pressure against a firmly closed glottis is always demanded. In other words, the greatest amplitude of glottal vibration is to be produced with the least possible air blast.[25] With proper adjustment of these pressure components, loud tones can be sustained as long as soft tones on any given breath.

5. Artistic singing, therefore, requires a relatively long expiratory effort with a constant or sustained compression of the lungs. For singing purposes, a refinement of dynamic controls must be made available in all types of crescendo, diminuendo, staccato, and legato patterns.

6. Since the inherent capacity to phonate loudly is acquired at birth, vocal loudness, per se, is not a product of direct training. Phonation and dynamics are, therefore, inseparable components of a normal vocal reflex. The refinement of this skill, however, involving dynamic nuance appropriate to musical context, is a result of guidance and intelligent practice under a teacher's watchful eye and ear.

7. The intensity of a tone will automatically increase by about one-third for each octave rise in pitch.[26] Within a rise of three octaves, therefore, the apparent loudness of the voice will about double itself without any increase in the initial energy of phonation. The untrained singer mistakenly judges that a higher tone demands a greater glottal effort. Thus, instead of maintaining the correct ratio of glottal firmness to subglottic air pressure, he strains needlessly at unrelated muscles in an all-

out attempt to attack or sustain his highest tones, thereby forcing his tone and wasting breath and muscular energy.

Quality-Controlling Factors

In the vocal tract we have a tone channel so individual in contour and composition that no two voices can ever be exactly alike. As previously stated, both fixed and variable resonators affect the singing voice. Fixed shapes are found in anatomical and structural components of the body, such as the nose, head, throat, and larynx. Variable elements are found in movable parts such as the lips, jaw, tongue, and palate.

It may be said that the keynote of artistic training is to avoid flabbiness in any part of the vocal passageway. Allowing for adjustments needed for diction, it is also important to prevent unnecessary movement of any of its parts. This assures equilibrium of the vibrator and optimal resonance and quality of the vocal output.

Furthermore, a firmly compressed tonal passageway provides a denser vibrating medium that is favorable to sonority and richness. This concept is contradictory to unwise directives that call for a condition of looseness, a moving larynx, an inert tongue, relaxation, and the open-throat feeling. Instead of these, muscular compactness without strain is needed so that all vibratory conductors can function at peak acoustical efficiency.

A stationary larynx prevents variations in subglottic air pressure during phonation. A relatively narrowed, compact pharyngeal and oral passageway is also conducive to tonal reinforcement.

In dynamic singing, the tongue root rises slightly and becomes firmer, since it is part of the extrinsic muscular chain that supports the larynx and all its adjustments. The cheek and lip muscles and the entire mouth cavity are also made firmer to add optimal resonance and acoustical support to the interior boundaries of the upper vocal tract.

All these conditions must be established without undue tension, clutching, or stiffness of unrelated muscles. Ideally, the responsiveness of the larynx and the various parts of the vocal tract, acting in combination, can produce a fundamental tone and as many as sixteen to twenty overtones for the singer's voice.

The complexity of this acoustical system is obvious, and all quality components are therefore closely related to the proper functioning of the entire interconnected system of muscles, cartilages, surfaces, cavities, and other structural elements in the vocal tract. The entire oro-pharygeal passageway, the nasal cavity, and cranium are also influential vocal resonators. Although of fixed shape and volume, they respond acoustically. Such anatomical fixtures help provide a basic quality formant for the vocal instrument.

A sensation of tonal vibrancy in certain cranial areas gives one the illusion of "head resonance," "tonal focus in the mask," and vibration in the "upper" resonance chambers. These sensations are the quality components that may be felt to predominate in the head, face, sinuses, nose, and mouth, especially when the singer is using the upper range of his voice. As pitch descends, the chest wall appears to respond with unusual vibrancy or *fremitus,* and this sensation continues throughout the lower pitch range.

The cultivation of optimal residual head resonance, known as the *head hum,* is considered the sine qua non of the well-trained artistic singing voice. Consequently, this type of technical training engages considerable attention in vocal pedagogy.[27]

Finally, the larynx itself is a type of resonator, its function being not only to generate tone (phonation) but to distribute tonal energy to outlying muscles, cartilages, and bones that are directly connected with it. Therefore, the intralaryngeal muscles can contribute much to the acoustical modulations of the voice. This service is also rendered by the muscles of the tongue, soft palate, pharynx, and all other extralaryngeal attachments and surfaces that border the vocal passageway.

The chief determinants of quality or timbre, then, are those factors that add overtones to the issuing sound wave. These factors include the size, shape, composition, and condition of the air passageways, muscles, bones, and resonators that comprise the entire vocal tract, including the larynx and the glottis itself.

The Tonal Response Reviewed as an Acoustical Product

In reviewing the foregoing discussions of *pitch, intensity,* and *quality,* it becomes apparent that these three acoustical properties are inseparable factors. All three are simultaneously embodied in the tonal product. The separation herein considered, therefore, is purely theoretical, to serve the purposes of analytical discussion.

In other words, tonal energy cannot be selectively controlled during phonation or directed at will. There can be no intentional head voice as opposed to chest voice, since both regions of the body vibrate simultaneously with the glottal tone. Nor can one consciously dampen chest tones and increase head tones, or vice versa. The laws of the simultaneous propagation of sound would preclude such acoustical anomalies. An indirect approach is therefore used, through esthetic ear training, to govern the control of acoustical elements.

Vocal pitch is primarily determined by such factors as the density, thickness, width, longitudinal tension, and contractile tensity of the vibrating glottal margins and by subglottic breath pressures.

Intensity and loudness are controlled by the compactness and force of breath pressure against the elasticity (resistance) of the glottal margins; by the mass, thickness, and width of the vibrating margins; and by the total area of all vibrating surfaces.

Quality or timbre is governed by the density and firmness of all the vibrating material, the acoustical response of resonators and adjacent structures, the shape and condition of the airway, and the size and composition of the channel of escape. Thus, through the acoustical efficiency of interconnected bones, muscles, ligaments, cavities, and surfaces in the route of acoustical transmission, the human voice receives both power and quality; and the term *vocal resonance,* as it is used in singing pedagogy, is loosely applied to a composite of all these effects. In optimal vocal development, even the texture and firmness of cheeks, soft palate, tongue, and lips can determine the acoustical response because of their larynx-connected parts and muscles. Likewise, the sternum, ribs, spine, shoulder blades, cranium, and other bones of the skeleton and their muscular attachments respond to the direct transmission of glottal pulsations through larynx-connected parts.

In short, glottal energy initiates pulsations that travel in all directions throughout the vocal tract, resulting in considerable reinforcement of tone, and imparting pitch, power, and quality to the singing voice. This entire complex adds resonance and beauty to the voice and the output for singing is considerably enriched thereby. The acoustical effects of a healthy muscle tonus, good posture, and physique are obvious.

Finally, it is well to bear in mind that the acoustical output is governed by a single response of the entire vocal tract in obedience to preconceived tonal *concepts* and that this tonal imagery is dictated by the impulse to express and communicate to a listener. It is a process of self-release which engages a complex mechanism automatically. The artistic functioning of this entire mechanism can be measured only by the perfection of tone that is audibly expressed in singing. Musical ear training is, therefore, a primary governing factor in the intonation, development, and control of the artistic singing voice.

REFERENCES AND NOTES

1. John Redfield, *Music, a Science and an Art* (New York: Tudor Publishing Co., 1935), p. 30.

2. H. Lowery, *A Guide to Musical Acoustics* (New York: Dover Publications, Inc., 1966), p. 15.

3. John Backus, *The Acoustical Foundations of Music* (New York: W. W. Norton & Company, Inc., 1969), p. 82ff.

4. Joseph Schillinger, *The Mathematical Basis of the Arts* (New York: Philosophical Library, 1948), p. 4.

5. L. S. Lloyd and Hugh Boyle, *Intervals, Scales and Temperaments* (New York: St. Martin's Press, 1963), pp. 88, 140.

6. Ibid., Chap. 16.

7. Schillinger, *Mathematical Basis,* pp. 5–9.

8. Backus, *Foundations of Music*, p. 44.

9. John Howard, *Expression in Singing* (New York: Erhard Kromer, Publ., 1905), p. 5.

10. Backus, *Foundations of Music,* Chap. 3.

11. J. W. S. Rayleigh, *The Theory of Sound* (London: Macmillan, 1896; reprinted, New York: Dover Press, 1945), 2: 120.

12. Juan G. Roederer, *Introduction to the Physics and Psychophysics of Music* (New York: Springer-Verlag, 1973), p. 55.

13. Lowery, *Musical Acoustics,* p. 31.

14. Redfield, *Music,* p. 27.

15. Carlo Meano, *The Human Voice in Speech and Song,* transl. Khoury (Springfield, Ill.: Charles C Thomas, Publ., 1967), p. 142.

16. Hermann, L. F. Helmholtz, *On the Sensations of Tone,* 2nd English edit, transl. Ellis (New York: Dover Publications, Inc., 1954), pp. 98, 104.

17. Harry Hollien, "A Laminagraphic Study of Vocal Pitch," *J. Speech & Hearing Research* 3 (Washington, D.C., 1960): 361–371.

18. Charles A. Culver, *Musical Acoustics,* 2nd edition (Philadelphia: The Blakiston Company, 1947), p. 88.

19. V. E. Negus, *The Mechanism of the Larynx,* 2nd edition (London: Heinemann Medical Books, 1957), p. 382.

20. Roederer, *Physics and Psychophysics,* p. 84.

21. Raoul Husson, "Special Physiology in Singing with Power," *The NATS Bulletin* (October 1957): 12–15.

22. Henry J. Rubin, "Experimental Studies on Vocal Pitch and Intensity in Phonation," *Laryngoscope* 73 (August, 1963): 973–1015.

23. Robert O. L. Curry, *The Mechanism of the Human Voice* (New York: Longmans Green, 1940), p. 57.

24. Husson, "Singing with Power," p. 12.

25. H. Holbrook Curtis, *Voice Building and Tone Placing*, reprint edition (Minneapolis, Minn.: Pro Musica Press, 1973), p. 40.

26. Douglas Stanley, *The Science of Voice*, 4th edition rev. (New York: Carl Fischer, 1958), p. 295.

27. Richard De Young, *The Singer's Art* (Chicago: De Paul University Press, 1958), p. 60.

IX

Ear Training for the Singer

An artist singer is primarily a musician. Like any professional, he must acquire a working knowledge of musical media and familiarize himself with the language of his art. Music is his stock in trade. Indeed, how much of music he knows can ultimately determine the success and longevity of his career.

Furthermore, the substance of music is *sound* and the singer's art therefore comprises those skills that are needed for capturing the *audible* language and logic of musical sound as it appears in printed form. Both audible and visual media are involved in this process. That is to say, the printed musical score is a lifeless symbol to the eye until dynamic and soul-stirring attributes are breathed into it by the performing artist. Thus, he translates and transmutes a printed symbology into audible and communicable patterns of sound.

Hearing is therefore as important to the musician singer as seeing is to the graphic artist. Like vision, hearing has its physical and mental aspects. The external organ perceives and the mind interprets. Together, these outer and inner agencies function as an integrated faculty, and the development of this faculty, both outer and inner, is the purpose of *ear training*. Since a singer's growth in musicianship is impossible without ear training, these two subjects are studied hand in hand.

Physiologically considered, *hearing* may be described as a

sensory-neural reaction to sound and the subjective appreciation thereof. The organ of hearing, in close association with the brain, is able to receive and interpret external sounds with remarkable acuity and at a considerable distance. But, although man's ear has a potential sensitivity for frequencies ranging from 20 to more than 20,000 Hz, or cycles per second (about ten octaves), the average individual uses only about ten percent of this auditory range.[1] For nonmusical purposes, he employs only about one octave (i.e., from 128 to 256 Hz). That octave corresponds to the approximate range of his conversational voice. Therefore, there are great possibilities for refinement and training in the hearing faculties of the average man and also in the hearing faculties of a student of singing.

In evolution, the sense of hearing is believed to have antedated the ability to phonate. According to Negus, in the absence of a hearing organ there is usually no sound-producing organ. There is also evidence in comparative anatomy that man acquired the ability to perceive sounds before he was able to produce them vocally. The ear is therefore older than the larynx in the evolution of man.[2]

It would follow that the cultivation of a singer's ear is essential to any voice-building program. Consequently, a knowledge of vocal pedagogy would be incomplete without a consideration of hearing and ear-training fundamentals. To this end, a nontechnical resumé and procedural overview are presented which will guide both teacher and student and tie in with the essentials of vocal acoustics previously discussed.

The Nature of Ear Training

Ear training is the process of becoming skillful in identifying, retaining, and recalling tonal images through the sense of hearing. In this development we have the experience of *thinking* music before we sing or play it. Since we hear ourselves and others through a complex and delicate air-and-bone conduction system, it is desirable to understand this process in both its physical and mental aspects.

Physical Hearing

Briefly described, when we hear externally, sound waves enter the *outer ear canal,* striking the *ear drum,* or *tympanic membrane,* and causing it to vibrate. These pulsations are initially air-borne but they are then mechanically transmitted through the middle ear via three tiny linked ear bones or *ossicles.*

Through the ingenious leverage system of these ossicles, sound waves are considerably augmented as they are conducted to a smaller membrane that covers an *oval window* at one end of the *inner ear.* The inner ear, which lies inside the oval window, contains a spiral-shaped, fluid-filled canal called the *cochlea.* In it are found the *basilar membrane* which contains auditory receptors or nerve endings of the *Organ of Corti.* The latter is a mechanism consisting of thousands of minute hair-like endings or fibers of the *auditory nerve.* These fibers are immersed in the *cochlear fluid.*

Each of these sensory nerve endings is probably responsive to particular frequency and intensity excitations. Thus, they can serve to differentiate and screen out the fundamentals and overtones of sounds that are received by the ears of a listener. They can also transmit neural impulses to the auditory centers of the brain, where nerve stimuli are identified and evaluated in terms of pitch, loudness, and quality. The Organ of Corti, in combination with the tympanic membrane and the ossicles of the middle ear, therefore acts as a transformer mechanism that converts outer air-borne vibrations into oscillating fluid waves in the inner ear and ultimately into neural stimuli.[3]

Of course, man hears his own voice *internally* by means of *bone conduction.* This is due to the direct transmission of pulsations that are generated in his *own* larynx to the nerve receptors and mechanisms in his *own* middle and inner ear. Hence, we do not normally hear ourselves as others hear us, unless the voice we use is first recorded and then listened to as external air-borne sound.

It will be recalled that the frequency or periodicity of the sound wave determines pitch; the intensity of the sound wave or sound pressure determines loudness; while quality or timbre is interpreted from a combination of frequency and intensity components. The resultant wave form consists of a spectrum of overtones. All are components of the impinging acoustical wave, the sensations of which are transmitted to the brain via the eighth cranial or auditory nerve. In the association and hearing centers of the brain, they are identified and interpreted as meaningful musical sounds. That, in brief, describes the *physical* process of hearing.

It is also interesting to note that the cavity of the middle ear is connected with the pharynx by means of the *Eustachian tube*. This tube, normally closed, is opened at intervals through the act of swallowing so that air pressure on either side of the tympanic membrane may be kept equalized. Obstruction of the Eustachian canal that prevents it from opening properly may be one of the causes of partial deafness. There are others. Sometimes there is a block in the middle-ear canal or transformer mechanism (tympanic membrane and ossicles) and a *conductive* hearing impairment results. If the defect is in the cochlea, auditory nerve, or brain, a *perceptive* impairment results.

People with conductive hearing defects tend to speak too loud because they do not fully hear their own voices. In certain individuals there is a partial organic hearing loss in some portion of the frequency range. Such a condition will impair the perception of tonal nuance and vocal quality, since only the upper partials may be lost to the ear. In any such case, audiometer tests and medical consultations are called for.[4] Naturally, in a musician, the neural response of the auditory mechanism must be more sensitive than in those who are non-musical. The optimal perception of tonal quality in singing, therefore, requires extreme sensitivity throughout the hearing range.

Mental Hearing

Psychologically considered, the recognition of sounds is a rather complex experience. Composite acoustical impulses received by each ear induce integrated auditory patterns in the brain that are interpreted as sound. If visual perception should accompany the act of hearing, these visual stimuli are simultaneously received by the appropriate brain centers. Here they are associated with the incoming sounds to create for the listener a single audio-visual impression of the hearing experience (e.g., the sight and sound of a person singing).

It is also in the nature of the brain to compare and contrast each new experience with related past experiences. Consequently, the memories of previously heard tones are unconsciously compared with those that are currently being heard. These associations are tinged with feelings, thereby producing esthetic evaluations and emotional responses to the voice that also form part of a musical experience.

One can, therefore, hardly dissociate the mental from the physical act of hearing, with its related esthetic responses. Indeed, when sounds are mentally imaged this same complex of associated values accompanies them. In other words, we are not conscious of each separate link in the chain of interactions that produce hearing. Furthermore, this entire response with all its interconnections occurs within an incredibly brief moment of time, and each such reaction becomes an inseparable part of the act of tonal perception which, in turn, governs the act of phonation in singing.

It is apparent, therefore, that the ability to perceive and interpret tone is primarily a function of the brain and, like every other function or faculty, is susceptible of training and improvement under systematic guidance. Tonal imagery is always a prime factor of vocal control. Indeed, the singer's mental image dictates the degree of muscular action needed for each sound produced. This obedience to the mental sense is quickened by ear training, which is a process of learning through repeated exposure to meaningful esthetic auditory experience.

Normal hearing, like normal vision, is devoid of conscious effort or sensation. Individual voices may differ, largely, because of differences in keenness of aural perception, and the essential difference between a good and bad voice lies more often in defective musical perception than in the structural condition of the larynx. It follows, therefore, that any block or defect in the auditory system results in impaired hearing which, in turn, restricts phonation in some noticeable manner.[5]

Functional Hearing Loss a Teaching Problem

Defects of hearing may be either organic or functional. The correction of organic deficiencies lies beyond the province of the teacher and would therefore be referred to an otologist or hearing specialist for medical advice. But when hearing deficiencies are not of organic origin, they may be caused by abuse, disuse, or neglect of the hearing function. Such conditions are amenable to instruction and will respond to ear training methods.

It is taken for granted that corrective exercises will strengthen the vocal muscles. But it should be as commonly accepted that the functions and faculties involved in tonal recognition and auditory visualization may also be trained regularly with good effect. The ear of the singer must be made highly impressionable to musical tone. Its possessor must have optimal hearing acuity and be able to appreciate and analyze the compositions performed by others. This ability combines with a fine musical memory, as well as with the ability to play or sing.

The ultimate efficiency and artistry of tonal expression can never exceed the acuteness of a singer's hearing perceptions and his ability to visualize tone. The point might also be made, in passing, that the persistent use of loud piano and other external instrumental accompaniments during voice lessons and practice periods is likely to drown out a student's perception of his own voice and thus gradually dull the functional sensitivity of his own ear. This form of auditory abuse would be detrimental to musical growth. During the early training period, therefore, much *unaccompanied* singing practice is adviseable.

Educating the Ear for Musical Expression

Numerous media for the cultivation of a fine musical ear are available to vocal students in the many ear-training texts and drill books now in print.[6] However, both teacher and pupil need to know how to use this published material. A systematic and compact study plan is therefore presented that will emphasize the peculiar needs of singers as artist musicians.

This resumé includes a brief discussion of preliminary ear-training methods in the categories of: *directed listening, tonal discrimination, auditory visualization,* and *aural perception of musical form and structure.* The integration and coordination of these four technical disciplines heightens aural sensitivity, keenness of perception, and tonal thinking. *Musical dictation, sight-singing,* and *score reading* are later acquisitions. All are required for musical understanding of the singer's art. Although discussed sequentially, they may be administered in any convenient combination suitable to the needs and competencies of the individual student.

Directed Listening

The recognition of tonal values is one of the first objectives of ear training. Therefore, typical illustrations may be presented to the pupil's ear in a graded sequence which uses all the song forms and conventional types of music as practice materials. In this discipline the following five phases of listening experience may be recommended and discussed:

1. What is tonality? It is the mental effect of grouping tones and chords around some governing keynote called the *tonic.* When the ear is once filled with the keynote, the first, third, and fifth notes of the diatonic scale are easily recognized as *strong tones;* the others are felt to be dependent or *leaning tones.* These effects of tonic dominance are modified by mode, pitch, harmony, quality of tone, accent, and speed. The pupil should learn that major chords have a *bright* effect; minor chords are more *dull* and *somber.* By listening to numerous compositional forms, the singer thus begins to recognize the function and importance of various tonal devices as a means of portraying character and mood in music. Especially is this true of song and operatic literature in which dramatic characterizations are paramount.

2. *What is the language of music?* In this approach, the teacher selects and presents for analysis typical illustrations of various musical patterns and moods, whether vocal or instrumental. Melodic designs, major and minor tonalities, inactive and active chord progressions, dynamic nuance, tempo changes, and the moods created by them are considered in a general way. The dormant sensitivity of the ear is thus awakened as it begins to understand and appreciate the basic language of music, which is also the language of song.

3. *Compositional forms* are next considered. The concepts of motives, themes, and phrases may be discussed. The *motive* may be explained as a melodic fragment or musical germ which is developed into a phrase or into a period. The larger germs are called *themes*. In fugue form they are called *subjects*. The language of song embodies all these materials.

The *phrase* is then presented as a short musical thought. It may be developed into a longer melodic pattern in numerous ways, i.e., by exact repetition, recurrence on a different scale step, reversing the direction of melodic intervals, inversion of an entire melody, the use of antecedent and consequent phrases to form a musical period, etc. The *period* is formed out of two or more contrasting or complementary phrases, ending with some kind of cadence. Such treatment is typical in conventional operatic and song literature.

The student then learns to recognize and trace the evolution of larger musical designs from the simple melody, on through the folk and art song forms, the rondo, march, dance, suite, overture, sonata, symphony, symphonic poem, and concerto. At first, common secular compositions are featured. Later, the melodic patterns in sacred music may be discussed as an introduction to the canon and fugue, the aria, motet, cantata, passion, oratorio, and mass.

4. Instrumental media should next be considered in conjunction with the foregoing. The composition of the orchestra is presented while listening to separate performances of strings, woodwinds, brass, tympani, percussion, and drums. The organ, with its tonal galaxies, might also be considered. Instrumentation is also important in operatic design and in vocal accompaniment.

5. Finally, *vocal parts* are introduced, including the aria, recitative, and dramatic episodes of opera. All need to be recognized and aurally identified before their function in composition and performance can be understood. The importance of directed listening is thus made apparent.

After he is properly launched on a voyage of tonal discovery, the pupil's further study of musical appreciation can be largely self-administered and it will continue throughout his lifetime. But implanting basic concepts is all-important and this becomes a matter of teacher guidance and instructional routine. These basic concepts aid in the initial recognition of musical language and form, and stimulate the cultivation of habits of concentration and analysis that make later musical thinking and artistic interpretation possible.

Illustrations worthy of appreciation and emulation will have maximum pedagogic value. Practice materials should therefore be selected because they embody worthy performance models and present archetypes of singing and instrumental artistry.[7] With such models before him, the student singer will unconsciously pattern his own expression after the best examples he has heard. In due time he will acquire individuality and freedom of style that will supplant all models. In other words, conventional forms and structures of music are to be the working tools of ear training until such time as creativity matures and artistic independence takes over.

Tonal Discrimination

Learning the names of things helps us recognize and identify a familiar experience in terms of previously learned attributes and thus we are able to reproduce it when necessary. A working vocabulary or standard terminology will therefore be needed in order to identify, differentiate, and describe the auditory experiences of ear training. This nomenclature would be applicable to tonal properties, as heard, in various patterns of pitch, dynamics, duration, and quality, as well as to the tones of voices, instruments, harmonies, and musical effects.

For practice purposes, therefore, pitch intervals and chord structures in rhythmic patterns should be identified and named as an introduction to the musical idioms later to be encountered. A standard harmony text may be useful for reference in this work.[8]

The piano keyboard will also help the singer illustrate for himself the simpler techniques of melodic harmonization, transposition, and modulation and thus provide an added stimulus to his tonal thinking. Skill in score reading and harmonic analysis will evolve from such procedures, and the analysis of piano and vocal literature for interpretative purposes may also be introduced.[9] This entire procedure will be spread out over many weeks of study and practice.

Auditory Visualization

Tonal imagery, also called *auditory visualization*, is an essential ear-training discipline. It may be defined as the preconception or mental expectation of sounds that are not actually present to the outer sense of hearing. It is our way of reproducing in memory or imagination the likeness of an auditory sensory experience, together with any feelings that might accompany it.

A singer must acquire the ability to retain the *memory* of all the foregoing characteristics of sound and develop the ability to recall them at will, *without* the aid of an instrument. The tones represented in a printed score must therefore be visualized instantly and listened to mentally and silently. This is invaluable discipline by means of which a singer learns to "hear" what he is reading without necessarily making a sound.

The *silent* memorization of meaningful fragments of music is therefore helpful, and this is achieved without the aid of an instrument. Many samples and types of instrumental and vocal literature may thus be explored. Ultimately, tonal recognition and auditory visualization become integral parts of every listening experience, much as the abilities to spell, articulate, and pronounce the words of the English language and to use them grammatically and expressively become inseparably linked to the interpretation and appreciation of English literature.

Aural Perception of Structure and Form

Form in music is the framework enclosing a musical design that establishes the relationship of all its parts. In visual art, form exists in space only. Hence it can be instantly viewed in its entirety. In music, however, form exists in time only, and unfolds itself as heard, beat by beat, so that it can be grasped only by the mental synthesis of its remembered elements. The singer who mentally hears the score he is silently reading enjoys an obvious advantage over the individual who must wait for a public performance or a recording to be able to make a tonal analysis of the music.

The study of musical structure and form is perhaps the most involved discipline in the ear-training program. However, three important items may be advantageously considered at this time. They are: a) *contrapuntal,* b) *harmonic,* and c) *stylistic* elements, and these will be briefly outlined as a guide to further study.

a. Contrapuntal analysis deals with the concurrent movement of interdependent melodic lines which are combined to create harmonic musical effects. The student starts with the *canon,* a simple but interesting composition in which all voices present and imitate the same melody successively. Then he is taught that the canon evolves into the *fugue,* in which several melodies are used successively to form euphonious combinations without sacrificing the individuality of each voice. Especially is this treatment evident in the works of composers like Palestrina and Bach, and in the prevalent polyphonic and contrapuntal vocal and instrumental styles of the sixteenth and seventeenth centuries. These may form the bases of extended study in this subject.

b. Harmonic analysis deals with essential chord progressions and the recognition of those tonal combinations that blend harmoniously when sounded together. Through directed listening, the singer's ear may become attuned to harmonic effects that accompany the vocal line. For example, in most classical music, melodic movement proceeds largely by means of supporting chords, rather than by single tones. They are the chordal and tonal relations that bestow an orderly beauty on music, which is further enriched by rhythmic values.

In this connection, concepts of dissonance and discord are worth noting. Dissonances enrich a melody by establishing rival harmonies whereas discords do not belong to any harmony. Also to be considered are the composition, progression, and modulation of chords, the function of chromatic and embellishing chords, the diatonic expansion or extension of chords and their harmonic effect as distinguished from mere melody, and so on.

The development and use of keyboard instruments brought about the gradual growth of harmonic and chordal forms of musical composition, as opposed to polyphonic or linear music. Thus, modulation, transpositions, and key systems came into being with a resultant evolution into the design of the *rondo, theme with variations, suite, scherzo, sonata, overture,* and *symphony.* A wide variety of these harmonic forms also found their way into religious music, along with the later development of the *hymns, chorales, cantatas, oratorios,* and the *anthems* of church literature which form a large part of existing vocal repertoire.

c. Stylistic analysis will be more fully discussed in a later chapter. It deals essentially with the idiomatic sequence and repetition of musical ideas and the peculiar arrangement of the content of a composition. The familiar A–B and A–B–A patterns, known as binary and trinary forms, are the simplest building blocks from which more elaborate musical designs are constructed.

Phrasing is also a dominant concern in the interpretation of song. The vocalist learns that musical ideas in singing are nearly always expressed in phrase units. In fact, the musical motive and phrase are basic melodic constituents of formal and stylistic development. Repetitions of these elementary units, with variations and extensions, develop into the song forms and other familiar structural components of modern vocal music.

Finally, special stress is to be laid on the development of the *song form*, because it is the most prevalent medium of vocal expression used in singing. A vast song literature exists in many languages, and the problem of setting words to music involves a special consideration of the techniques of diction and interpretation, later to be discussed.

The analysis, through sight and sound, of all the foregoing stylistic elements of structure and form will provide a rich cultural background for the singer. It will also provide a varied knowledge of musical, and especially vocal literature. It is the teacher's function to guide and direct this study so that it will parallel and match the pupil's technical vocal development and keep pace with the expressional needs and interpretational demands of the vocal literature he is studying.

Reviewing the Essentials of Ear Training

In summation, a singer's musicianship in performance depends, in large measure, on the possession of a well-trained ear and also on general cultural musical development. Both are equally important. Silent tonal thinking of melodic passages and unaccompanied audible singing practice are recommended. Giving intelligent attention to the *listening* part of each vocal lesson is also important. Outside listening experience will further stimulate and improve hearing alertness.

The physiological processes of auditory perception may be summed up in five steps:

    1. Atmospheric vibrations or sound waves impinge upon the outer ear (tympanum) to produce nerve impulses in the inner ear.
    2. These impulses travel along nerve pathways to specific areas of the brain.
    3. Various centers of the brain associate each incoming stimulus with a previous hearing experience and produce a recognition or intellectual and emotional evaluation of the new experience.
    4. The elements of tonal experience, past and present, thus recognized, are integrated into a tonal memory pattern for present or future use. These memory patterns may be recalled at will.
    5. An appropriate action or motor response is initiated which flows out through the organs of vocal expression together with appropriate facial and body movements.

Complex neurophysiological mechanisms are thus involved in the sensory perception of sound. Each such perception contributes to memory patterns which, in turn, help the individual singer form judgment values for the esthetic performance of music and song.

The four primary stages of ear training should be remembered as: *directed listening, tonal discrimination, auditory visualization,* and *aural perception of form and structure.* Together they constitute a preliminary program for the cultivation of professional musicianship.

Finally, because artistic singing demands eloquence of delivery and the ability to interpret and communicate, an artist's convictions must be transmitted through his singing as surely as they are through his speech. The empty, technically perfect voice is as unconvincing to an audience as the expressions of a lifeless robot. Warm enthusiasm, deep understanding, and keen sensitivity are expected. These qualities add to the joys of musical expression and are part of the art of singing.

To command this language of music a singer must do more than learn to vocalize a song. He must acquaint himself with the architecture of music, learn to play an instrument, master the principles of internal form and structure, study harmony, develop an appreciation of good music, and become sensitive to the modulations and moods of fine instrumental and vocal compositions.

He must also possess the ability to sing or play unfamiliar intervals with ease and precision, must understand unusual harmonic progressions and be able to sing at sight from any vocal score that is placed before him. Through patient and persistent study he thus acquires the inner sense which transmutes the dots and lines of a printed score into artistic and intelligible singing of varied tone color and expressive mood.

Thus, by a cycle of mental and mechanical disciplines, creative vocal expression is brought to life in a communicable art form. The open door to this esthetic realm is the faculty of hearing, a natural endowment of man and an indispensable part of his musical culture. It is through the exercise of his musicianship that a singer becomes capable of lifting up his audience. For musical entertainment is based largely on the joy of listening to a realm of beauty and purity of sound that is governed by order, rhythm, harmony, and melody.

REFERENCES AND NOTES

1. John Backus, *The Acoustical Foundations of Music* (New York, W. W. Norton & Company, Inc., 1969), p. 111.

2. V. E. Negus, *The Mechanism of the Larynx,* second edition (London: Heinemann Medical Books, 1957), p. 274.

3. Georg von Bekesy, *Experiments in Hearing* (New York: McGraw-Hill Book Company, 1960), p. 100.

4. Harold M. Kaplan, *Anatomy and Physiology of Speech* (New York: McGraw-Hill Book Company, 1960), Chap. 13.

5. Jorgen Jersild, *Ear Training* (Copenhagen, Denmark: Wilhelm Hansen, 1966).

6. Douglas S. Moore, *Listening to Music,* rev. ed. (New York: W. W. Norton & Company, Inc., 1963).

7. André Hodier, *The Form of Music,* transl from the French by Noel Burch (New York: Walker and Company, 1966).

8. Robert W. Ottman, *Elementary Harmony; Theory and Practice* (Englewood Cliffs, N.J.: Prentice-Hall, Inc., 1961).

9. Kenneth Simpson, *Keyboard Harmony and Improvization* (London: Alfred Lengnick & Co., Ltd., 1963).

X

The Singer's Musicianship

As our survey of ear training continues it becomes increasingly apparent that an artist singer will need to learn the principles of notation and acquire the ability to read and interpret all the important elements that appear in a printed musical score. These include dozens of conventional symbols such as: staves, ledger lines, clefs, key signatures, notes and rests in their different values and various groupings, holds, single and double bar lines and repeats, tempo expression and dynamic markings, brackets, slurs, accents, key changes, accidentals, appogiatura and grace notes, tremolo and trill signs, and dots.[1]

Also needed is a working familiarity with Italian and German musical terms and abbreviations, rehearsal letters, score patterns, movable clefs, spacing conventions, and the names, designations, and range of the various orchestral instruments and vocal parts.[2] This, in itself, is a long-range development and should not be hurried.

The materials used in ear training, as previously presented, lay the foundations for this growth. However, three essential disciplines remain that will round out the study program. These are reviewed briefly as: *musical dictation, sight singing*, and *score reading* in the discussions which follow.

Musical Dictation

In dictation work, the appeal is to both eye and ear. The teacher plays intervals, chords, phrase excerpts, etc., and the student, after a brief interval of silence, writes them down accurately with suitable notation. Retentive capacity and a mental-visual-aural development are thus achieved.

A complete dictation program will include: 1) learning the elements of notation; 2) beginning the study of harmony; 3) approaching one-, two-, and three-voice writing with a simple piano accompaniment; 4) considering chords in the order of their functional importance, i.e., triads, inversions, seventh chords, etc.; 5) introducing the recognition of nonchord tones and modulations as forms of embellishment and as connecting links in the continuous development of a musical idea; 6) using figured bass as a type of musical shorthand in which harmonies are indicated by numerical subscripts placed beneath a melody; and 7) counterpoint.[3]

At appropriate intervals the keyboard may be used to confirm the growing powers of mental hearing. The keyboard should not be struck, however, until a pupil has had the opportunity to hear mentally what he is about to play or sing. Dictation is thus used indirectly to promote sight-singing ability.

Sight-Singing Procedures

Sight singing has as its purpose reading music silently and reproducing it vocally. This program is especially important to singers and it, too, is available in many published texts on the subject.[4] Learning techniques usually revolve about the use of the tonic note as an orientation center from which we perceive the movement of melodies, harmonies, and rhythms. Out of this, the following ear-training disciplines are evolved:

  1. *corrective listening:* the pupil is taught to recognize the difference when music is deliberately altered or

marred by the teacher to show the effects of such alterations.

2. *linear listening:* the simple melodic lines used in two-voiced counterpoint are studied.

3. *harmonic listening:* the moods of chords and cadences and their functions in expounding a musical idea are aurally observed and analyzed.

4. *contrapuntal listening:* the simple melodic lines simultaneously used in two-voiced counterpoint are studied.

5. *analytical listening:* being able to recognize and write down specific conventional tone patterns, chords, and cadences of various types, using musical notation.

6. *silent reading,* with audible utterance at predetermined points in the score to check pitch and timing: this discipline is especially helpful for choral and ensemble singing.

7. *solfeggio:* the application of *sol–fa* syllables to the audible sight-reading of tones, melodies, and other parts of the printed score.

The *tonic sol–fa* system uses a letter notation, as distinguished from a staff notation. The initials of the seven familiar musical syllables are employed to designate the diatonic notes of the octave: *do (ut) – re – mi – fa – sol – la – ti (si) – do.* Higher octaves use a small figure above the note letter (d') and the lower octave uses a small figure below the note letter at the right side (d_1). A notation for time is also adopted and duration is represented by varied spacing.[5]

By this means, a given tune can be represented with the same syllables, in whatever pitch or key it is sung. Thus, soprano, tenor, alto, or bass would all sing the same syllabic representation of a melody. Tonic sol–fa may, therefore, be used for ear training before staff notation is attempted. Rhythmic beat is also analyzed and simplified by the use of time names. Thus, the tonic sol–fa method leads directly into sight singing without the aid of an accompanying instrument.

Score Reading to Improve Eye and Ear

Reading a score at sight is really a form of memory work in which the reader rapidly photographs complete measures of music and executes them aloud while he is busy memorizing at sight the music that lies ahead. Each measure is therefore anticipated before it is sung or played. The vocalist can thus instantly translate what he sees into sounds, with correct timing, musical value, rhythmic effect, and expression.

Vocal score-reading practice involves the development of five new senses. They are: *pitch sense, key sense, time sense, rhythmic sense,* and *visual sense.* To these may be added the instrumentalist's *tactile sense,* which is necessary for sight reading on the piano keyboard. The mind is thus occupied with many simultaneous actions, all of which occur with ease, accuracy, and speed in the habitually trained sight reader. Each of these items will be briefly described.

1. Pitch sense or note grasp is the ability to sing any note in a score with accurate pitch. It is a type of musical spelling. Begin with the naming of single notes on the staff and immediately locate them on the keyboard. As speed improves, instead of naming the note sing it aloud before playing it and continue this practice until considerable proficiency is acquired. Do the same with intervals and groups of notes. Then try chord-naming, from bottom up, using the same procedure. Do this with broken chords or arpeggios and other note groupings. Be patient but thorough, and learn to memorize with mind, eye, ear, and muscle.

2. Key sense. The harmonies within a given key are studied and practice is continued in the same key for a few days at a time, until the sight and tonal feeling of it are developed. Familiarity with all keys (both major and minor) is thus cultivated. Simple transposition work may also be practiced, using melodies and chords of simple hymn tunes. When using the keyboard, one must learn it by touch alone so that it is not necessary to glance at it to locate a note or chord.[6]

3. Time sense. Music is a transitory phenomenon because tonalities are always in motion. This motion is measured in three dimensions at once as *time, tempo,* and *rhythm. Time* is the indication of single note values or their duration. *Tempo* suggests the mechanical speed of tonal movement or the frequency with which tones occur in a measured period of time. *Rhythm* depicts the forward urge and movement of an entire piece of music.

It is better to *think* time or tempo than to count it aloud. The end in view is the inner realization of musical pulse and its metrical subdivisions. A single melodic part should first be studied. Then gradually introduce the juxtaposition of two or more parts. Practice on one staff at first; then train the eye to read two staffs together. Playing and singing duets is an excellent time-sense developer, remembering, however, that stopping to correct errors is not to be tolerated while the time sense is being developed.

4. Rhythmic sense. Rhythm is the horizontal motive power that creates the overall effect of continuity, coherence, and unity in musical expression. In vocal, as in other types of music, ideas are usually communicated in phrase units rather than note units. The rise and fall of tonalities and melodic line, the speed of this movement, the delineation of form, and the use of accents, drawn-out emphases, pause and tonal contrast, surge and sweep of dynamic nuance—all these constitute the language of music and song.

The ear learns to recognize this tonal language in all its details and ultimately interprets its expression as a message conveyed from the heart of the performer to the heart of the listener. When this tonal idiom becomes intelligible to the singer, his rhythmic sense is born. He then interprets *wholes,* not parts, and the overall scheme is never violated by mechanical display, overemphasis, carelessness of detail, a sluggish beat, or any other irregularity that would attract unfavorable attention to itself.

5. Visual sense. This is the ability to relate printed notation to vocal utterance. It includes the ability to associate notes instantly with the *image* of the sounds, as *heard*. Conversely, as each tonality is mentally heard, its notational aspect is simultaneously visualized. The pupil should memorize, at a glance, a few notes at a time and then play or sing them from memory. Next, he should try this with short phrases, then longer ones. Chords should also be memorized in this fashion, then played or sung in the same manner. When reading a group of notes or a chord, visualize their position on the keyboard before playing them. In due time, the hands will automatically follow the dictates of the mental image, if it is clearly perceived in the mind's eye and ear, just as the voice will easily reproduce the notes that are mentally heard. Thus, in developing visual memory, we coordinate mind, ear, eye, and muscle.

Practicing for Speed and Accuracy

Each of the foregoing skills (i.e., *note grasp, key sense, time sense, rhythm sense,* and *visual sense)* should be practiced separately until proficiency in each is assured. Then they may be practiced in various combinations, using the literature of simple music as drill material. Although absolute precision and accuracy are ultimate objectives, the time and rhythm of the music should never be interrupted by minor corrections. It is best not to think of individual notes in the advanced stages of sight-reading practice but, rather, to maintain the movement and flow of the music at all costs. Later on, problems arising out of errors may be isolated, analyzed, and drilled separately.

The primary purpose of sight reading is to establish quick observation of details *before* they are needed so that their technical or vocal execution may be anticipated. The mind is thereby released for the broader purposes of musical interpretation. The sight reader must learn to look ahead as far as possible and also to think ahead.

The following six steps are recommended for attaining visual speed. Use a piece of music that is written in 4/4 time.

First step: Sing (or play) only the notes that fall on the *first* beat of each measure. Silently count out the remaining beats of the measure while preparing eye, ear, and hand for the initial beat of the next measure, and so on. Thus relieved of intermediate details, the mind will be trained to think ahead.

Second step: Sing (or play) only the *first* and *third* beats of each measure while silently counting in the remainder as mind and eye leap ahead to the next measure.

Third step: Sing (or play) first notes only, as before, but allow the voice to render lightly (or the fingers to touch lightly) the remaining beats so that the forward movement of the eye is unimpeded.

Fourth step: Sing (or play) all notes in the complete piece as written, but never stop to correct an error. Never interrupt the time as you read forward. Go back later to determine the cause of errors.

Fifth step: Think the piece through *silently,* but hear it mentally as you do so, imagining dynamic changes and other indicated expression marks.

Sixth step: Now, sing (or play) it through *audibly,* with complete musical interpretation, as a finished product.

Practice one step at a time. Form each habit separately until all details are executed with ease and precision. Then combine habits. In the last stage, think of *phrase* units rather than single notes. Now, try a variety of time signatures in the practice material, using this method with adaptable scores.

Using Vocal Improvization

Improvization is a visualization process in which original, unplanned tone patterns are mentally heard *before* they are actually sung. Five steps are recommended:

1. Silently create a short original melody. Think it through again and again until it is etched in the memory. Then visualize it note by note and tone by tone until it can be men-

tally repeated at will, without uttering a sound.

2. Now, sing aloud as you improvize. Don't use a keyboard. Sing the improvized melody first. Then write it down. Then sing what you have written. Pitches and rhythms should always be accurately observed. Practice creating and writing single tones at first, then grouped tones, then melodic-phrase patterns. Always write down what you have created, however crude or elementary it may seem.

3. While reading a short literary poem, vocally improvize a melodic or recitative tonal line for it, without instrumental accompaniment. This may seem aimless, at first, resembling an ad lib musical soliloquy. But it will help promote the free expression of thought in song and it is also a stimulus to vocal and artistic growth.

4. Next, write down any original vocal or instrumental melodies that may occur to you. Disregard their form or quality. As written, they represent the free expression of musical ideas, uninhibited by intellectual self-analysis.

5. Finally, try composing the types of short song forms with which you are familiar. These written pieces need not be construed as musical gems but, rather, as practice devices that stimulate the faculties of creative expression and spontaneous thinking.

Continue this type of improvizational practice as a daily discipline. A few minutes a day will suffice, at first. Later, longer periods may be thus consumed until musical thinking, writing, and vocal improvization become as easy as thinking, writing, or speaking one's native language.

Materials for Self-Study Reviewed

In the final analysis, a well-rounded musical development for the singer will also include the study of such areas as structural forms, rules of composition and the description of the instruments, a basic knowledge of conducting, music pedagogy, harmony, counterpoint, orchestration, instrumental playing, and music history. It takes all of these, and more, to make a first-class musician, whether he be vocalist or instrumentalist.

To achieve these ends, the student should have access to many sources of practical musical information. These include dictionaries,[8] histories,[9] encyclopedias,[10] and an extensive bibliography of vocal, operatic, and song literature.[11] A program of reading and self-study will also cover numerous areas of related bibliographical, musicological, and educational information.

The scope and intensity of such a program will, of course, depend on the interests and aptitudes of the individual and the amount of spare time that is available for cultural pursuits. But the teacher must be ready to counsel and guide the pupil in all these studies.

Topics for Self-Study

As a way of cultural enrichment and improving general technical knowledge, topics like the following should also be investigated by the student singer:

1. Accent
2. Accidentals
3. Accompaniment
4. Acoustics
5. Anthem

6. Appoggiatura
7. Aria
8. Ballad
9. Cadence
10. Canon

11. Cantata
12. Chromatics
13. Clef
14. Counterpoint
15. Diatonic

16. Dissonance
17. Dynamics
18. Enharmonic

19. Figured Bass
20. Fixed Do

21. Form
22. Fugue
23. Grace Notes
24. Harmony
25. Hymn

26. Imitation
27. Intervals
28. Inversions
29. Key
30. Leitmotiv

31. Mass
32. Melody
33. Meter
34. Mode
35. Modulation

36. Mordent
37. Motet
38. Notation
39. Opera
40. Opera Comique
41. Operetta
42. Oratorio
43. Orchestra
44. Orchestration
45. Organ
46. Ornaments
47. Overture
48. Phrasing
49. Pianoforte
50. Recitative
51. Rhythm
52. Rondo

53. Scale
54. Score
55. Signature
56. Sonata
57. Song
58. Suite
59. Suspension
60. Syncopation
61. Temperament
62. Tempo
63. Thematics
64. Time
65. Tonality
66. Tonic Sol-fa
67. Trill
68. Turn
69. Variation

Musical Terms Frequently Encountered

The accomplished vocalist will also need to become familiar with the exact meanings of the following musical terms and abbreviations, and with the various names of at least thirty musical instruments. These provide a better knowledge of the proper terminology of music that is found in vocal and instrumental literature.[12]

1. a, al, alla
2. accelerando
3. adagio
4. ad libitum
5. affetuoso

6. affrettando
7. agitato
8. allargando
9. alla breve
10. allegro

11. allegretto
12. alto
13. amabile
14. amore
15. ancora

16. andante
17. andantino
18. animato
19. animando
20. appoggiatura

21. appassionato
22. arco
23. arioso
24. arpeggio
25. assai

26. attacca
27. basso
28. battuta
29. ben
30. bis

21. bravura
32. brio
33. buffa
34. calando
35. calmando

36. canzone
37. cantabile
38. canto
39. capo
40. cappella

41. coda
42. con, col, colla
43. come
44. commodo
45. concerto

174

46. continuo
47. contra
48. corda, corde
49. crescendo
50. da, dal, dai

51. deciso
52. decrescendo
53. del, della
54. destra
55. diminuendo

56. divisi
57. dolce
58. dolcissimo
59. doppio
60. due, duo

61. energico
62. espressivo
63. fermata
64. feroce
65. fine

66. forte
67. fortissimo
68. forza
69. fuga, fugato
70. fuoco

71. furioso
72. giocoso
73. glissando
74. giusto
75. grandioso

76. grave
77. grazia, grazioso
78. grosso
79. indeciso
80. inquieto

81. istesso
82. largo, larghetto
83. largamente
84. legato
85. leggiero

86. lento
87. lo, il, la

88. lontano
89. lunga
90. ma

91. maestoso
92. marcato
93. mano
94. marcia
95. meno

96. mezzo
97. missa
98. maggiore
99. minore
100. misurato

101. moderato
102. molto
103. morendo
104. mosso
105. moto

106. movimento
107. nel, negli
108. non
109. nota
110. obligato

111. ossia
112. ostinato
113. ottava
114. opus
115. parte

116. pastorale
117. pausa
118. per
119. perdendosi
120. perpetuo

121. pesante
122. piacere
123. piacevole
124. piano
125. pianissimo

126. pizzicato
127. piu
128. poco
129. poco a poco

130. pomposo
131. ponderoso
132. portamento
133. primo
134. presto
135. quasi

136. quieto
137. rallentando
138. recitativo
139. replica
140. rinforzando

141. risoluto
142. ritardando
143. ritenuto
144. ritmo
145. rubato

146. scherzando
147. secco
148. secondo
149. segno
150. segue

151. semplice
152. sempre
153. senza
154. sereno
155. sforzando

156. simile
157. sinistra
158. smorzando
159. solo, soli
160. sopra

161. soprano
162. sordino
163. sostenuto
164. sotto
165. spiritoso

166. staccato
167. stesso
168. strascinando
169. strepitoso
170. stretto

171. stringendo	179. tenore	186. tutti
172. sul, sulla	180. tenuto	187. troppo
173. subito		188. un, uno
174. tacet	181. testa	189. vivace
175. tanto	182. testo	190. vive
	183. tranquile	
176. tema	184. tre	191. voce
177. tempo	185. trio	192. volta
178. teneramente		

Musical Abbreviations Frequently Used

1. accel.	21. M.D.	41. sf., sfz
2. cad.	22. mf	42. sim.
3. cantab.	23. M.G.	43. smorz.
4. cl.	24. M.M.	44. sord.
5. cres.	25. mp	45. sost.
6. D.C.	26. M.S.	46. S.P.
7. decres.	27. Ob.	47. stacc.
8. D.S.	28. 8va	48. string.
9. dim.	29. op.	49. ten.
10. div.	30. p, pp	50. Timp.
11. dolcis.	31. Ped.	51. tr.
12. espress.	32. pianiss.	52. trem.
13. f, ff	33. Pf.	53. Tromb.
14. Fag.	34. Picc.	54. Tromp.
15. Fl.	35. pizz.	55. unis.
16. fp	36. rall.	56. V⁰, VV
17. forz.	37. recit.	57. Va., Vla.
18. H., Hr.	38. riten.	58. var.
19. leg.	39. ritard.	59. Vcl.
20. marc.	40. rf., rfz	60. V.S.

The Orchestral Instruments Named in Four Languages

English	Italian	French	German
1. Harp	Arpa	Harpe	Harfe
2. Violin	Violino	Violon	Geige: Violine
3. Viola	Viola	Alto	Bratsche
4. Cello	Violoncello	Violoncelle	Violoncell
5. Double Bass	Contrabasso	Contre basse	Kontrabass

6. Flute	Flauto	Flûte	Flöte
7. Piccolo	Flauto Piccolo	Petite Flûte	Kleine Flöte
8. Oboe	Oboè	Hautbois	Hoboe
9. English Horn	Corno Inglese	Cor Anglais	Englisches Horn
10. Clarinet	Clarinetto	Clarinette	Klarinette
11. Bass Clarinet	Clarinetto Basso	Clarinette basse	Bassklarinette
12. Bassoon	Fagotto	Basson	Fagott
13. Double Bassoon	Contrafagotto	Contre-Basson	Kontrafagott
14. Horn	Corno	Cor	Horn
15. Trumpet	Tromba	Trompette	Trompete
16. Trombone	Trombone	Trombone	Posaune
17. Tuba	Tuba	Tuba	Tuba
18. Kettledrums	Timpani	Timbales	Pauken
19. Bass Drum	Gran Cassa	Grosse Caisse	Grosse Trommel
20. Cymbals	Piatti, Cinelli	Cymbales	Becken
21. Side-drum	Tamburo militare	Tambour militaire	Kleine Trommel
22. Triangle	Triangolo	Triangle	Triangel
23. Tenor Drum	Tamburo rulante	Caisse roulante	Ruhrtrommel
24. Glockenspiel	Campanetta	Carillon	Glockenspiel
25. Celesta	Celesta	Céleste	Celeste
26. Bells	Campanelle	Cloches	Glocken
27. Xylophone	Zilafone	Xylophone	Xylophon
28. Gong	Tamtam	Tam-tam	Tam-tam
29. Organ	Organo	Orgue	Orgel
30. Piano	Pianoforte	Piano	Klavier

The Study of Song Literature

Obviously, a thorough preparation in musicianship is no easy matter. A singer's taste and appreciation must be cultivated through years of systematic exposure to the finest music of every description, performed by the finest artists. Many compositions should be heard, analyzed, and discussed until the potential singer is on speaking terms with most of them. Frequent attendance at concerts, recitals, operatic, and dramatic performances provide access to the best works of musical art as presented by the foremost conductors, orchestras, soloists, and ensemble performers. Excellent recordings are also available.

As a concurrent development, hundreds of vocal compositions are to be studied and reviewed. These comprise the standard song literature of the professional singer. They include vocal gems of American, British, French, German, Italian, and other composers. They are listed in categories for voices in all ranges and qualities, with composer's names, etc., in published anthologies and in the libraries, bibliographies, and catalogues of well-known music publishers. Many of them are also available on phonographic recordings.

Likewise, the oratorios, masses, and other sacred compositions of Scarlatti, Pergolesi, Handel, Bach, Haydn, Gounod, Liszt, Mendelsohn, and others are not to be overlooked, since they provide interesting and challenging musical and dramatic content for the seasoned vocalist. The basic song materials that can be studied and used for solo repertoire are listed in a later chapter. Materials thus covered will furnish an invaluable proving ground for voices at all levels of development and will encompass all the problems that the average pupil encounters in the vocal studio.

Operatic Repertoire

Finally, for the more advanced student, vocal assignments include arias, recitatives, and dramatic studies in operatic repertoire. Both teacher and student will, therefore, need to be familiar with standard operatic works and the vocal training resources contained therein.

The singer's operatic repertoire derives mainly from more than one hundred operas. Most of them are composed in one of four main languages: English, German, French, or Italian. Some of these operas are rarely performed in public, but they are all rich in training material for vocal repertoire.[13]

There are well over 1600 characters in opera to choose from in a singer's repertoire, covering every type and range of voice: soprano, mezzo-soprano, contralto, tenor, baritone, and bass. Over 200 characters may be found in each main category. It is therefore virtually impossible for any one singer to exhaust all the possibilities of operatic study.

The choice of assignments would, of course, depend on the type of personality and voice the pupil has. The teacher would have to know what roles to assign after testing out the capabilities, tessitura and range, personality, vocal quality and vigor, physique, temperament, endurance and agility, knowledge of language, clarity of diction, musicianship, age, and maturity of each student.

As a convenient reference, the world's noteworthy and most familiar operas are given here under their composer's names. Obsolete and little-known works are excluded in this listing:

Balfe
1. Bohemian Girl

Beethoven
2. Fidelio

Bellini
3. La Sonnambula
4. Norma
5. I Puritani

Berlioz
6. La Damnation de Faust

Bizet
7. Carmen
8. Les Pêcheurs de Perles

Boito
9. Mefistofele

Charpentier
10. Louise

Debussy
11. Pelléas et Mélisande

Delibes
12. Lakmé

Donizetti
13. Don Pasquale
14. L'Elisir d'Amore
15. La Favorita
16. La Fille du Regiment
17. Lucia di Lammermoor

Flotow
18. Martha

Giordano
19. Andrea Chenier
20. Fedora

Gluck
21. Alceste
22. Orfeo ed Euridice

Gounod
23. Faust
24. Romeo et Juliette

Halevy
25. La Juive

Handel
26. Rinaldo

Humperdink
27. Hänsel und Gretel

Leoncavallo
28. I Pagliacci

Mascagni
29. Cavalleria Rusticana

Massenet
30. Hérodiade
31. Le Cid
32. Manon
33. Thais
34. Werther

Meyerbeer
35. L'Africaine
36. Dinorah
37. Les Huguenots
38. Le Prophète

Monteverdi
39. La Favola d'Orfeo

Mozart
40. Così fan tutti
41. Don Giovanni
42. Entführung aus dem Serail
43. Idomeneo
44. Le Nozze di Figaro
45. Die Zauberflöte

Moussorgsky
46. Boris Godounov

Offenbach
47. Les Contes d'Hoffman

Pergolesi
48. La Serva Padrona

Peri
49. Euridice

Ponchielli
50. La Gioconda

Puccini
51. La Bohème
52. La Fanciulla del West
53. Gianni Schicchi
54. Madama Butterfly
55. Manon Lescaut
56. La Tosca
57. Turandot

Purcell
58. Dido and Aeneas

Rossini
59. Il Barbiere di Siviglia
60. La Cenerentola
61. La Gazza Ladra
62. Guillaume Tell
63. L'Italiana in Algeri
64. Semiramide
65. Tancredi

Saint-Saëns
66. Samson et Dalila

Smetana
67. The Bartered Bride

Strauss, J.
68. Die Fledermaus
69. Der Zigeunerbaron

Strauss, R.
70. Ariadne
71. Elektra
72. Der Rosenkavalier
73. Salome

Thomas
74. Hamlet
75. Mignon

Verdi
76. Aida
77. Una Ballo di Maschera
78. Don Carlo
79. Ernani
80. Falstaff
81. La Forze del Destino
82. Luisa Miller
83. Macbeth
84. Nabucco
85. Otello
86. Rigoletto
87. Simon Boccanegra
88. Traviata
89. Il Trovatore

Wagner
90. Der Fliegende Hollander
91. Götterdämmerung
92. Lohengrin
93. Die Meistersinger von Nürnberg

94. Parsifal
95. Das Rheingold
96. Rienzi
97. Siegfried
98. Tannhaüser
99. Tristan und Isolde

100. Die Walküre

Weber

101. Euryanthe
102. Der Freischütz
103. Oberon

Summary and Conclusions

In summation, singing is a multidimensional art. Therefore, all the foregoing sources of information have to be available if students of singing are to be successfully guided through a well-rounded program that leads to artistry, interpretative skill, sight-reading ability, ear training, and general musicianship.

An accomplished singer must know something of the rich musical culture of his civilization. This includes sacred and secular music, operatic tradition, folklore, the lives of great artists, a survey of vocal and musical bibliography, the aims and ideals of a composer, and the style of his period.

A vocalist must acquire the ability to read music fluently at sight, both silently and audibly. A page of music should be as easy for him to read and understand as the page of an interesting novel. In short, a singer's musical understanding comes mainly through the cultivation of a rich musical background, the use of a finely sensitized and discriminating ear, and much experience in expressing himself both vocally and instrumentally in the idiom of his art.

Such a development is a life-long accomplishment, to be sure. But out of it emerges a breadth of understanding and the mellowed expressiveness and interpretative maturity of the finished artist. That is the essence of scholarship and self-mastery in any art. It is the difference between amateur and professional, and it is achieved by means of a program of cultural growth and discipline that includes general education, technical studies, ear training, and musical knowledge. As Emerson wisely stated: "To be well educated is to be at home in the world."

REFERENCES AND NOTES

1. Karl W. Gehrkens, *Music Notation and Terminology* (New York: Laidlaw Brothers, Inc., 1930).

2. Roger E. Chapman, *Essentials of Music* (Garden City, New York: Doubleday & Company, Inc., 1967); Jack Sacher, editor, *Music A to Z* (New York: Grosset & Dunlap Inc., 1963), p. 176.

3. Bruce Benward, *Teacher's Dictation Manual in Ear Training* (Dubuque, Iowa: William C. Brown Co., 1961).

4. Gabriel F. Berkowitz and Leo Kraft, *A New Approach to Sight Singing* (New York: W. W. Norton & Co., Inc., 1960); Wilhelm Keilman, *Introduction to Sight Reading* (New York: C. F. Peters Corporation, 1973).

5. *Grove's Dictionary of Music and Musicians,* 5th edition (New York: St. Martin's Press, Inc., 1959), q.v., "Tonic Sol–Fa."

6. Kenneth Simpson, *Keyboard Harmony and Improvization* (London: Alfred Lengnick & Co., Ltd., 1963), Chaps. 8, 9.

7. Frederick Schlieder, *Lyric Composition Through Improvization* (New York: C. C. Birchard & Co., 1927).

8. Willi Apel, *Harvard Dictionary of Music* (Cambridge, Mass.: Harvard University Press, 1945).

9. Paul Henry Láng, *Music in Western Civilization* (New York: W. W. Norton & Co., Inc., 1941); Harman and Wilfred Mellers, *Man and His Music* (New York: Oxford University Press, 1962); Wallace Brockway and Herbert Weinstock, *Men of Music* (New York: Simon & Schuster, 1958).

10. Rupert Hughes, *Music Lover's Encyclopedia,* revised and edited by Deems Taylor (New York: Doubleday & Co., Inc., 1954); Nicholas Slonimsky. *Baker's Biographical Dictionary of Music,* 5th edition (New York: G. Schirmer, 1958).

11. Berton Coffin, *Singer's Repertoire,* 2nd edition (New York: Scarecrow Press, 1962); Sergius Kagen *Music for the Voice* (New York: Rinehart & Company, Inc., 1949).

12. W. J. Smith, *A Dictionary of Musical Terms in Four Languages* (London: Hutchinson & Co., Ltd., 1961); Parks Grant, *Handbook of Musical Terms* (New York: Scarecrow Press, 1967); Sacher, *Music A to Z,* pp. 352, 357.

13. David Ewen, *Encyclopedia of the Opera* (New York: Hill and Wang, Inc., 1963); Harold Rosenthal and John Warrack, editors, *The Concise Oxford Dictionary of the Opera* (London: Oxford University Press 1964); Milton Cross, *New Complete Stories of the Great Operas,* edited by Karl Kohrs (Garden City, New York: Doubleday & Co., Inc., 1955).

XI

Vocal Intonation and Its Problems

Intonation is the act of initiating and sustaining musical sound. It is the vocalist's physical response to his aural image. This is not just a matter of sounding voice. The output must include distinguishing basic properties that are embodied in every singing tone, properties of *pitch, duration, dynamics,* and *quality.* The resultant expression must also be musically acceptable and esthetically satisfying.

In this discussion, therefore, principles and procedures that relate to tone production in its essential attributes are reviewed. Such topics as *tonal attack, extending the range,* and factors of *pitch, duration, dynamics, quality,* and *resonance* are considered from a singer's point of view. Illustrative drills and exercises are suggested, when necessary, to supplement material already in use, to sharpen the tools of instruction, as it were, and to enhance the usefulness of the countless teaching devices and vocal exercises that are already available to every singing teacher.

The Tonal Attack

The *attack* is the clear and distinct commencement of vocal tone. It is the synchronization of glottal closure and chest pulse. The latter term denotes the breathing movement needed to build up adequate subglottal breath pressure for the activation of the vocal folds.[1]

Under normal conditions, the pupil's ear governs the output. However, when bad habits are noted, the pupil's ear is not a reliable monitor and the teacher's judgment must prevail. Correct attack, therefore, starts with a mental image right on the desired pitch, and it does not waver in pitch, quality, or intensity as long as the tone lasts. The beginner's approach embodies three preparatory objectives, and appropriate corrective exercises like the following are used, when needed, to achieve them.

1. *A clear mental image must be formed.* This may be acquired by listening to good vocal models, by imitation, and by instrumental guidance. An interval of *silent* visualization on correct pitch is also helpful before actually singing each note or series of notes in a song. Strong intonation concepts are thus inculcated as mind action precedes physical action.

2. *The glottal closure must be strengthened,* as in the following procedure:

a. At medium pitch level, unaccompanied, sound the vowel "ah." Repeat it in a light glottal staccato several times, with even intensity.

b. Now, *gradually* increase the repetitive frequency of these light staccato tones until the glottal "ah" attains a rapidity that resolves itself into a single prolonged vowel. Practice several times in this manner before proceeding.

c. *Next,* repeat this drill on different vowels, using the very light staccato glottal attack throughout.

d. Try this rapid staccato sequence on different pitches and on regular scale intervals, using the repetitive approach of (a) and (b). Swallow slowly after each exercise, to relax the glottal muscles.

This practice group is used for conditioning muscular responses at the level of the glottis. It is not a singing technique.

The attack is always light, firm, detached, and precisely on pitch. The drill may be continued intermittently, for several lessons, until a clean-cut tone is achieved and every trace of breathy emission is eliminated.

e. Now, practice a staccato *aspirated* laughing attack for each tone within the pitch range. In doing this, think of the action of the chest rather than the glottis. Each tone will seem to be bounced off the stomach and out of the mouth as if it were impelled by staccato laughter (hah-hah-hah; ho-ho-ho; hee-hee-hee; etc.).

f. Next, use the centripetal chest action described in (e) above, to produce a sighing groan on a sustained pitch. A groaning "ah" is heard that appears to emanate from the abdominal region. Repeat several times; then repeat with a *humming* sound.

g. Next, start at a moderate pitch level and sing a *descending* arpeggio or scale sequence of three, four, or five tones, on any vowel, using the same approach (i.e., nonvigorous sighing and groaning). Continue in this manner, on different vowels and pitches, until mild compressive breath support for each tone can be captured and remembered for later use in sustained singing.

h. Continue this approach with scale passages, melodic fragments, rhythmic and dynamic tonal patterns, staccato or legato, until basic coordinations have been established and habits are well under way. Thereafter, the attention can be gradually diverted toward tonal imagery, rather than mechanics. The high-chest posture is maintained throughout.

3. *Sustained breath compression* against the *closed* glottis must be acquired. Proceed as follows:

a. Inhale comfortably, not extremely. After inhalation, apply a threefold (dorsal, lateral, and abdominal) contraction of the thorax. This is achieved *silently,* against a *closed* glottis, as if about to cough or grunt lightly. Repeat this action several times, *without* making a sound. Then relax and swallow.

b. Now, perform the same breathing action with a very

light but slightly prolonged glottal tone, on various vowels and pitches (ah—, ah—, ah—; aw—, aw—, aw—; oh—, oh—, oh—; ee—, ee—, ee—; etc.).

c. Next, place a slightly aspirated "h" before each tone. (hah—, hah—, hah—; haw—, haw—, haw—; ho—, ho—, ho—; etc.). Renew the breath slowly after each trial but do not drop the chest. Be careful not to jerk the abdominal wall inward on the tonal attack. Spasmodic action of any part of the breathing apparatus is faulty. The larynx is always stationary.[2]

These preliminary exercises are put to use gradually and repeated under a teacher's supervision so that gentle, not spasmodic, action and proper balance between breath compression and glottal closure are gradually established. It is important to rest frequently between trials by swallowing gently and then pausing.

More specific intonation problems of *pitch, duration, dynamics,* and *quality* may now be considered. These embody principles and procedures previously discussed.

Pitch Factors: Extending the Range

In its early stages, a singer's training consists of awakening an aural awareness of the vocal range he possesses. Unused pitches must become familiar to the pupil's ears through practice. Aural preconceptions and physical experience will then dictate their freer use in singing. To this end, the teacher guides the pupil into a gradual extension, note by note, of his unused range until his own ear has learned to recognize his own capabilities.

It is considered best *not* to start at the bottom and work upward. Thus, the range is never strained upward from below but, rather, each initial tone is attacked squarely on pitch, then followed by a *descending* legato sequence of tones.[3]

1. Begin at a point near the middle or most comfortable pitch level. Sing a simple three-, four-, or five-note descending

legato sequence on the vowel "ah." Use a short arpeggio or scale fragment.

2. Next, with each repetition of the foregoing, attack the *initial* note of each descending sequence on the next *higher* pitch level. Proceed thus, step by step, until the highest comfortable pitches are reached.

3. Other vowels and syllables may now be practiced in this manner. The ear thereby develops a sense of tonal initiative and the dragging or "sliding up into pitch" tendency is prevented.

4. Later on, longer arpeggi and moderate downward interval leaps may be attempted. But in every case, each *initial* attack is on the next *higher* pitch level than its predecessor. The initial tone is thus always followed by a *downward* legato scale fragment or short arpeggio.

5. Although lower portions of the vocal range do not usually present a serious pitch problem, they may be practiced in similar fashion, starting at any point in the lower range and proceeding *downward* with each initial note of a descending scale fragment.

6. During several weeks of patient preliminary work, melodic exercises may be gradually introduced that move in any direction and that more nearly resemble the inflectional patterns of a spoken song text. Short songs or song fragments of graded range may be added as exercise material. An effortless melodic pitch range is thus gradually acquired.

Using the Inflectional Approach

As a supplement to the above exercises, pitch range may also be extended by following the inflections of the *speaking* voice.

a. For example, try using the word "alright" as an exercise. Attack the *first* syllable of this *spoken* word at a comfortable pitch level. Then immediately dip the inflection downward and slide it upward again on the second syllable. The result will resemble a spoken expression of exaggerated cheerful assent as the word "alright" is being spoken. Repeat this exercise several times.

b. Now, with each inflected repetition of the same word, attack its first syllable on the next *higher* pitch, again dipping all the way downward and sliding upward again on the second syllable. Continue this sequence of cheerful-sounding inflections of the *spoken* voice until the highest pitches are reached. Use a s-l-o-w rate throughout.

This quasi-singing exercise, if performed in s-l-o-w motion, illustrates the naturalness of spoken inflection for reaching relatively high pitches in the vocal range.

c. Now, try the same type of *spoken* inflections with words like "*cer*-tainly," "*I'll* do it," "*give* it to me," "*please* come here," "*tell* me about it," "*I'm* feeling *fine*," etc. With each repetition, the initial attack on each first syllable is always to be one scale step higher than its predecessor. The syllable then dips downward, as before, and then inflects upward on the next syllable or word.

d. Similar inflectional exercises may be devised to accompany any melodic pattern in a song. First isolate the pattern desired, then match it to a *spoken* phrase taken from the text of the song, or use an original *spoken* phrase that will best lend itself to that type of inflection. Always *speak* the phrase *very* slowly and attentively until accuracy of inflection on desired pitches is captured.

e. Simple melodic exercises that are derived from actual songs may now be used. These melodies should lie within the pitch limits previously rehearsed, so that no unfamiliar pitch level is experienced by the student.

f. Light legato, staccato, and sustained tonal patterns may next be introduced as part of melodic training. At this stage it is best to focus the attention on freedom of production, smoothness, and flexibility of tonal movement, while feeling at home in all portions of the vocal range. This graded approach covers many types of song fragments. Even recitative may be used (with light chordal accompaniment).

g. Unaccompanied, then accompanied, versions of a song may next be practiced. When singing unaccompanied, the piano is touched lightly, from time to time, to guide the mental ear.

h. Similarly, an opening chord may be given at the beginning of a familiar song. The pupil is then allowed to think through the entire melody *silently*. At any point, on signal, he should be able to sing aloud the tone he is thinking with exact correspondence to the pitch and timing in the score. This type of mental-pitch training will serve to build aural acuity and melodic freedom within the enlarged range of the speaking and singing voice. Rhythmic and dynamic factors may be ignored at this stage.

One should not attempt singing that is overloud, forced, or intensely dramatic during the early stages of this developmental program. If a pupil becomes impatient to try more dramatic songs, he may be transferred to *spoken* declamations in poetry and prose that will help give vent to his pent-up histrionic abilities without doing violence to the vocal-training program. *Spoken* song texts and other classical selections of worthwhile literary or dramatic content may be used for this temporary diversion.

Register Breaks: Physiological Causes

In the process of extending the singing range, references to vocal registers and register breaks should be avoided. The *prevention* of a "register break" is more important than its cure; and to clarify the pedagogical problems involved a brief discussion of causes may be helpful.

It will be recalled that during phonation for singing, the anterior ends of the glottis are being pulled in a *forward* direction by the contraction of the cricothyroid muscles. Simultaneously, the arytenoid muscles exert a *backward* pull at the posterior ends of the glottis. Thus, for any given pitch, each set of end muscles acts in opposite directions against a resisting *internal* contraction and stiffening of the glottal ledges themselves. In this muscular synergy, the degree of contraction varies with pitch and intensity. Since a state of equilibrium is thus normally maintained between opposing forces, nothing moves appreciably and no part of the larynx will be pulled out of position.

On the other hand, if either end of the glottis should yield due to faulty action or imbalance of opposing connecting muscles, cordal tension will be momentarily affected. If the arytenoid muscles yield, the thyroid cartilage will rock forward in a downward arc until, at about the time the note f above middle c is reached, the anterior cricothyroid notch will be closed. Then, as ascent of pitch continues, a spasmodic readjustment takes place. The thyroid cartilage rocks upward suddenly because extrinsic muscles have been brought into play. When the thyroid cartilage thus rebounds the vocal cords will momentarily relax and an audible pitch *break* will occur. The voice then continues upward into its so-called higher "register." A sensation of relief is experienced by the singer during this transition.[4]

The so-called "passagio" is that segment of the ascending pitch range in which the thyroid cartilage tilts forward until it closes the cricothyroid notch and then rebounds to its former position. To correct the resultant register break, a so-called "covering" action is consciously used by the ill-advised singer. The "covering" action prevents closure of the cricothyroid notch during pitch transit by activating delinquent supralaryngeal muscles so as to correct the forward-tilting tendency and thus prevent a "register break."

Our problem, however, is to maintain a *constant* balance of the entire laryngeal musculature, both intrinsic and extrinsic, during pitch movement. If this balance is maintained, with the larynx kept in a retracted position in the throat, the thyroid cartilage will *not* rock forward and the anterior cricothyroid notch will not become closed at any pitch level. Consequently, a readjustment of the thyroid position with a resultant pitch break will *not* occur.

Therefore, in cultivating the singing voice, progressive

technical and melodic exercises affecting the entire singable range are used, with expressional motivation as a constant factor; and the concept of registers and register breaks is never mentioned. In other words, the glottal musculature will be most likely to act correctly for singing when posture is correct; when the ear governs vocal output; and when expression rather than technique is a motivating factor.[5]

Psychological Causes

In singing performance we *will* the result, not the means. In everyday use, vocal utterance is normally motivated by communicative intent rather than self-conscious tonal display, and intonation reflexes are normally governed by the ear. The vocal instrument will therefore be predisposed to correct action, provided it is *allowed* to act. The usual obstructions to vocal action are inhibitions or restraints from within and conscious strivings from without.

In other words, preoccupation with limitations in the voice creates a mental roadblock. The very reminder of registers builds a fear of breaks, and this fear is augmented when the pupil is improperly taught to "cover" certain pitches and manipulate the "passagio" for tones that are needed to bridge so-called register gaps.

The "high" and "low" illusion is also a potential cause of register breaks. The very thought of pitch elevation can cause a conscious reaching upward, with attendant muscular striving and straining. As a temporary palliative, therefore, the pupil may be directed to think *descent* while singing up the scale. That is, he may be instructed to imagine himself descending a flight of stairs, or moving downward on an escalator, as he sings higher and higher in his vocal range. Since thought governs action, breaks will not occur when this counteracting exercise is properly performed. Ultimately, the vocalist learns to think *straight ahead* on all tones, especially in ascending passages.

In *falsetto,* the vocal ledges vibrate at their outer margins only.[6] That is to say, because of a slackened musculature, there is little or no synchronous vibratory response of contiguous areas of the vocal tract. Falsetto tones are due to weaker efforts of all intrinsic and extrinsic muscles of the larynx.

The *messa di voce* exercise is recommended as a further training procedure, but only after pitch and breathing fundamentals have been mastered. This method provides a gradual strengthening of the entire glottal mechanism, with all its supporting muscles, in coordination with proper breathing controls. Thus, it becomes possible to learn how to control a gradually prolonged crescendo on any pitch, in all dynamic gradations from falsetto, through mezza voce, to full voice. More of this later.

Duration Factors

Briefly put, the *will* to make a sound induces a pulmonary-glottic synergy that causes phonation. The expressional impulse of the singer directs nervous energy into all relevant laryngeal and respiratory muscles, regulating their firmness, adductor and longitudinal tension, and also regulating the breath support needed to assure sustained phonation at any dynamic level. A complex coordination thus occurs which is apportioned over a complex musculature in a manner that brings about the perfect distribution of energy and the equilibrium of all parts.

During phonation, the vocal lips are not sealed but merely sucked together in a sustained kissing action. Constant breath pressure induces a minute, intermittent pulsating separation of the glottal lips which permits an infinitesimal amount of air-escape during each vibratory swing. It follows, therefore, that sustained phonation would eventually deplete the lungs, calling for replenishment of breath at appropriate intervals during the song.

The duration of tone, therefore, calls for four stages of breath control: *intake, retention, compression,* and *economic release*. These may be described as follows:

Intake must be swift and silent, adequate but not excessive. Each thought takes its own breath, appropriate to the expressional needs thereof. Only intense, long-sustained, and dynamic climaxes demand maximal intake. Therefore, breath-budgeting to suit the phrase length is paramount. The trained singer never exceeds these requirements.

Retention may be described as a feeling of "not breathing" while singing. Although the lungs are adequately filled, there is never a pushing of breath against tone. Quite the contrary, the breath is almost withheld during phonation, an apparent paradox, but one that makes the difference between the flute-like, floating legato production of an artist and the harsh breathy or metallic tone of the unskilled amateur. Correct intonation oftens reminds one of the sensation of yawning, since all vocal sound is cushioned by a cavernous breath restraint, an illusory feeling of "not breathing" throughout.

Compression, as previously described, is the centripetal contraction of the thorax that always accompanies artistic tone production. Except for dynamic passages or unusual dramatic climaxes, this compressive action is continuous and firm but gentle, not convulsive or maximal. Good posture is always maintained.

Economic release is a product of the preceding three factors. Although the breath is being slowly depleted, escape is so gradual as to seem nonexistent. Breath renewal is dictated either by oxygen hunger or by the interpretational pattern of the song.

All in all, the duration of tone is largely governed by sustained breath support applied to a sustained glottal closure. Expiratory breath thus acts in conjunction with the elastic resistance of the adducted vocal folds to produce a sustained tone without muscularity or needless tension. To improve this breath support, the exercises in the chapter on "Breathing Methods and Mechanisms" should be reviewed.

Control of Vocal Dynamics

Subglottal air pressure is also employed to increase the *power* of the phonated tone. Vocal dynamics are, therefore, closely related to breath support. During a *crescendo,* as previously explained, glottal resistance is increased proportionately as breath pressure increases. The gradual added firmness of vocal muscles during a crescendo improves their elasticity and thus augments the amplitude of each glottal swing. A resonance factor is also present in that the augmented vibratory energy that is generated would be transmitted over wider areas of the singer's body. This would produce a synchronous vibratory response in these areas, much as the bridge, sound post, and body of a violin vibrate synchronously with the strings thereof. The larger the vibratory area thus engaged, the louder (and richer) the sound. Resonance thus becomes a factor in controlling vocal dynamics.

A helpful corrective for lack of tonal energy is suggested. It is called the *intensive whisper*. Proceed as follows:

1. First, project the words of any song text in a loud, *spoken* whisper, without phonation.
2. After several repetitions of this whispered text, suddenly resume the full voice, using the same intensity for vocal utterance that was used for the preceding intensive whisper. That is to say, try to project the spoken *voice* as far as you projected the voiceless *whisper*.

An immediate improvement in breath support for phonation, dynamics, and resonance will be forthcoming. Repeat the entire intensive whispering exercise at frequent intervals, so as to energize all tonal projectors and build subglottal breath pressure for normal singing purposes. Distinct articulation should always be used when whispering and correct singing posture should be maintained.

When the singer's breath is properly managed, its emission remains nearly constant at all dynamic levels.[7] To test this, hold a lighted candle close to the mouth while prolonging an "ah" vowel. Now, *gradually* augment the voice during a slow crescendo. The flame should not flutter, even for loudest tones. A flickering flame indicates breath wastage and improved retention is then called for.

Vocal dynamics in singing are also governed by psychological factors. They are: a) idealized hearing concepts; b) intensity of feeling and its effect on muscular tonus; c) communicative urge, i.e., conscious awareness of the distance between singer and audience; and d) the degree of dynamics called for in the expressional interpretation of the score.

Awareness of the presence of a listener will help motivate projection. It is suggested, therefore, that the student always practice as if he were standing before an imaginary audience, as an act of *communication,* rather than as a self-contained vocal exercise.

Messa di Voce

This exercise consists of swelling a continuous tone from pianissimo to maximum power, and then diminishing the voice gradually to its starting point. The *crescendo* is very gradual and the *diminuendo* equally so. The accomplished singer must be able to achieve this control for every note in his vocal range.

Begin with single singing tones of short duration. Gradually increase their length with each trial. Reach out with your singing voice as if trying to maintain contact with an imaginary listener who is slowly receding and then approaching you. Be careful to budget the breath so that a singing crescendo can be made to last as long as a diminuendo on the same tone.

The three stages of *messa di voce* are: 1) swelling to maximum volume *(formare il tuono);* 2) sustaining at the maximum level *(fermare il tuono);* 3) diminishing to the vanishing point *(finire il tuono).* The singer learns to control this process through a thousand degrees of intensity, from softest to loudest and back again, without interruption or the slightest deviation in pitch, quality, or breath support. A basic breath and tone coordination will thus be acquired which, in time, becomes habitual.[8] Weeks of supervised practice may be needed to accomplish this result.

Breath Renewal

The replenishment of breath is also an important factor in singing, especially in dynamic tone production. Such renewal must provide adequate oxygen supply at all times. Therefore, the act of ventilating the lungs becomes a learned technique. Renewal must be swift and silent, and strategically placed where it will be least obtrusive. At phrase intervals, dramatic pauses, and wherever expressional intent permits, a swift gulp of air may be needed.

Very little breath is required for vocal intonation if retention is adequate and the phrase length moderate. But if the phrase to be sung is overlong and loaded with explosive diction, a greater need for oxygen arises. This will dictate a quicker expulsion of *unused* breath followed by a swift but silent refill at more frequent intervals. The artist always anticipates his needs, skillfully budgets his breath, and unobtrusively gulps in just the right amount of air needed to sustain a given tone or phrase—no more, no less. Too much breath is as bad as too little.

In summation, the following factors of breath control are related to vocal dynamics in singing:

1. Closure of the glottal chink must be firm, and this is achieved, in part, by glottal resistance against suitable compression of the subglottal breath chamber.

2. Breath is thereby better retained and sparingly released during the minute intermittent vibratory excursions of the glottal lips.

3. The entire chest boundary, including the abdominal wall, activates a *constant* subglottal compression chamber which improves tonal support and adds sonority to the voice.

4. After inhalation takes place, abdominal muscles move *gradually*, not fitfully, with a steady *inward* lift as tone increases in volume or rises in pitch.

5. For singing purposes, the rib cage moves alternately outward and inward, denoting *lateral* expansion and contraction. The breathing effort during phonation is always inward, or *centrally directed*, not upward toward the glottis. Especially is this true as pitch ascends, or during crescendos and in vigorous passages.

6. Renewal of breath must be swift, silent, and unobtrusive, without disturbing the flow of tone. Either mouth or nose may be used. Expediency, comfort, and speed are the determining factors.

7. A high-chest position is always to be favored, and at no time should the clavicles, shoulders, or breastbone be heaved.

When all these controls have become habitualized, the entire breathing effort will become automatic and properly coordinated with the act of sustained phonation.

Vocal Quality and Resonance

Intonation is not exclusively a glottal phenomenon. Each vocal tone is also influenced acoustically by the conformation and composition of the airway lying above and below the glottis. The upper tone passage is open, the lower one closed. Some parts are rigid and immovable. Others can be varied in size and shape. The muscle tonus of the body, responding as it does to health, posture, and mental attitude, also affects the acoustical response of the entire system.

It will be remembered from a previous discussion that an air chamber provides better conductivity for sound when it is compacted than when it is expanded and its contents rarified. Optimal breath *compression* is therefore essential for maintaining vocal quality and resonance during phonation for singing.

Breath support, good posture, and muscle tonus promote a favorable transmission route for all glottal pulsations as they radiate into outlying areas of the singer's body. Under ideal conditions, a vocal *fremitus* may be felt by the singer himself as he places his hand on his chest while he is humming. Fremitus is a vibratory sensation that is perceptible to the touch. Likewise, there is palpable vibration in the mask and bones of the face during phonation.

The term *head hum* is used to differentiate a perceptible vibration in the mask from a chest fremitus, since the terms *chest resonance* and *head resonance* in their broader connotations are too often misunderstood.

The following exercises are recommended:

1. Establish a head hum initially by prolonging "m-m-m" on a comfortable pitch level. Gradually swell this humming sound. Note the increasing vibratory sensation in the mask as the humming sound is continued and gradually augmented, without forcing, until maximum sonority is reached.

2. Now, practice opening and closing the mouth *very gradually* during the prolongation of each of these head hums, first using "m," then "n," then "ng." A vowel sound emerges as the mouth is being opened and the vowel is then sustained until the mouth is *gradually* closed again. However, the accompanying sensation of resonance in the mask must not be allowed to diminish or vary during the transition from closed to open mouth, and return (e.g., m-m-m-ah-ah-m-m-m; n-n-n-ah-ah-ah-n-n-n; ŋ-ŋ-ŋ-ah-ah-ah-ŋ-ŋ-ŋ). Full sonority and resonance is thus nurtured, without forcing, for each exercise.

3. After the head hum or head resonance has been captured, apply it to each vowel in the language. Use the techniques described above (e.g., m-m-m-ah-ah-ah; m-m-m-ee-ee-ee; m-m-m-oh-oh-oh; m-m-m-oo-oo-oo; etc.). Repeat each item several times with an optimal head hum accompanying it. Always practice s-l-o-w-l-y.

4. Now, use the vowel-attached sequence of (3) with the "n" and "ng" (ŋ) hums. Slow practice is essential.

5. The exercises recommended above may now be practiced in *messa di voce* style. Maximum volume is thus gradually attained without diminuation of the head hum. It is essential that every trace of forcing be eliminated and that there be no constriction whatever in lip, mouth, or throat muscles.

The "ng" hum is especially important because it lifts the back tongue muscles out of the throat. For this reason, it is always helpful to prefix a silent "ng" mentally, to any vowel that is being sounded. Optimal head resonance or head hum must become part of every intonation technique in singing. Optimal vocal fremitus is likewise nurtured in similar fashion.

Summarizing Intonation Problems and Their Correctives

Correct intonation, the ability to sing in tune, adequate sustaining power, control of dynamics, and breath support are all fundamental requirements of the singer's art. The following ten criteria provide observable evidence of correct intonation for singing. Marked deviations from these norms are warnings of improper adjustment, muscular imbalance, and faulty posture. Remedial exercises are then called for.

1. The chest is always high and stationary.
2. Slow but firm lateral and dorsal chest contraction is used with an accompanying gradual inward and upward lift of the abdominal wall.
3. The larynx remains positioned against the spine and it is motionless during phonation at any pitch level.
4. Under-chin muscles are always limp and flaccid to the touch during tone production.
5. The jaw opens easily, without strain or forcing, and always retains its natural orbit of movement. It is never thrust forward or unduly retracted.
6. During ascent of pitch the soft palate is practically stationary.
7. The uvula may rise and gradually disappear as

pitch ascends the scale, especially in dynamic singing.

8. The faucial pillars may be gradually narrowed and they may appear to approach each other during ascent of pitch, especially during dynamic singing.

9. With sustained vigorous intonation the tongue may stiffen gradually. It may widen, curl slightly upward at the tip, and hump *upward* at the rear.

10. Optimal head hum (felt in the mask) is uniformly evident at any level of intonation, especially during sustained, dynamic or high-pitch singing. A chest fremitus is always present.

No attempt should be made to force any of the above conditions, since most of them will serve as instructional signposts for the teacher, not the pupil. The maintenance of correct posture and the elimination of localized or conscious physical effort will often suffice to restore the vocal apparatus to the correct conditions indicated above. Open-throat and relaxation nostrums should be avoided, and the possibility of register breaks should not be discussed.

There are, of course, innumerable intonation exercises and vocalizes for low, medium, and high voice already in use by teachers everywhere. They are to be found, for the most part, in the many singing tests now in print and they need not be repeated here.[9] The remedial drills suggested above are relevant to less familiar instructional procedures and are intended, therefore, to illustrate specific principles of performance as outlined in this text.

In general, the following twelve tonal patterns are most often included in all vocalizes now in use by the singing profession: 1) sustained tones; 2) scale fragments; 3) arpeggios; 4) diatonic legato scales (major and minor); 5) chromatic scales and intervals; 6) staccato notes; 7) repeated notes; 8) equal and dotted slurs; 9) portamenti; 10) trills, turns, and grace notes; 11) syncopation; and 12) dissonances.

Of course, all vocal exercises may be modified to suit individual needs. However, emphasis should be laid on accuracy of intonation, legato note connection, sustained intonation with dynamic gradations, and flexibility, agility, and speed in developing any part of the vocal range. Thus, the pupil gradually acquires the freedom, self-confidence, and ease needed for expressing the familiar tonal idioms found in song literature.

In general, five different types of intonation are most often required of singers. In all of them, tone is never attacked with the glottis but with a lateral stroke of the chest and the abdominal lift for breathing support, as heretofore explained. These intonation types may be described as: *aspirato, staccato, marcato, legato,* and *portamento.*[10] In singing performance, each of these types of intonation requires a different style of execution, but the basic method of breath support is the same. Each should be practiced separately in the aforementioned sequence, since mastery of one leads to mastery of the others. Working backwards, a perfect *portamento* demands a perfect *legato*. Perfect *legato* emerges from its predecessor, the *marcato* technique, and so on. The initial state, therefore, is the *aspirato*, i.e., singing with an imaginary "h" in front of each tone until all symptoms of glottal clutching have disappeared. A perfect *sostenuto* or *messa di voce* emerges from the ultimate mastery of the foregoing types of intonation.

Persistent off-pitch tendencies and other abnormalities may be caused by faulty breathing, poor tonal imagery, lack of ear training, forced tonal attack, and postural strains. The following general correctives are beneficial:

1. *Spasmodic breathing.* Apply the remedial techniques described under breath control in chapter five.

2. *Faulty perception.* Drills should be devised that will promote tonal visualization. For example, the teacher sings or hums a tone; the pupil imitates after an interval of silence. Over an extended period, the scale may be thus delineated, note by note, in different intervals, rhythms, and groupings, by the slow, pause-and-imitate singing of simple pitches. Variations of this procedure depend on individual needs. It will also be helpful to re-

view the discussion on ear training.

3. *Aural dependency.* When practicing for pitch perception, the vocal response should always be unaccompanied. This enables both teacher and pupil to perceive the vocal effort clearly. If used at all, piano accompaniment should be light and it should not drown out the singer's voice. In other words, the pupil needs to hear himself, always, until pitch acuity and aural independence are established.

4. *Strained attack.* After throat tensions and stiffness are eliminated by posture exercises, the *head hum* is promoted. Regular intonation patterns should then be introduced and practiced in a light, unforced manner. Both the "m" and "ng" hums may be recalled from time to time, and the light abdominal staccato attack of laughter may be used repetitively.

Finally, keep in mind that, in singing, the strength and endurance of all vocal muscles in a continuity of action is called for. For this reason, the continued use of short fragments of light music may not always be desirable. A longer composition is needed occasionally, one that will challenge the ability to sustain the flow of tone with adequate breath support.

The Relaxation Fallacy

It is worth repeating that, in most normal habituated physiological processes, correct function is practically sensationless. In fact, the use of the wrong muscles often excites greater sensation than the use of the right muscles.

Artistic performance, therefore, does not necessarily involve conscious control of vocal mechanisms. Intrinsic elements of the larynx impart little or no physical awareness of their action during correct intonation. Nor do muscles of breathing and those of the vocal tract report their exact coordinations to the conscious mind during the singing act.

Supposed sensations are therefore illusory, since they do not match the actual efforts involved. For this reason, the practice of holding the throat "perflectly relaxed" is ill-advised, since the functioning muscles of the throat cannot be consciously relaxed during phonation.

Muscular contractions throughout the vocal tract are necessary to support any singing tone. Contraction of the entire chain of laryngeal elevators opposes the downward-pulling action of the laryngeal depressors with resultant equilibrium of all parts. All are powerfully contracted for intensified tone production, especially in the upper part of the pitch range.[11] In short, artistic singing is the result of unconscious but nevertheless significant muscular efforts.[12]

In conclusion, both teacher and pupil will realize that in any technical training procedure the mastery of intonation for singing first entails a posture-building program, a strengthening of the muscles of breathing and phonation with a retraction, correct positioning, and stability of the larynx, a conditioning of the vocal tract and its resonators, and a parallel process of esthetic ear training and musicianship. Beyond this, the mastery of intonation comprises a sevenfold objective: 1) correct attack; 2) pitch accuracy; 3) perfect legato at all speeds and for all intervals; 4) breath support, flexibility, and endurance for longer florid passages; 5) perfect *messa di voce* (swelling and diminishing) and control of dynamics for any tone; 6) uniformly good quality or resonance (fremitus and head hum) in all pitches and intensities; and 7) purity of vowels and good diction, or the clear and exact pronunciation of vowel-attached syllables and words in any text.

It is well to bear in mind, also, that there is a network of delicate nerve endings located in the minute fibers of the vocal tract that deliver, with supersensitivity and lightning speed, all the efferent energies needed to activate the vocal cords and the entire supporting laryngeal and respiratory musculature. These impulses are differentiated and coordinated by the brain, according to need, so as to induce and control all the subtle variations of pitch, duration, dynamics, and quality needed for artistic intonation. The singer's mental image governs this output.

After preliminary intonation problems have been solved, and vocalizes with legato, staccato, conjunct, and disjunct scale intervals, and remedial exercises have served their purpose, graded song literature may be used as practice material. The gradual building of the singer's repertoire is thus evolved. In this connection, due consideration should first be given to the classification of the pupil's singing voice and the voice-training implications of a singer's diction. A preliminary survey of these two areas will help pave the way for artistic fulfillment in assuming the later responsibilities of public performance.

REFERENCES AND NOTES

1. William Vennard, "The Bernoulli Effect in Singing," *NATS Bulletin* (February 1961): 8.

2. Raoul Husson, "Special Physiology in Singing with Power," *NATS Bulletin* (October 1957): 20.

3. Louis Bachner, *Dynamic Singing* (London: Dennis Dobson, 1947), p. 81.

4. Raoul Husson, "Registers and Register Passages in the Human Voice," *Nature* 89 (No. 3312, Paris, 1961): 152–160; Wilhelm Ruth, "The Registers of the Singing Voice," *NATS Bulletin* (May 1963): 2.

5. Victor A. Fields, "Review of the Literature on Vocal Registers," *NATS Bulletin* (Feb/Mar 1970): 37; A. A. Soninen, "Is the Length of the Vocal Cords the Same at All Different Levels of Singing?" *Acta Oto-Laryngol.* Suppl. 118 (1954): 219–231.

6. Henry J. Rubin and Charles C. Hirt, "The Falsetto. A High-Speed Cinematographic Study," *Laryngoscope* 70 (1960): 1305.

7. Paul Moore and Hans von Leden, "Dynamic Variations of the Vibratory Pattern in the Normal Larynx," *Folia Phoniatrica* 10 (No. 4, 1958): 205.

8. Ida Franca, *Manual of Bel Canto* (New York: Coward-McCann, Inc., 1959), pp. 8–11.

9. Typical orthodox training procedures are found in: Manuel Garcia, *Hints on Sing-*

ing (New York: Edw. Schuberth & Co., Inc., 1894), pp. 20–44; Nicola Vaccai, *Practical Italian Vocal Method* (Leipsig: Peters Edition); Dame Nellie Melba, *Melba Method* (London: Chappell & Co., Ltd., 1926); Franca, *Manual of Bel Canto*, Chap. 1.

10. Garcia, *Hints on Singing*, p. 20.

11. Raoul Husson, "Special Physiology in Singing with Power," *NATS Bulletin* (Oct. 1957): 14.

12. Vennard, Hirano, and Fritzell, "The Extrinsic Laryngeal Muscles," *NATS Bulletin* (May/June 1971): 22.

XII

Classifying the Singer's Voice

The classification of a pupil's voice involves a diagnostic analysis in which the teacher estimates innate vocal qualities and characteristics with all the foregoing elements of tone production in mind. Special emphasis is laid on personality, cultural background, age, and maturity factors, and the pupil's potential for artistic growth.

Classifications are made mainly for the purpose of prescribing suitable practice materials and the type of song literature that is most adaptable to a particular voice at a given level of development. Such judgments are temporary, at best, since it is obvious that as a pupil continues his training he may improve the range, quality, and scope of his voice to such a degree that reclassifications will be necessary.

First lessons should be fairly simple and the beginner should be allowed to sing a variety of song materials so that he may reveal his strong and weak points before he is made aware of the technical requirements of good singing. In this way, instruction will be administered in terms of revealed abilities and needs, rather than as an arbitrary pedagogical routine.

Preliminary Observations

The first lesson could be the singing of a simple song that the pupil already knows, or one that can be easily followed on the piano. Use a light accompaniment. If the melody is familiar, stop suddenly and have him continue singing it by ear. This will test his sense of pitch and rhythm, his feeling for text, his ability to handle phrase lengths in breathing, innate expressive quality, and, in general, how he handles his voice.

Is it effortless or strained? weak or strong? Is it throaty, nasal, strident, hoarse, or breathy? Is it metallic or mellow? What about its characteristic quality and range? Is it superficial, mechanical, and matter-of-fact, or sensitive and expressive? Is it on pitch all the time? Is it exaggerated and bombastic, energetic and bold? or timid, tremulous, self-conscious, and restrained?

Is diction clear and are words correctly enunciated? Is the meaning intelligible? Is the tonal line smooth and uniformly clear, or are there rugged portions of the range that reveal special weaknesses? Are the highest pitches forced? What part of the range has the richest quality? Does the male voice sound like a tenor or baritone? the female voice like a soprano or contralto?

What about posture, stance, facial expression, bodily poise, physique, and general health? Are breathing abnormalities noticed? An alert teacher notes the assets and limitations of the pupil's singing voice, his personality and diction, and his musicality in the singing of one or more of these preliminary and, if possible, unaccompanied songs.

Next, have him sing with full piano accompaniment. This will also reveal his ability to keep strict time, stay on pitch, and balance a melodic line with the harmonic background provided by the accompanying instrument. Hearing sensitivity is also to be noted.

After all these preliminary observations have been made, a systematic procedure may be planned and administered for furthering the ultimate objectives of the vocal training program. These objectives are now restated in general terms as follows[1]:

1. To develop good posture and good breathing habits.
2. To attack each note firmly and accurately, at first in disjunct, then in legato, sequences and in phrase groups.
3. To sustain any pitch in the score to any desired notational length without wavering or blurring its quality.
4. To move from pitch to pitch, or from note to note, smoothly, effortlessly, accurately, and with unimpaired vocal quality.
5. To be able to handle intervals slowly and smoothly, then quickly, both in legato and staccato combinations.
6. To handle tones or phrases of any length, at all dynamics and with good breath support.
7. To energize and strengthen the vocal organs so that an unfaltering vocal line can be sustained in any key, without strain or fatigue.
8. To be able to swell or decrease the volume of tone throughout the pitch range with uniform quality.
9. To develop a pitch range that is needed for average song repertoire.
10. To develop flexibility, mobility, agility, endurance, and precision in all sorts of melodic movement, both in conjunct and disjunct tonal combinations.
11. To improve diction or distinctness of verbal enunciation at all pitches, dynamics, and tempi.
12. To improve sincerity and depth of expression along with good vocal technique and a declamatory or dramatic sense for interpreting recitative and song lyrics.
13. Finally, to develop poise, stage presence, and style in the execution of a suitable but varied singing repertoire of musical literature for actual performance before an audience.

Naturally, these general aims may be broken into innumerable specific tasks as the exercise materials are marshalled for use in early lessons. Although many of these objectives can be pursued simultaneously, the teacher's adaptation of practice exercises and song materials will have to be governed, largely, by the type of voice that is being trained, and by problems of technique that arise out of a preliminary diagnosis of the pupil's vocal shortcomings. Vocal classifications also serve this purpose.[2]

Diagnostic Problems

For diagnostic purposes, therefore, vocal training may be viewed as the combining of five body actions into a synergic response that is perceived as singing. These are: *posture, breathing, phonation, resonation,* and *articulation*. Corrective training demands adequate control of all relevant structures and a musical achievement in the artistic use thereof.

Every impaired vocal tone is an effect. It has a cause. Therefore, the specific cause must first be located and removed through corrective exercises. Mere repetition of the faulty tone will not improve it. Basically, what is needed is a rounded-out coordination of the entire system of extrinsic and intrinsic laryngeal muscles accompanied by a suitable breathing response and monitored by faultless tonal imagery.

With this in mind, vocal training should also provide for ear training, the strengthening of all pitch regulators, and a commensurate increase of breath support until all voice-related muscles are equal to any demand made upon them. To this end, the teacher administers a routine of technical exercises and vocalizes, following patterns suggested in the chapters on "Breathing," "Ear Training," "Intonation," and elsewhere throughout this text. Typical exercises may also be found in the references cited at the close of each chapter.

The entire body, chest, abdomen, neck and throat, larynx, tongue, palate, and spine must be viewed as an integrated unit with no part or parts overlooked in this development. A single weak link can destroy effective action of the entire chain. Therefore, what is important is the constant reminder of the *wholeness* of the vocal response and the intricacy of its operation.

Obviously, no panacea can be offered as an infallible guide to perfection, for technical proficiency varies with each individual. Nevertheless, a diagnostic survey like the following can, when needed, indicate desirable intructional paths to be followed. It should be remembered, also, that all instructional procedures have the ultimate purpose of achieving proficiency in the art of *singing* and the performance of song literature, and not merely technical skill in vocal tone production.

The main *categories of instruction* may now be classified as follows:

1. diagnosis of obvious faults (if any);
2. beginning exercises (legato note connection in familiar range, slow scales, intervals, melodic passages, and simple songs);
3. posture (stance, chest, head, arms, shoulders, etc.);
4. breath control (intake, retention, compression, attack, support, economy, phrasing, dynamics, renewal, etc.);
5. intonation problems in attack, legato, and staccato and sustained tones (check posture, laryngeal position, tongue, jaw, etc.);
6. timbre and resonance (use of the head hum);
7. dynamics (attack, projection, messa di voce, breath support);
8. ear training and tonal imagery;
9. diction (vowels, consonants, distinctness, fluency, speech habits, foreign languages, etc.);
10. voice classification (as to age, sex, range, quality, power, temperament, etc.);

11. home practice methods and materials (exercises, drills, songs);

12. practice materials for studio use (vocalizes, scales, etudes, ornaments, etc.);

13. health and hygiene (diet, rest, exercise, recreation, living habits, mental attitudes, etc.);

14. musicianship and background studies in notation, keyboard harmony, sight singing, dictation, score reading, music theory, terminology, etc.; and

15. song analysis, recitative, sacred and secular song literature, problem songs, repertoire, characterization, operatic studies, etc.

Checkpoints for Position and Technique

1. As previously explained, when technique is good, the general effect is to *compress* the chest and the entire tonal passageway from lips to larynx, and to maintain a *stationary* condition of all laryngeal supports, without straining or striving, and a firm, *compact* subglottal breath chamber during sustained voice production.

2. It should also be noted that model singers, instead of opening the throat, as is often erroneously advised, tend to *narrow* the entire tonal passageway slightly as they deliver higher and louder tones. As previously explained, this narrowing tendency is not a conscious action but, rather, a result of the correct action of thyroid-tilting, cord-stretching muscles which also form the pillars of the fauces. The comparative expansion of the rear of the mouth in delivering low tones is not indicative of relaxation of these parts but of efforts that are less powerful than those made for high tones. Advising a high position of the soft palate so as to enlarge the resonance cavity at the back of the mouth is also fallacious for physiological and acoustical reasons already explained.

3. The chest is always *high;* shoulders and clavicles rest

downward; the body posture is upright but never backward, and firm without stiffness.

4. The elbows are slightly *removed* from the sides of the body.

5. For tonal breath support, the abdomen gradually lifts *inward* with accompanying lateral *compression* of the chest.

6. The larynx remains *backward, downward,* and *stationary*.

7. Under-chin muscles are always *relaxed* during phonation at any level.

8. The soft palate remains *stationary* at any pitch level, but the uvula may gradually disappear with rising pitch of the voice.

9. The faucial arch (fauces) *narrows* slightly with ascending pitch and during increase of vocal intensity.

10. During intensive sustained phonation at any pitch level, the tongue may stiffen slightly with its tip curled upward and the *posterior* lingual surface arched *upward,* never downward. A groove at the back of the tongue is evidence of weak laryngeal (hyo-stylo-glossic) support and should be corrected.

11. The lower jaw drops easily when it moves, without jutting forward.

12. The lips and cheeks may become slightly narrowed and stiffened during dynamic singing passages, but rigidity in any part should be avoided.

Diagnosis of Obvious Faults

The chronic misuse of a function calls for long-range remedial procedure. This is administered in small doses and in a graded sequence of exercises embodying the principles already discussed. Melodic fragments of simple songs may also be practiced. Materials are used that encourage the use of corrective techniques and strengthen weak controls of unresponsive muscles without upsetting the balanced coordination of the entire vocal apparatus.

1. *Off-pitch singing* may be caused by:

   a. defective or impaired hearing;
   b. lack of ear training or tonal imagery;
   c. exposure to or imitation of faulty models;
   d. local effort and forced intonation;
   e. weak glottal muscles;
   f. excessive breath pressure or poor breath support;
   g. laryngeal instability or a rising larynx;
   h. lack of tonal initiative (too much accompaniment).

Possible *correctives* for these symptoms are: 1) thinking the tone before attacking it; 2) vigorous singing within a moderate pitch range that will energize and strengthen enfeebled glottal muscles; 3) light *coup de glotte* exercises at any pitch level; 4) rapid repetition of a light staccato tone on every pitch within the singable range; 5) the *messa di voce* exercise to enforce suitable breathing controls; 6) corrected posture with a high chest and a stationary larynx.

2. *Breathiness* may be caused by:

   a. faulty attack;
   b. forced breathing or shallow breathing;
   c. poor posture;
   d. abdominal tension (lack of breath support);
   e. physical inertia or fatigue;
   f. glottal inflamation (hoarseness);
   g. excessive breath intake;
   h. weak glottal muscles (poor adduction).

Possible *correctives* for these symptoms are: 1) physical culture and body-building exercise; 2) chest position should be properly elevated and rib-cage muscles strengthened; 3) laughter will strengthen the diaphragm; 4) vocal endurance tests on a timed hum or "ah" vowel, or a slow, long, legato phrase will build economy of breath emission; 5) the lighted candle test may be helpful (q.v.); 6) think breath *retention* during sustained intonation; 7) eliminate spasmodic breathing effort; 8) use the glottal exercises suggested under off-pitch singing (above).

3. Impaired vocal quality may be caused by:

    a. nasality (malfunctioning soft palate);
    b. throatiness (collapsed tongue muscles or constriction);
    c. harshness (forcing, muscle fatigue, local effort);
    d. shrillness (nervous tension and forcing);
    e. voix blanche or whiteness (loss of vibrato, mechanical effort, lack of interest or warmth);
    f. fatigue (caused by intemperance or lack of rest);
    g. poor posture, inertia, lack of motivation, etc.;
    h. laryngeal instability;
    i. poor breath support;
    j. lack of tonal imagery or impaired hearing.

Possible *correctives:* 1) glottal muscles need to be invigorated as indicated under *off-pitch singing* and *breathiness* (above); 2) use the swallowing exercise followed by a light, repetitive *glottal* attack of tone; 3) body-building and posture exercises to strengthen the extrinsic musculature in the vocal tract; 4) use breath-retention exercises and sustained *messa di voce* at different pitch levels; 5) the *head hum* should be practiced to induce optimal resonance with minimal effort; 6) rest is often indicated; 7) practicing mental or *silent* singing and ear-training exercises are also helpful; 8) listening to and emulating model singers will also help create a sense of tonal values; 9) singing easy songs will help.

4. Tremulous, weak or feeble voice may be caused by:

    a. wobbly larynx;
    b. weakened laryngeal muscles;
    c. lack of breath support;

d. unstable tongue position;
e. weariness or fatigue;
f. timidity, nervousness, worry, or fear;
g. ill health;
h. local effort.

Possible *correctives* include: 1) body-building exercises; 2) posture correctives; 3) a light glottal cough to strengthen the glottic closure; 4) raising the posterior lingual surface during a strong, sustained whisper, alternated with sustained phonation in the same position; 5) staccato scale passages; 6) spoken declamations and energetic commands using a loud whisper alternated by a sudden change to full voice; 7) breath compression exercises which include candle-blowing, gasping, loud yawning, sighing, laughter, and crescendo controls; 8) linear vocal projection to an imaginary listener (distant); 9) using the head hum; 10) more frequent exposure to an audience; 11) strong motivation; 12) rest.

After diagnostic preliminaries and routine correctives have been launched, the beginner should be given an opportunity to express himself musically in rendering several simple songs. It is better to select music that lies well within a pupil's range so that a sense of accomplishment may accompany any performance thereof.

Once the instructional program is well established, it would seem unwise to attempt song literature that lies beyond the scope of a pupil's expression, however beguiling its musical qualities might be. There is nothing more frustrating to a singer than the unfulfilled desire to sing a high note or a passage that is just beyond his own capabilities. Such frustrations build up fear complexes and invite chronic tensions that can spell ruination to the entire program.

We do not attempt to make a voice "big" unless it shows natural signs of developing that way. There is no virtue in shouting or bellowing. What the voice needs is tonal purity and mellowness, endurance and flexibility, not sheer volume. Easy fragments of a requested song or aria may be sung, however, as a sampling of what is to come. Thus, an incentive to work toward future rewards is substituted for the disappointments of unfulfilled ambitions.

This does not necessarily mean that the vocal diet should be all pap. Rather, it would contain only those difficulties that may be overcome with diligent practice within a reasonably short period of time. Some elements of the finest repertoire of classical, romantic, and impressionistic song literature could thus be included in the practice schedule. But selections would always be made with the purpose of exercising present abilities. Thus, the student's vocal artistry would grow, through correct use, by gradual stages of unfoldment.

Pitch Range

Each well-developed voice should be able to sing from two to three octaves in order to handle the music that is written for it. A preliminary classification will therefore be determined, in part, by the series of pitches that can be sung with comfort, adequate power, expressiveness, and good quality.[3]

About two octaves defines each basic vocal range, as indicated in the following table. However, since most beginners feel at ease in only a small segment of the assigned classification, practice work should lie well within the pupil's range where it may gradually develop its full potential, without strain.

1. *Soprano:* c^1 to c^3 (middle C to C above treble clef).

2. *Mezzo Soprano:* g to g^2 (fourth space G on bass clef to G above treble clef).

3. *Contralto:* e to e^2 (third space E on bass clef to fourth space E on treble clef).

4. *Tenor:* A to a^1 (low A on bass clef to A on treble

clef). Tenor parts are usually written an octave higher than sounded.

5. *Baritone:* F to f¹ (F below bass clef to low F on treble clef).

6. *Bass:* D to d¹ (D below bass clef to D above middle C).

This chart is approximate, to be sure, since individual differences must be accounted for; but it will give the teacher a starting point for launching a suitable study-training program.[4]

The normal range of these voices may be approximately described as an octave (more safely a seventh) below and above the notes d, f, a, e¹, g¹, b¹, as shown below. Trained vocalists frequently exceed these ranges.

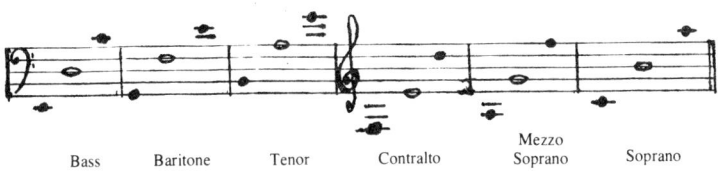

Bass   Baritone   Tenor   Contralto   Mezzo Soprano   Soprano

If the voice cannot reach a full two-octave span, its classification would nevertheless be determined within the approximate scope of the above two-octave table. A safe procedure would be to practice within a conservative range during the first few months of the training program. Extensions should never be forced, and the upper half of a beginner's range should be practiced *mezzo-forte,* whenever possible, to avoid strain.

Temperament and Timbre

Psychological factors are also important in voice classification.[5] In women, as in men, tonal expression is largely an outpicturing of the peculiar physical and mental character of the individual. The so-called temperament of the singer is therefore a product of his predominant frame of mind which, in turn, determines the characteristic mental and emotional responses with which he faces life. This internal constitution may produce a peculiar balance or mixture of mental and emotional reactions which affect disposition, personality, and character. Furthermore, it determines how a person meets situations and overcomes difficulties, and it also affects the predominant timbre or quality and range of his speaking and singing voice.

Consider the female voice. A light, airy, cheerful, and genteel but characteristically feminine quality in the coloratura soprano represents one type of temperament. This kind of voice is to be contrasted with the contralto, which tends to possess nearly opposite temperamental characteristics, inasmuch as the contralto voice darkens and deepens toward a firmer and more aggressive type of expression.

In the transition from one extreme to the other, we often observe that preset conditions of mind and mood in the nature of the person tend to influence the vocal type. Any voice usually expresses the emotional makeup and character of the individual. In terms of these gradations of prevailing temperament, the female voice may be classified into at least five distinctive types as: *coloratura soprano, lyric soprano, dramatic soprano, mezzo-soprano,* and *contralto.*

A comparable emotional and temperamental spectrum is depicted in the male voice, which ranges from an approximation of light, buoyant, melodious quality in the high *lyric tenor,* through a deeper, darker, and more ponderous masculinity in the *dramatic tenor, baritone, bass-baritone,* and *bass.*

Vocal timbre is basically a sex characteristic,[6] determined, in part, by glandular activity in the body. Nevertheless, variations in temperament and timbre are by no means to be construed as sex deviations. Rather, they are influenced by prevalent or predominant patterns of thought, feeling, and expression in the average individual. Through habitual use, these mental or emotional traits set an aural-vocal texture in the range of human expression, much as the characteristic predisposition toward cheerfulness or gloom might carve the lineaments and frown lines of character into the facial features of an adult.

For the foregoing reasons, it is obvious that, as an individual grows toward maturity and adulthood, more and more of the true nature of that person will be released into audible expression. Furthermore, as poise and self-confidence and maturity become manifest in varying degrees, there will be corresponding changes in the timbre of the voice.

Thus, chronic timidity, restraint, or fear might produce tremulous, high-pitched lightness in vocal expression. Self-reliance, self-assertion, and boldness of spirit would produce a deeper, more commanding voice with a characteristic firmness and clarity of timbre that suggests freedom from restraint or fear.

Likewise, a predisposition toward cheerfulness would tend to promote vocal buoyancy and, on the other hand, chronic gloominess or pessimism would make for a more stolid or heavy-sounding and nonresilient type of voice. All these differences in temperament effect a perceptible change in the inherent vocal quality of any individual.

Tessitura

In bel canto terminology, *tessitura* (It.: *texture*) originally referred to natural quality or timbre of the singer's voice.[7] However, the wider application of this term embraces all inborn vocal attributes, as opposed to the cultivated product which results from a training program. As now used, *tessitura* is appraised in terms of three principal tonal components: *pitch, intensity,* and *quality*. This is to be, largely, a hearing judgment, since the teacher must use his own ear to discern those properties that are characteristic of each vocal type.

Pitch is the overall compass, range, or singable portion of the voice from the lowest to the highest point on the musical scale. *Intensity* is the inherent magnitude or strength of the voice, its carrying power and dynamic scope. *Quality* or timbre is the characteristic richness and purity of tone including its harmonic constituents, resonance, and overtones. Ease of expression in any or all of these three acoustical dimensions determines vocal *tessitura*.[8]

In other words, the purest, most facile and singable portion of the vocal range in which its most useful and most powerful tones lie is the *tessitura* of that voice. A combination of flexibility or ease of expression, a full use of pitch, intensity (dynamics), and quality values in all tones of its natural range is considered the hallmark of the artistic singing voice.

A more objective, supplementary use of the term *tessitura* sometimes refers to the structure of the song itself. In this sense, barring extremes, it denotes that part of the pitch range of a vocal composition or piece of music in which most of its easily singable tones lie. When thus used, the term does not indicate the range of a voice, but rather the adaptability of a given voice to a certain piece of music.

To help determine vocal properties by tessitura standards, a twenty-one-level guide is given at the end of this chapter. This classification is listed in condensed form and is based, largely, on a preliminary hearing judgment which employs the criteria previously discussed. Such descriptions are impressionistic, at best, since they relate to subjective hearing evaluations, rather than to physical or structural aspects of vocal equipment. In making this judgment, the teacher must possess sensitive hearing and a superior auditory memory of tonal and vocal values.

Of course, some classifications overlap. Some lyric sopranos may sing a lower range than some mezzo-sopranos; an occasional mezzo may sing higher than some lyric sopranos, etc. Therefore, a hard-and-fast rule cannot be applied to the classification of any singing voice.

Acoustical Factors

A musical instrument is usually enriched by the low partials and overtones that are built into its tonal range. When these are screened out or dampened, a thin, hollow shrillness results. Fundamentals and overtones give life and dimension to a musical instrument.[9]

The human voice, likewise, needs the support of its fundamentals and overtones. Those who have not fully developed their lowest singable tones will lack the hearing perception of this vocal dimension. Their voices will seem to possess pitch and volume with little or no variation in quality. A monotonous sameness results.

For this reason, the fanatical preoccupation with high notes can have a weakening effect on the tonal foundation of the singer's voice, thereby producing a tenor-like timbre in an otherwise baritone range for the male voice, with analogous results for the female. Eventually the entire vocal structure suffers because of a one-sided development.

In most beginners, vocal texture or timbre varies slightly with pitch movement. Quality may, therefore, gradually lighten as pitch ascends, until an impression of thinness or transparency is produced in the uppermost tones. This change is basically an acoustical one and is largely due to weak auditory perception of unused or little-used tonalities. Although these changes are scarcely noticed in adjacent tones of the scale, the transition from "heavy" to "light" may become apparent in more widely separated areas of the vocal range. As the voice continues to mature and strengthen through correct use and ear training, such changes gradually lessen until they become imperceptible.

It would be erroneous to insist that each tone in the vocal range have identical timbre. The end in view is freedom of production, consistent with a responsive fluency and flexibility of expression. Most of all, vitality and richness are needed at all levels of pitch and dynamics in the singer's voice. The pupil's ear must learn to recognize and monitor these acoustical results at any level.

The primary purpose of vocal training for singing is to elicit natural, human-sounding tones inherent in a freely functioning voice, rather than a mechanized tonal product. Consciously produced muscular techniques that develop rigidly established tonalities resembling those of a musical instrument are therefore to be avoided.

Male and Female Vocal Differences

Male and female voices may be said to differ from each other in pitch range for five reasons. *First,* the male vocal cords are inherently longer and thicker throughout the vocal range. *Second,* the resonance cavities of the adult male vocal tract are generally larger than those of the female. *Third,* there are structural differences between male and female in the texture and composition of all boundaries, walls, and supporting muscles, bones, and surfaces of the vocal instrument. *Fourth,* a female voice possesses a smaller larynx in proportion to the air spaces above it and therefore would tend to sound its overtones, rather than its fundamental tones (e.g., French horn). *Fifth,* the wider spread of the thyroid cartilage in the female instrument causes a thinning-out of the glottal muscles as they reach to the midline when adducted for phonation, and this may cause a difference in the basic pitch and quality of the tone emitted.

The average spread of the thyroid lamina in the adult female larynx is approximately 120 degrees, while that of the adult male larynx averages about 90 degrees.[10] All these structural characteristics can account for differences in the overtone spectrum produced by male and female voices, and these are the variations we recognize as contrasts in vocal quality. In short, the ratio of the size of the larynx to the size of the vocal resonators could account for some of the acoustical differences between male and female voices and determine some of the distinguishing characteristics in the vocal classifications hereafter listed.[11]

Pedagogical Implications

As a music-making instrument, the human voice is classified into four conventional groupings: *soprano, alto, tenor,* and *bass.* All known subdivisions are derived from these basic categories. Voice classifications for singers are, at best, approximate since it is difficult to assign a fixed category to a growing human phenomenon. Individual differences always occur, and the gradual prolonged development of any particular voice may readily outreach the limits of its assigned class.

When an exceptional voice demonstrates a brilliant superiority in range, vitality, and dramatic potential, it is called a *spinto* voice (It., *spingere:* to push or urge forward). Thus, there are *spinto sopranos* and *spinto tenors.* A spinto may be assigned a more challenging repertoire than is usual for the average voice in that classification. Thus, a florid soprano with unusual dramatic qualities may be called a *lyric-spinto soprano.* Likewise, a flexible lyric tenor voice with robust or vigorous quality and unusual range may become a *lyric-spinto tenor.*

The teacher is reminded, however, that an incompletely developed voice need not necessarily be classified differently from one that is more fully developed in the same category, since both voices might possess the same potential for future growth. When subdivisions are used, splintered designations such as *tenor-baritone* and *bass-baritone* come into being.

Limitations in range, dynamics, or quality may become chronic with singers if their full vocal resources are not challenged by the type of training they receive. Because of over-conservative teaching methods, they often reach a plateau of development and remain there for a lifetime, never daring to continue to exercise or explore their full vocal potential. Such half-grown voices, may, with proper training, at any time grow out of an assigned category. Indeed, individual performers have been known to change both range and quality of voice even relatively late in life.

Unusual Voices

History records many musical "greats" of the nineteenth and early twentieth centuries who possessed full voices of unusual versatility and range. For example, *Maria Malibran* (1808–1836) was both soprano and contralto. *Marianne Brandt* (1842–1921) sang soprano, mezzo-soprano, and contralto roles. *Lilian Nordica* (1859–1914) was known as a soprano but she excelled in both coloratura and dramatic repertoire.

Adelina Patti (1843–1919) was a distinguished coloratura who sang many lyric and even dramatic soprano roles with great success. Her unusual vocal range was amazingly even and flexible throughout. *Ernestine Schumann-Heink* (1861—1936) sang both mezzo-soprano and contralto roles.

Lilli Lehmann (1848–1929) began her career as a lyric and coloratura soprano, and later developed into a dramatic soprano. *Emma Calvé* (1858–1942) was both soprano and mezzo-soprano. Olive Fremstad (1872-1951) was a mezzo-soprano of extraordinary versatility who possessed a dramatic voice of unusually high range, meeting all the requirements of the high soprano.

Margaret Matzenauer (1881–1963) distinguished herself in contralto, mezzo-soprano, and soprano roles in a long and brilliant operatic career. More recently, *Maria Callas* (1923–) has a voice of unusual range combining the flexibility and brilliance of a coloratura with the style and intensity of a dramatic soprano. *Joan Sutherland* (1926–) is also a leading contemporary coloratura and dramatic soprano. These are all spinto voices.

Among the men, *Jean de Reszke* (1850–1925) made his debut as a baritone and later became a successful tenor. *Mattia Battistini* (1857–1928) possessed a high baritone voice of exceptional range and could sing florid music with the agility of a tenor. *Italo Campanini* (1846–1896) was an outstanding spinto tenor, as was *Enrico Caruso* (1873–1921). There are many others.[12]

It is apparent, therefore, that a superior voice could, in time, lend itself to masterful development beyond its present tonal range. In other words, there is potential for marked improvement in every individual. That is his birthright. It is therefore not desirable for a teacher to decree permanent limits of development in terms of arbitrary vocal classifications, since he may thereby irreparably stunt his pupil's growth. The present dearth of great voices in the singing world may be attributed, in part, to this type of limited training. Flexibility of method and means of training should always be maintained.

The teacher is advised, therefore, to find song literature that can best be expressed at the pupil's stage of development. This affords a temperamental outlet in singing, one that is best suited to a pupil's physical and mental makeup. His voice can then grow in the direction of his greatest need.

Vocal classifications should be used for temporary guidance and for purposes of selecting a practice repertoire, with the reservation that experimental changes can be made, from time to time, in order to explore the possibilities of further development as the pupil matures and grows in artistic stature.

Resumé of Vocal Categories

For guidance, review, and ready reference, a descriptive list of the standard classifications currently in use is here given. The average singing range in each main category is also indicated. Exceptional voices may reach beyond each of these arbitrary limits.

1. *Soprano* (It., *sopra:* above): a general classification denoting the highest treble female voice. It differs from alto, which is considered a woman's voice but is also found in boys;

b-flat to a^2 is the average range, but it may reach to c^3 or higher, and with unusual voices, as low as f or e. (Boys' voices usually cover two octaves, from a to a^2, of the soprano range.) Soprano voices are now subdivided into four, possibly five, types as follows:

2. *Coloratura Soprano:* a high, pure tonality, lighter than lyric or dramatic soprano, the latter type being more sonorous and full-toned by comparison. *Coloratura* denotes brilliant and facile vocalization with special competence in florid and ornamental passages such as runs, trills, arpeggios, elaborate cadenzas, etc. It is a voice of clarity, agility and flexibility which extends with ease to f^3 or higher.

3. *Lyric Soprano:* a smooth-flowing melodious voice of medium soprano range, possessing good substance and rich quality, especially adapted to the fluent and expressive movement of melodious song literature.

4. *Lyric Spinto Soprano (soprano lirico-spinto):* a versatile lyric soprano voice of unusual scope and range, with the potentialities of a dramatic soprano.

5. *Dramatic Soprano:* a more powerful and more resonant voice suited to declamatory and operatic roles. Emotionally expressive, it carries well and is rich in resonance and quality. The dramatic soprano range is somewhat higher than the mezzo-soprano and somewhat lower than the lyric soprano.

6. *Mezzo-soprano* (It., half-soprano): a voice of full, deep, or dark quality, lying between soprano and contralto, and possessing some of the characteristics of each. Its range is not quite as high as soprano and it lacks the flexibility, scope, and variety of a full soprano range.

7. *Alto* (It., high): This general term was originally used to denote certain high voices of men, which were also called *countertenor* or *male soprano,* and of women, which were called *counteralto* or *contralto.* The male alto or countertenor has to be able to sing from about f^1 to c^2, mainly by the use of falsetto, his natural voice being either tenor or bass. It is a voice used principally in cathedral choirs. In four-part men's choirs, this voice sings the highest part, hence the name *altus*

or *alto*. In the female alto voice, the range extends somewhat lower than soprano and is now almost exclusively described as *contralto*, without subdivisions.

8. *Contralto* is therefore the deepest and lowest female voice, with an average range of two to two and one-half octaves, from e to about a^2. It possesses a peculiarly resonant, deep, and weighty quality which gives it rich, dramatic, and sonorous character.

The *combined* range of all the female voices (contralto, mezzo-soprano, and soprano) is from e upwards for about three octaves to e^3.

9. *Tenor:* the general term used for the highest natural male voice (B to a^1). A lighter, more flexible voice in this category is called *lyric tenor* (d to c^2). The more powerful tenor is almost a baritone and is called *dramatic tenor, helden tenor,* or *tenor robusto* (c to a^1). A descriptive listing of tenor subdivisions would be as follows:

10. *Countertenor:* A male alto, also called *contra tenor* or *alto-tenor*. As explained above, he sings with a skillfull use of falsetto, overlapping the contralto range.

11. *Lyric Tenor:* a light, high, melodious tenor voice of rich quality.

12. *Lyric Spinto Tenor (tenore lirico-spinto):* A more versatile lyric tenor with wider expressive range and a bolder quality that approximates the robust characteristics of the dramatic tenor.

13. *Dramatic Tenor:* a robust and vigorous tenor with a powerful, deeper, and emotionally expressive voice approaching a baritone in timbre and especially suited to declamatory or operatic singing.

14. *Helden Tenor:* a heroic tenor voice possessing the agility, unusual brilliance, and expressive power suited to Wagnerian roles.

15. *Tenor Robusto:* a hearty dramatic tenor voice with an especially rich, vigorous quality. It is typically used to suggest vitality and strength in characterization.

16. *Bass:* a general term describing the lowest or deepest male voice (E^b to d^1). Employing a full gamut of fundamental tones, overtones, and resonances, it possesses unusual richness and vibrancy. Special types of bass voice have certain designations to describe unusual flexibility, higher or lower than usual range, or somber quality. These are itemized as:

17. *Baritone:* a high bass voice. If unusually high in range and brilliant in timbre, it is called *tenor-baritone*. If it is a melodious, flexible, high bass voice, but not quite as rich as the bass, it is called *lyric baritone*.

18. *Bass-baritone* (sometimes called *lyric baritone* or *basso cantabile):* a flexible lyric bass voice but somewhat richer, more sonorous and somber in quality than the baritone.

19. *Basso-profondo:* a deep, powerful bass whose range can extend half an octave or more below an ordinary bass range, as low as A^b_1.

20. *Contra-bass* (double bass): a very rich bass timbre that can reach downward to FF or F_1. An extraordinarily deep voice.

21. *Basso-buffo:* an agile bass voice suited to comic operatic roles. A bass clown or comedian in any of the above bass categories.

REFERENCES AND NOTES

1. Victor A. Fields, *Training the Singing Voice* (New York: Columbia University Press, 1947), Chap. 2.

2. Weldon Whitlock, *Facets of the Singer's Art* (Champaign, Illinois: Pro Musica Press, 1967), Chap. 3.

3. Fred'k Husler, and Yvonne Rodd-Marling, *Singing, the Physical Nature of the Vocal Organs* (New York: October House, Inc., 1965), p. 86.

4. Victor A. Fields, *The Singer's Glossary* (Boston: Boston Music Company, 1952).

5. Van A. Christy, *Expressive Singing* (Dubuque, Iowa: Wm. C. Brown Co., 1961), 2: 79.

6. Harold M. Kaplan, *Anatomy and Physiology of Speech* (New York: McGraw-Hill Book Company, Inc., 1960), pp. 47, 61.

7. Cornelius Reid, *Bel Canto: Principles and Practices* (New York: Coleman-Ross Co., Inc., 1950), p. 58.

8. William S. Drew, *Singing: The Art and the Craft* (London: Oxford University Press, 1937), p. 169.

9. John Redfield, *Music, a Science and an Art* (New York: Tudor Publishing Co., 1935), Chap. 18.

10. V. E. Negus, *The Mechanism of the Larynx,* 2nd edition (London: Heinemann Medical Books, 1957), pp. 444, 446.

11. Redfield, *Music,* p. 273.

12. Henry Pleasants, *The Great Singers* (New York: Simon and Schuster, 1966).

XIII

The Singer's Diction

Although singing is usually defined as a tonal art, the tonal output of the singer is always implemented by the techniques of language. In a practical sense, therefore, singing may be regarded as a form of communication and, as such, it embodies the verbal expression of ideas as well as tones. Its verbal media must be intelligible to an audience and it must convey meaning as well as mood. In this respect, it resembles speaking.

Speech is defined as the faculty of uttering articulate sounds to express thoughts. But speech is devoid of formal musical design. We learn the language of speech at an early age and, by the time the esthetic values of living are appreciated, deep-rooted habits have already been established. When pedagogically viewed, therefore, many aspects of singing impinge in some degree upon the speech function. Song may even be regarded as a sublimation of speech, and for pedagogical purposes we can summarize their basic interdependence and their differences as follows:

    1. The transitory vowel utterances of speech become precise, measurable vocal vehicles when sung.

    2. Impromptu inflections of speech become definitely prescribed melodic contours of song, the pitch

range being wider in singing than in speaking.

3. Unnoticed irregular rhythmic factors of speech become prominent metrical features in song.

4. Pauses are whimsical and variable conveniences of the speaker, but in singing they are always standardized and fixed by musical notation.

5. Impromptu variations in the loudness of the speaking voice become a fixed formula for dynamics in singing.

6. The quality of voice imparts mood and feeling values, both in speaking and singing. But the singer's use of vocal quality attains esthetic prominence through the sustained and somewhat intensified nature of vocal expression in song.

7. There are no indeterminate sounds in singing; speech is full of them. Nearly every verbal utterance in song has musical impact on the listener and is therefore governed by definite laws which affect dynamics, pitch, quality, and other musical factors.

8. The singer's art is consistently poetic, lyrical, or declamatory in nearly every measure of the musical score; speech may be mundane, coarse, matter-of-fact, and may even serve simple utilitarian purposes.

9. In speech, tonal values are incidental to the logical communicative intent of the message. On the other hand, tones in singing are all-important elements of musical structure which in themselves provide a type of auditory language and impart esthetic pleasure to the ear.

10. In short, the purely intellectual and scientific values of speech as a means of exchanging ideas are exalted to a musical plane of technical precision and soul-inspiring beauty by the effective songwriter.

Speech, of course, has its own esthetic dimensions. The spoken word holds an important place in the arts of drama and declamation, both in poetry and prose. There is also a definite beauty in the spoken word. The Gettysburg Address, a psalm from the Bible, the wit and wisdom of Will Rogers, Shakespeare, Emerson, Wordsworth—the entire culture of man is spread before us in the art of oratory and declamation and no one would intend to disparage the spoken word as an art form. Indeed, there is scarcely a phrase in the English-speaking repertoire of published masterpieces that does not also lend itself to textual setting for song when blended to a musical score.

The song maker, the operatic composer, the writer of oratorios, sacred, and religious scores is fully aware of the close relationship between the spoken word and the verbal text of a musical composition. One could hardly exist without the other. All resemblances and differences indicate this close relationship, and it is this relationship that is a matter of pedagogical concern to both teacher and pupil for it is obvious that each medium of oral expression supports the other.

Verbal utterance provides a moving vehicle for the singing voice and, conversely, the voice provides audibility, dynamic range, inflectional, and other expressive qualities for the spoken word. Therefore, the study of singing really includes a careful consideration of diction and its relation to the art of tone production.

Singing is, therefore, a product of both voice training and speech training, combined to be expressed in a musical medium. Voice is inherent; speech is acquired. Song is the medium or form of expression of both. Our formula may be stated thus: *voice* plus *speech* plus *music* equals *singing*.

If we started in infancy, we could cultivate both singing and speaking habits simultaneously. But since the study of singing is usually begun long after basic speech habits have been acquired, the teacher of singing is often confronted with the need to reeducate these early habits, to uplift or rechannel them into musical media suitable for expression in the singing art. This reeducative process is achieved by the use of a speech-song approach to the study of diction.

Improving Vocal Values
Through a Speech-Song Approach

In this transfer from speech to song, certain questions arise:

1. If the student's speaking voice is inadequate, should it be strengthened separately before we attempt to use it for singing?

2. If the pupil's speech is careless, how can his speaking diction be converted directly into singing diction?

3. If the pupil is unfamiliar with a foreign language in the song he is learning, how can he be expected to transfer everyday speech patterns into a foreign-language song pattern?

4. What if the pupil is predisposed to inert, languid, or vocally indolent speech? How can we energize his voice for singing purposes?

These and other problems suggest that the training of the singing voice should be closely related to a parallel speech-training program. A deficiency in one will inevitably reflect incompetence in the other and, conversely, with a musical ear to guide it, a well-developed speaking voice will readily transfer into vocal preparedness for singing. Therefore, the following sequence of events is recommended for the beginner:

    a. Begin with a diagnosis or analysis of the pupil's everyday speaking personality.

    b. Commence a *speech*-improvement program that emphasizes both clear enunciation and voice.

    c. Introduce poetry reading and the declamation of song texts and dramatic prose gems in *spoken* form, accentuating both voice and diction as you go.

    d. Make appropriate corrections of vocal inflection, posture, facial expression, body movement, and action patterns in these spoken declamations as a preparation for later use in expressive singing.

    e. Add an impromptu musical accompaniment for some of the more rhythmic spoken declamations and poetry readings. Emphasize intelligibility and meaning throughout.

f. Begin to pay more attention to the *sound* of the voice. Work on the prolongation of the syllabic vowels in each word, on sustaining vowel pitches, and on the use of prolonged vowels for more important words.

g. Finally, speak the words of any song text and match each word to the notational values of the musical score, gradually adding piano accompaniment, as needed. Then, repeat this step and *sing* the words instead of speaking them.

With this preliminary approach, the concept of singing as verbalized vocal expression is related to its spoken antecedents. Thus, we become aware of singing as a vocal art that evolves from the artistic use of the speaking voice.

Intonation in singing concerns itself with the sounding of vocal tones on the musical scale. Spoken intonation, on the other hand, is the meaningful rise and fall of the inflectional pitch of the speaking voice. Ideally, the expressive melodic patterns of a song may be considered the outgrowth of the inflections used in speaking its text. Therefore, it may be said that any verbal text lends itself best to a singing rendition if its melodic contours approximate the inflectional patterns that normally accompany an expressive reading of its *spoken* text.

To test this further, proceed as follows:

1. Speak the text of a simple song in declamatory style, ignoring the melody. Say the words aloud with expressive earnestness and sincerity of meaning.

2. Now *sing* the same song and note whether the incidental rise and fall of your spoken voice in the previous reading approximates or resembles the melodic line used by the composer.

If the melody seems artificial and unrelated to the meaning of its spoken text, the song is unsuited to the beginner's training program and should be discarded. If, on the other hand, the unstudied *spoken* inflections of the text closely approximate the vocal line of the musical score, the composition will lend itself readily to a speech-song approach.

3. Now, chant any improvised spoken statement and note whether it can be made to resemble a singing rendition of that statement. Recitative may be used for this purpose, as a teaching device. In fact, both teacher and pupil may hold extended conversations in a type of improvised quasi-musical recitative. More of this later.

4. Say "ah!" carelessly, using a nondescript vocal sound. Now prolong it, even slightly, and it approximates a singing tone. Its musical value lies in the use of a sustained pitch and in the definite time value assigned to it. Try similar *sustained* spoken intonations on any other vowel *(ah, eh, ee, oh, oo,* etc.), then on prolonged monosyllables containing these vowels *(how, may, I, know, you, well, my, own, true, love,* etc.) and you have a better glimpse of the verbal or vowel aspects of singing.

Obviously, then, the key to expressive diction for singing lies in the sublimation of speech values for singing purposes. That is to say, the voice of singing must never be divorced from its verbal message or communicative intent during the early training program and, vice versa, we must insist that pupils learn to sing, at the outset, by *saying* something with every tone produced. "Sing it as if you were saying it" is a constant watchword for the beginning songster.

In summation, we draw these four conclusions:

    a. Good diction in singing identifies itself with good tonal line. However, the tonal output of the song is imbedded in the verbal symbols themselves and these verbal-tonal patterns constitute the very essence of singing. The true service of a singer's diction, therefore, is to provide a suitable tonal vehicle without sacrificing the communication of meaningful ideas through song.

    b. Diction is verbalized vocal expression as distinguished from pure voice production. The study of a singer's diction, therefore, relates to the study of *words* as vehicles of vocal utterance.

c. In a more practical sense, diction also refers specifically to the production of intelligible *sounds* of language, considered either phonetically or in syllabic and verbal forms. In this connection, diction also includes the correct pronunciation, usage, and communication of words that contribute meaning and mood to the song.

d. Artistic interpretation and expression in singing are closely related to diction because singing utilizes the resources of both language and music.

The review of English diction for singers presents no significant problem if the pupil's daily speech is standard. But if his articulation is careless and distorted, or handicapped by faults that require remedial treatment, it will be necessary, first, to diagnose such faults in terms of acceptable speech norms.

What are these norms? The pedagogical approach to this problem requires a careful review of fundamentals. These include the articulation of consonants and vowels as a basic technique for use in speech or song. Correction manuals and articulation drill books are available for intensive study in this subject, when needed.[1] But the following resumé involving the basic function of English vowels and consonants will help give direction to the corrective program at whatever level it is pursued.

The English Consonants Summarized

Three main categories of English consonants are used for the singer. These are determined by characteristics of *sonancy*, *duration*, and *position*.

In the first or *sonancy* grouping, consonants are subdivided into two categories called *sonants* and *surds*. The sonants are the voiced or vocalic sounds. They include: *w*, *m*, *v*, *z*, *b*, *d*, *th* (as in *th*is), *zh* (as in a*z*ure), *n*, *l*, *r*, *g*, *ng*, and *y* (as in *y*es). The *surds* are unvoiced (nonvocalic) sounds and are made with breath alone. They include: *f*, *p*, *t*, *s*, *sh* (as in *s*ure), *k*, *h*, and *th* (as in *th*in).

The second or *duration* category is subdivided into *stops* and *continuants*. The stops are the nonprolongable sounds. They are: *p*, *b*, *t*, *k*, *g*. The continuants are prolongable sounds. They are: *w*, *f*, *v*, *m*, *s*, *sh*, *z*, *zh*, *th*, *n*, *l*, *r*, *ng* (as in si*ng*), *h*, and all the vowels.

In the third classification, only *positional* designations are indicated and the following nomenclature is therefore widely used:

1. *labials*, or lip sounds *(p, b, v, w)*;
2. *labio-dentals*, or lip-to-teeth sounds *(f, v)*;
3. *lingua-dentals*, or tongue-to-teeth sounds *(th)*;
4. *alveolars*, or tongue-to-gum-ridge sounds *(t, d, n, l, r)*;
5. *sibilants*, where the anterior tongue is raised toward the alveolar ridge *(s, z, sh, zh, ch, j)*;
6. *velars* (also known as *palatals)*, or back-tongue-to-soft-palate sounds *(k, g, ng)*; and
7. *aspirates*, or breath-friction sounds *(h)*.

These positional categories should be practiced or demonstrated individually until all the English consonants can be located and accurately produced. In a sense, the consonants serve only to define or delineate the vowel sounds to which they are attached. The organs of articulation thus act as valves that modify the breath stream and they also determine the size and shape of the vocal orifice and the rate of release of the phonetic elements of language, be they *vowel* or *consonant*, *sonant* or *surd*, *stop* or *continuant*. When deficiencies occur, the following procedural hints may be helpful:

a. Test the various sounds for sonancy by saying or singing *pairs* of words like the following. Use a monotone. In this procedure, consonants should be slightly exaggerated and all vowels prolonged (e.g., *rag – sack; lad – fat; dove – tough; judge – catch;* etc.). It will be noted that the first word of each pair contains sonants only, while the second word contains contrasting surds. Similar pairs of sonant-surd contrasts may be prepared and practiced until the qualitative or sonancy factor in consonants and vowels is easily recognized.

b. Note that the *stops* are consonants that arrest the breath, hence their name. They make no appreciable sound, although the slight plosive release following each of them is audible. The vocal line in singing would all but obliterate the stops unless they were *slightly* emphasized. Therefore, they need to be more distinct in singing than in speaking.

c. Sing the following syllabic contrasts in a monotone: *pa – ma; day – lay; cad – man; keep – lean;* etc. Observe that the stops are not prolongable. Therefore their occurrence in the words of a song text affects the continuity of the vocal line. Similar contrasting syllables may be paired and used for practice until the ear learns to distinguish *stops* from *continuants* in both spoken and song forms.

d. Independent *anterior* lingual action is a *must* for singers. That is to say, the front of the tongue is required to move more actively and extensively than the back of the tongue. However, jaw movement must be minimized, especially in the production of alveolar and velar consonants.

e. The alveolars are produced with the raised tongue tip contacting the gum (alveolar) ridge at the spot where the arch of the palate begins. However, minor deviations from this position are admissable to accommodate transitional or *sandhi* movements of the speech organs during fluent utterance.

f. The *th* (either sonant or surd) is the only consonant requiring lingua-dental contact. For all other English consonants, the tongue is in a relatively retracted position with respect to the teeth. Therefore, except for *th*, the tongue never touches the teeth. This does not apply to foreign languages like Italian, Spanish, or German wherein dentalizations or dental contacts are more numerous.

g. Since all the *sonants* are vocalized (e.g., *v, z, m, l, zh,* etc.), they usually take the pitch of the vowel immediately following them, except at the end of a phrase.

h. For carrying power and clearer definition in a large auditorium, it may be necessary to exaggerate the initial attack of each of the consonants. This should not be overdone.

i. The English *r* is not usually trilled, although the *r* is rolled or trilled in foreign languages. The *r* should be sounded a little stronger in song than in speech, and it should be sung in pitch. Never exaggerate the *r* sound.

j. The *l* takes a full voice. The anterior tongue contacts the roof of the mouth lightly while the singer sounds a full tone, as though no consonant were expected.

k. Continuant surds like *f, s, sh, th* (as in *th*in) require a slight interval of toneless breath in their production. However, they should never be noisy or conspicuous.

l. At the foundation of our study of diction is the inseparability of vowels and consonants. That is to say, vowels require consonants for clear definition, and consonants become meaningless when produced without vowels. Each is linked to the other, and the combination of the two forms the *syllable* which lies at the root of all verbal expression. It is obvious, therefore, that to cultivate good diction for singing, vocalizes should embody entire *syllables* rather than isolated vowels.

m. Finally, although consonants may be subordinated to vowels in singing, they are not sacrificed to the latter. Consonants are the necessary boundary sounds which help identify the vowels. Consonants must therefore be accurately positioned, and lightly, quickly, and clearly executed. The prime consideration in diction is economy of movement in all working parts of the articulatory apparatus. Furthermore, since many consonants are, at best, nonvocal obtrusions or vocal interrupters, they must not be allowed to attract attention to themselves. Nevertheless, consonants should always be distinctly sounded, for intelligibility would be impossible without them.[2]

Also to be considered are the elements of muscular

movement needed in articulation. If exaggerated, these movements of the speech organs may constrict and muffle the voice. Therefore, an economy-of-effort principle governs all articulatory action and it is necessary to learn to minimize transitional movements *between* sounds, especially during speedy utterance. The *sandhi* factor enters here.

The Sandhi Effect

Articulation in speaking or singing is not a sequence of detached phonetic elements like the letters on a printed page. Rather, the *sounds* of language are always joined together in a flowing phonemic pattern. That is to say, although each sound has its phonetic identity, it always occurs in fluent legato conjunction with other sounds that form the syllabic structure of words.

Each phonetic element in vocal diction therefore serves as a *connecter,* and is always in transition as it glides from its own identity to that of its neighbor. These tiny transitional glides produce minute blending or assimilatory changes that are called *sandhi effects (sandhi:* from Sanskrit, a placing together).[3]

Sandhi effects in fluent diction must be compensated for by using greater precision and exactitude in the placement of the organs of articulation. Phonetic accuracy is therefore mandatory because the slightest deviation from standardized lingual norms can produce audible distortions which mar the intelligibility of words. The sandhi effect in diction is a feature of all legato singing.

English Vowels and Their Function in Singing

Obviously, vowels are the principal vocal elements of the language. They convey the characteristics of the singer's voice and determine basic quality, resonance, pitch, and other distinctive features of vocal tone. It is axiomatic, therefore, that the vowel is the vehicle of the singing voice; that your singing voice is only as good as your vowel; that vocalization is essentially *vowelization*.

In vowel production, the vocal channel is relatively open or unblocked at all times. Vowels, therefore, derive their phonetic identity from the varying combinations of size and shape in the resonators that produce them. These spatial configurations generate a distinctive overtone spectrum or *formant* for each vowel that is sung. That is to say, certain partials become accentuated, others subdued or dampened, as the mouth and pharyngeal cavities change their relative size and conformation in various combinations.

Vowel formants are influenced by at least three factors: a) the volume, size, or shape of the resonance cavity; b) the area of the openings into and out of the cavity; and c) the number of interrelated cavities that are joined or coupled together into a unified system, with their combined effect on the resonance characteristics of the system.

Through acoustical analysis it is possible to tabulate the characteristic vowel formants of speech and song.[4] But the exact methods of producing them is not easily perceived. Furthermore, individual anatomical variations in the vocal tract would preclude a rigid standardization of tongue positions or other positional controls for the vocal (vowel) resonators.

How then are the vowel sounds to be produced by the singer? The answer to this question is complicated by the fact that vowels are formed by the *combined* influence of at least eight different organs or segments of the vocal tract. These include the pharyngeal and laryngeal vestibules, the epiglottis, the tongue, jaw, fauces, velum, and lips. The flowing movements of all these interrelated elements combine to affect the vowel formant.

When a particular muscular adjustment is only externally observed, the position of that organ is often erroneously considered as the only index to vowel production. But there are other parts, both visible and hidden, that are simultaneously coordinated in the production of each sound.

Vowel production is, therefore, necessarily governed by hearing concepts. That is to say, the tongue and the various pharyngeal muscles are taught to respond unconsciously to the *hearing* concept of the sound desired, thus controlling the requisite subtle modifications of the oral passageway and the entire complex of resonating cavities.

Like the consonants, vowels must always be intelligible in a singer's diction. They must support, not distort, the resonance characteristics of the individual's voice. It is therefore considered necessary to establish a *hearing* recognition of optimal vowel-vocal resonance at all levels of pitch and dynamics and in legato, staccato, syllabic, and verbal forms. In this connection, the intonation problems and exercises of chapter eleven may be reviewed.

Finally, there are potentially as many vowels as there are cavity shapes, that is to say, an infinite or unlimited number. However, phoneticians distinguish at least thirteen standard vowels in the English language, and these must be learned with accuracy, for they comprise the tonal spectrum of all intelligible singing diction.

Unlike the consonants, it is difficult to establish standardized positions of the organs of articulation for each vowel. Rather, the entire vocal tract must automatically adjust itself to produce each characteristic vowel as a concomitant of sensitive hearing.

In short, when habits of diction are at fault, vowel techniques can be reeducated by freeing the tongue and throat from erroneously preconceived placement rules and by learning to rely primarily on the tonal judgment of the educated ear. Repetitive and imitative practice will prove this to be so.

Vowel Rotation Exercises

To thus reeducate his ear, the pupil learns to move his voice through a slowly gliding legato sequence of all the basic vowel patterns. While making these transitional glides he mentally associates each vowel with a monosyllabic key word that contains that vowel. The sequence will sound somewhat like an extended cat's *miaow* because it encompasses all the vowels in a continuous sustained wail.

a. Sing the following thirteen standard vowels on a continuous monotone, at a comfortable pitch level. The voice should glide slowly but smoothly from one prolonged sound to the next, without pausing, allowing two counts for each vowel, or long enough to permit the aural identification thereof. This vowel rotation series is phonetically represented as follows[5]:

$$i \rightarrow \text{\textsc{i}} \rightarrow e \rightarrow \varepsilon \rightarrow æ \rightarrow a \rightarrow ə \rightarrow ɑ \rightarrow ʌ \rightarrow ɔ \rightarrow o \rightarrow ʊ \rightarrow u$$

The appropriate key word for each vowel in this sequence may be listed as follows:

*e*ve – *i*ll – *a*te – *e*nd – *a*m – *a*sk – *a*lone –
*a*rm – *u*p – *o*rb – g*o* – p*u*ll – p*oo*l.

(See "Comparative Phonetic Chart" on page 249 of this chapter.)

b. After several trials, repeat the *miaow*-sounding series, or any part thereof, with slow crescendo and diminuendo variations (messa di voce) at different pitch levels.

c. The same series may now be practiced in a reverse sequence, in a continuous drawl resembling a protracted "W-Y-E" sound, as follows:

$$u \rightarrow ʊ \rightarrow o \rightarrow ɔ \rightarrow ʌ \rightarrow ɑ \rightarrow ə \rightarrow a \rightarrow æ \rightarrow \varepsilon \rightarrow e \rightarrow \text{\textsc{i}} \rightarrow i$$

and with similar dynamic variations in messa di voce style.

d. Repeat this legato series of vowel sounds at different pitch levels and with different inflections, always bearing in mind that optimal vocal resonance (head hum) is to be maintained throughout.

This rather weird-sounding exercise is not to be thought of merely as a prolonged feline wail, but, rather, as a sensitive vowel-adjusting ear-training device. It is a method of strengthening the transitional adjustments of all the vowel resonators while disciplining the ear. In other words, as the voice glides continuously through thirteen recognizable sounds, the ear mentally associates each vowel identity with its appropriate key word. At the same time, a constant aural vigil is maintained toward timbre and quality. When deviations are noted, the teacher isolates the fault, presents a model for imitation, and prescribes a repetitive drill until the error is corrected. Syllabic vocalizes, verbal, and other diction exercises may follow this preliminary vowel tune-up.

e. Monosyllabic words in various vowel patterns may now be practiced. At first, use a loud unvoiced whisper for each word, then full voice, as a way of focusing attention on comparative vowel and vocal values, e.g., *e*ve – br*i*ngs – d*a*y's – *e*nd – *a*nd – c*a*sts – *a* – ch*a*rm – l*o*ve's – c*a*ll – gr*o*ws – f*u*ll – m*oo*n; and, in reverse series: wh*o* – w*ou*ld – kn*o*w – n*au*ght – d*oe*s – st*a*rt – *a* – t*a*sk – *a*nd – th*e*n – t*a*kes – h*i*s – *ea*se.

Following this series, the diphthongs may be practiced in similar fashion. A *diphthong* is a gliding monosyllabic junction of two dissimilar vowel sounds occurring in the same syllable, e.g., m*ai*n – m*ou*nd – m*i*nd – m*oi*l – m*oa*n – m*u*le. Ideally, any isolated vowel sound is always mentally associated with the model syllable or key word that contains it.

In practicing vowel rotation drills, two objectives are achieved. *First,* the various muscular boundaries of the vocal (vowel) tract are limbered up through tone-connected exercises. *Second,* the aural recognition of each vowel is strengthened as it is being practiced in a slow, legato tonal sequence.

These synthetic vowel drills are for guidance in the conscious reeducation of bad habits. They should be continued only until correct habits of intonation and diction have been firmly implanted. The ear then takes over. In other words, after the pupil has acquired habitual precision, intelligibility, and flexibility in all actions of the organs of articulation, his attention may be directed to the overall effects of expressive diction in song. He then proceeds with the interpretation of song literature and the preparation of a suitable repertoire. The study of diction thus becomes a corequisite of song study, rather than a detached discipline in the vocal-training program.

The Technical Problems of Foreign-Language Study

Although it is assumed that the pupil's native language is English, a study procedure in foreign languages may be launched early in the voice-training program. By this means, the mastery of foreign diction can keep pace with the growing linguistic demands of a gradually enlarging song repertoire. The use of textbooks is, of course, necessary.[6] When obtainable, phonetic song texts and English translations of song texts that parallel the original words can also be helpful in mastering the foreign language idiom.[7] A preliminary study of foreign syntax, grammar, and sentence structure is also corequisite.

Basically, the study of foreign diction includes three dimensions that deserve special attention. These deal with *sounds, syllables,* and *words.* For convenience they are here considered in reverse order as: *vocabulary building, pronunciation problems,* and *methods of articulation.*

Building a Vocabulary

Traveling or living in a foreign country is, of course, ideal. But, considering the vast resources in our libraries and museums, it is possible for anyone to dip into any foreign culture for purposes of linguistic study without actual residence abroad. After the mood, temperament, and historical, artistic, and literary background begin to be understood, the actual study of a foreign *vocabulary* may be commenced. A systematic threefold procedure encompasses a) pronunciation; b) synonymy or the formulation of meanings; and c) usage. Each of these will be briefly described, for the guidance of students.

a. Pronunciation. This includes skill in combining the sounds of the language into syllabic and verbal patterns with special attention to correct accent. This calls for the use of a dictionary and requires frequent oral drill on classified vocabulary lists. At first, only words accented on the first syllable may be practiced, then those accented on the second syllable, then the third, and so on. Accentual patterns of words are thus more systematically committed to memory for later use in reading the spoken texts of songs. The interpretation of song rests, in large measure, on the meanings of words and ideas.

b. Studying Synonyms. At first contact, pronunciation lists are rehearsed for accent only. Later on, an English synonym may be supplied for each word. The dictionary is consulted for proper definitions and synonyms until the original word is brought into sharp relief and its exact meaning grasped. Firm associations are thus built between the word, its pronunciation, and its meaning.

c. Usage. As a next step, each newly acquired word is to be used in an impromptu sentence each time it is pronounced. *Usage* may be defined as the customary practice which dictates the way that words or phrases are made serviceable in a language community. Therefore, as soon as a group of new words is learned, short impromptu conversations may be tried by practicing five or six new words at a time in appropriate conversational sentences.

Next, reading aloud from foreign literary song texts may be practiced, with special attention to the usage of words contained therein and their correct pronunciation. This final procedure involves three stages: *first,* translating aloud as you read; *second,* translating silently or mentally as you read aloud; *third,* thinking the word in its correct context, without the necessity of translation, as you read silently. Thus, vocabulary skills are acquired in any language by the threefold mastery of *pronunciation, synonymy,* and *usage.*

Methods of Articulation

The study of the *sounds* of the language or the formation and articulation of its phonetic elements is of major importance. Because of its complexity, this aspect of diction is here considered last, although the order of study might very well be reversed in actual procedure. In many instances, the teacher will find it convenient to administer all three departments of diction simultaneously so that a parallel attainment in each may keep pace with the mastery of the other spects of vocal training. It would be appropriate, at this point, to introduce the study of phonetics as an approach to the mastery of articulation in a foreign language.

Phonetics as a Teaching Tool

Phonetics is a system of notation for representing speech sounds by means of symbols that have *one* value only. The symbol always represents the same sound and it is thus possible to spell any word phonetically as it is actually heard and to minimize confusion as to the pronunciation of silent letters and variants.

All silent letters are, of course, omitted in phonetic spelling. This audible representation is called the *ear word*, to distinguish it from its visual counterpart, the *eye word* (e.g., in English phonetics, tΛD is the ear word; *tongue* is the *eye word*). The pupil must learn to distinguish between the two. The *International Phonetic Alphabet* is, therefore, widely used as a teaching tool because it is adaptable to both English and foreign-language study and comparative phonetic analyses between languages are thus made possible.

It will be helpful if the student learns the phonetic alphabet from some standard text on the subject[8] in much the same manner as he would study musical notation from a suitable textbook. Fluency in sight reading of English phonetic notation then becomes transferable to foreign languages, with the addition of several unique sounds and symbols in each language.

The *International Phonetic Alphabet* consists of more than fifty symbols, many of which are the already familiar letters of the English alphabet. It will be necessary to memorize these symbols, especially those that are not already familiar and those that represent the unique sounds of each foreign language. A comparative chart is here presented to afford a survey of the symbolic representation of the typical sounds of *English, Italian, French,* and *German,* since these four languages encompass the greater part of a singer's repertoire. It is to be noted, however, that the comparisons represented in this phonetic chart are necessarily approximate, for there are some sounds in each language that closely resemble, but are not identical with, the comparative sounds of English. By studying comparative phonetics, however, the ear will gradually find its way from the already familiar English sounds to the unfamiliar variations and approximations of these sounds that exist in the other languages. The ultimate mastery of the more refined phonetic distinctions in each foreign language is necessarily a product of intensified ear training and much repetitive drill therein.

Comparative Phonetic Chart

Words contain approximate sound of phonetic symbol listed at left

VOWELS

Symbol	English	Italian	French	German
1. i	eve	mi	fine	wie
2. ɪ	ill			bist
3. eɪ	ate	che	des	Spät
4. ɛ	end	ecco	neige	Herz
5. æ	am			
6. a	ask		patte	Lamm
7. ə(*)	alone		ce	Gewiss
8. ɑ	arm	casa	âme	Vater
9. ʌ	up			
10. ɔ	orb	corda	fort	Wort
11. oʊ	go	voce	beau	Tod
12. o	pull			und
13. u	pool	luce	goût	gut
14. ʊ			neuf	Götter
15. ɸ			bleu	
16. y			lune	kühl
17. y̨			puis	
18. ã			sans	
19. ɛ̃			rien	
20. ɔ̃			non	
21. œ̃			un	

(*) unaccented schwa is an indeterminate or neutral vowel

DIPHTHONGS

1. eɪ	cave	Dei		
2. ɑʊ	house	aura		Baum
3. ɑɪ	nice	laico		rein
4. ɔɪ	toy			heute
5. oʊ	tone			
6. ɪu	suit	chiusa		
7. eʊ		eureka		
8. ɪə		lieto		
9. ɪo		odio		

CONSONANTS

Symbol	English	Italian	French	German
1. b	bib	botte	bon	Blume
2. d	deed	addio	dans	Dorf
3. f	fife	fatto	boeuf	offen
4. g	gay	gola	gare	gehen
5. h	how			Haus
6. j	you	ieri	bien	Jahr
7. k	cook	cosi	café	Kalt
8. l	lull	legge	malle	liebe
9. m	maim	come	mon	machen
10. n	noon	buono	ne	nein
11. p	peep	pesca	pain	Paar
12. ɹ	ray	rosa(*)	rue(*)	rein(*)
13. s	see	sette	sait	lassen
14. t	taut	terra	matte	Tag
15. v	Eva	venti	wagon	Wasser
16. w	away	questa	oui	
17. z	zoo	rosa	pose	sagen
18. ŋ	young	ancor	anglais	Ring
19. ʃ	she	scena	chat	Schule
20. tʃ	each	voce		
21. dʒ	edge	oggi		
22. ʒ	azure		je	
23. θ	thin			
24. ð	this			
25. nj	onion	ogni	agneau	
26. lj	million	gli		
27. ç				ich
28. X				auch

(*) foreign r may be trilled, uvular, or flipped with a single tap of the tongue

Special Notes on the Phonetic Chart

It is often best to begin foreign-language study with Italian because all the Italian vowels and consonants occur in the English language, although they are, of course, spelled differently. In Italian, the stressed vowel is slightly lengthened when it is followed by a single consonant. Otherwise, it is shortened.

Certain difficulties will be met in French because there are a number of exceptional sounds in that language. Special problems include the y or *ü* (as in l*u*ne); the *eu* as in n*eu*f); and all the nasal sounds (e.g., *an, en, on, un)*. The rolled *r* in French requires not only a trilled tongue but also a light quivering action of the soft palate accompanying it.

In spoken French, the final consonant of a word is often elided with the vowel that begins the word following it. This is called *liaison*. Otherwise, French consonants do not differ essentially from their English equivalents.

In German and French, a peculiar adaptation of the oral cavity is effected by simultaneously raising the tongue and narrowing the oral aperture at the lips. This combination produces the *umlaut*, which is not heard in English. For the French *ü* (as in l*u*ne), the tongue is a little lower than for the German *ü* or umlaut.

In German, a glottal attack is used for words beginning with a vowel sound, especially after a word that ends with a consonant.

German and English consonants are similar, except for gutteral sounds, which include two kinds of *ch (ich* with the high-tongue aspirate and *ach* with the low-tongue aspirate) and the fluttering *r*. These and other phonetic problems and peculiarities will be found set forth in greater detail in any foreign-language study text.

Conclusions for Singing

The curse of the amateur is unintelligible diction. Therefore, the student singer should be guided by the axiom that *the word is father to the tone.*[9] It is rather foolish to sing songs to an audience who cannot understand them. Hence, mastering the communicative intent of the text actually precedes the musical interpretation of a song. Although this approach reverses common procedure, it guarantees a type of rendition that imparts the true intention of the composer, namely, to convey textual content along with the musical content of a song.

Speaking and singing are governed by the same basic laws of expression. Differences between the two relate primarily to musical pitch and time values. Therefore, in a sense, vocal education really begins when children are first taught to speak.

Of course, the blending of tone and word is not always easy to accomplish. But the teacher will realize that it is much easier to develop voice and diction side by side than to endure the later impatience and frustration that result from a delayed development of one or the other. If the singer will bite into the words decisively, he will find that they vitalize the tones of his singing voice and help impart meaning to the song. Observing and correcting the habits of everyday conversational diction is therefore part of this program in which spoken declamations and impromptu recitatives in full voice can be helpful.

The mastery of the language he is using is, of course, fundamental to the needs of a professional singer. In fact, to speak or sing any language intelligibly, whether native or foreign, a thorough-going review of fundamentals is called for. These are set forth in seven different aspects of word study. 1) *Spelling* peculiarities must be learned so that the printed language, or eye word, may be read with ease. 2) *Articulation* problems are to be mastered, that is, the formation of correct speech sounds. 3) *Pronunciation* of word lists is next recommended and these must be practiced with special attention to correct syllabic accent. 4) Word derivations and *definitions* are studied in order to arrive at correct meanings. 5) *Syntax or grammar* must be learned and understood. 6) *Idiomatic usage* is next considered, along with other structural peculiarities of the language for everyday speaking or for literary purposes. 7) Finally, *conversational fluency* is practiced so that euphony, rhythm, and style may be coordinated with correct usage.

The resultant knowledge and skill should be adequate for both speaking and singing purposes. Several years may be involved in this study procedure, and few singers have the time or patience to master each language thoroughly. But while the student is gaining mastery over his singing voice and learning to overcome bad habits and express himself vocally in his native tongue, he may at the same time be at work studying the essentials of three or four foreign languages.

The following correctives are suggested for unintelligible English (or foreign) diction:

1. Ultraforceful (nonvocal) whispering of the text of a song. This will serve to energize the consonants while also projecting the vowel shapes without straining the vocal organs.

2. Chanting the text in a musical monotone as a device to divert attention from music to diction and the meaning of words.

3. Slowly speaking or declaiming (not singing) the text with a musical accompaniment on the piano. This will serve to accentuate the meanings of the words of a song.

4. Subordinating tone to text while singing. This is a good temporary device used to correct an imbalance when the pupil's diction is indistinct. The vocal tone is to be subdued while the diction is to be exaggerated throughout the song. Continue this type of practice until the imbalance is corrected. Thereafter, diction and tone are to be regarded as equally important.

5. Conversational singing. Sentences, either impromptu or from a song text, are spoken very slowly at first, then *intoned* in a form of improvised musical chant or recitative. Teacher and student may converse in any language in this manner, while correct diction is being emphasized.

The teacher may devise similar correctives to offset the

pupil's sluggish diction. It is well to begin by memorizing the words of a new song so that the original meaning of the text may be grasped. In this way, deeper interpretative insights will be developed. The singer also grasps the larger implications of language mastery as he approaches the study of interpretation and prepares himself for the role of the performing artist.

In the last analysis, diction is a distinguishing characteristic of the singer's personality. It conveys the verbal concepts that make the language of song intelligible to ourselves and to others. Since the distinct statement of an idea begins any process of communication, it is also the first step in bringing a singer's thoughts and feelings into communicable form. Intelligible diction is, therefore, an essential vehicle of vocal expression, whether in speech or in song.

REFERENCES AND NOTES

1. Madeleine Marshall, *The Singer's Manual of English Diction* (New York: G. Schirmer, Inc., 1953).

2. Harry Plunket Greene, *Interpretation in Song* (London: Macmillan and Co., Ltd., 1956), p. 104.

3. Victor A. Fields and James F. Bender, *Voice and Diction* (New York: The Macmillan Company, 1949), p. 228.

4. Peter B. Denes and Elliot N. Pinson, *The Speech Chain* (Baltimore: Bell Telephone Laboratories, Inc., 1963), p. 64.

5. Fields and Bender, *Voice and Diction,* p. 179.

6. Texts like the following may be used:

Jones, Smith, and Walls, *Pronunciation Guide to French, German, Italian and Spanish* (New York: Carl Fischer, Inc., 1965).
Paul Passy, *The Sounds of the French Language* (London: Oxford University Press, 1948).
Eva Wilcke, *German Diction in Singing,* trans. and ed. Bainbridge Crist (New York: E. P. Dutton, 1930).
Theodor Siebs, *Deutsche Bühnenaussprache-Hochsprache* [German Stage Diction] (New York: Frederick Ungar Publ. Co., 1944).
Joseph Louis Russo, *Present Day Italian* (Boston: D. C. Heath Co., 1947).

Ralph Erolle, *Italian Diction for Singers,* 3rd edition (Boulder, Colorado: Pruett Press, 1963).

Richard G. Cox, *The Singer's Manual of German and French Diction* (New York: G. Schirmer, Inc., 1970).

Kurt Adler, *Phonetics and Diction in Singing* (It., Fr., Span., Ger.) (Minneapolis: University of Minnesota Press, 1967).

John Moriarty, *Diction: Italian, Latin, French, German* (Boston: E. C. Schirmer Music Co., 1975).

7. Berton Coffin; Ralph Erolle; Werner Singer; and Pierre Delattre, *Phonetic Readings of Songs and Arias* (Boulder, Colorado: Pruett Press, 1964); Philip L. Miller, *The Ring of Words* (Garden City, New York: Doubleday & Company, Inc., 1963).

8. R–M. S. Heffner, *General Phonetics* (Madison, Wisc.: University of Wisconsin Press, 1950).

9. Philip A. Duey, *Bel Canto In Its Golden Age* (New York: King's Crown Press, Columbia University, 1951), Chap. 10.

XIV

Interpretation in Singing

Interpretation in singing is essentially a clarification process. The singer penetrates external aspects of the score and attunes himself to its underlying throught, mood, and musical value. In doing this, he becomes a creative artist rather than a mere technician, and he reads into his expression of the song as much of its original purpose as he can. Although interpretation is intuitional and inspirational, it also requires intellectual insights, technical virtuosity, and communicative intent.

Three major factors emerge. They involve a synthesis of mental operations that support the interpretative process, and they are described as *absorption, assimilation,* and *expression.* Together they constitute a formula for growth in artistic stature, and they also make for musical understanding and effective performance before an audience.

Absorption is largely a perceptive process. That is to say, the perceptive singer recognizes and absorbs the musical and other meaningful elements of a song and makes an accurate appraisal of the controlling idea of a composer's work. He then responds not only to tonality and text, but also absorbs underlying musical values and understands the character to be portrayed in the song. He knows exactly what to look for, where to look for it, and how to recognize and identify what he is looking for. His perception helps him identify experience and thus makes possible further comprehension of the musical content of a song.

Assimilation may be described as a process of comprehension or mental synthesis which relates that which is presently perceived to previously acquired knowledge. A singer must know what to accept or reject, how to tell what is excellent from that which is spurious or misleading. He must possess not only an awareness of musical values, but a sensitive feeling about their suitability for expression and a quick recognition of their practical effects in performance. Assimilation, therefore, comprehends and evaluates experience.

Expression is a communicative process. It is the act of imparting one's understanding to an audience by appropriate audible and visible means. In other words, a singer begins with an intelligent recognition of the true nature of a musical experience or a clear perception thereof. Then, he attaches individual values to it and correlates it with his own judgments, thoughts, and feelings; and his mental activity reaches fulfillment in the vivid and meaningful communication or outpicturing of his personal reactions. Thus, he *absorbs, assimilates,* and *expresses,* and thereby achieves an interpretation based on his own understanding.

To recapitulate, a singer who merely performs musical notes, however skillfully, may be called a perceptive technician. If his rendition is both technically skillful and meaningful in a conventional sense, he may be said to have an evaluative grasp or comprehension of his subject, but without originality. If he imparts personal values and original nuances that arise out of his own creative thinking, in short, if he expresses *himself* and contributes something new to individualize and vitalize an otherwise orthodox subject matter, he becomes, in fact, a real interpreter.

Perception may be improved by culture, education, rational thinking, and other mental disciplines, and by exercising keen awareness of all the experiences of life itself. *Com-*

prehension is developed by imaginative thinking, by the association of ideas, by recognizing relationships between events past and present, and by learning to visualize that which is not seen. *Expression* may be improved by practicing initiative, originality, and creativity in one's own behavior, by adjusting oneself to environmental circumstances, and by individualizing all creative endeavors through the practical media of voice and language, whether in speech or song. These are the singer's tools, both mental and physical.

In order to translate these theoretical concepts into more practical terms, many avenues of training will have to be considered. These include such items as: *the role of language in creating a musical vehicle for song; building artistic stature for performance; personality growth; the use of dramatic discipline, declamation, exaggeration, and recitative; how to win and hold an audience; using creative imagination; creating the illusion of the first time; the importance of empathy; creating atmosphere and mood; the artist's attitude and stage presence; unity of effect; style in singing;* and finally, *principles of characterization* and *the preparation of an operatic role.*

The subject of interpretation is therefore complex, at best, and it has many facets. The discussions which follow in this and the following chapters are necessarily brief, but they will serve to give both teacher and pupil certain insights into the varied training program that is essential for every performing artist.

The Role of Language

To the interpreting artist the text of a song is deeper than words. It is also a vehicle of tone, form, and communicative intent. Therefore, although a singer does not usually create the words of a song, he must understand their meaning and grasp the motives of the composer in using them. He is responsible, in a sense, for the matching of words to music in that he channels all these materials through his own mind before interpreting them, and he therefore clothes them with the characteristics of his own creative expression.

Building Artistic Stature

What does the singer express? Himself, of course, since there is no other possibility. He is the center of all he creates. Whether he is original or imitative depends largely on whether he has the freedom and facility to create new forms out of materials available to him or whether he merely seeks to imitate standardized modes of expression. If his tools are skillfully handled, he achieves clarity, coherence, and independence. If he is obscure or inept, much of his intention will be lost, frustrated, or misshapen in the vocal and verbal forms that emerge.

Therefore, in building artistic stature, the singer must clarify and enrich his knowledge of the musical world and his awareness of its cultural resources. He must sample the technical tools and materials that are available to him, learn to use them effectively for musical purposes, practice until he attains speed, flexibility, and skill, and thus lays a firm foundation of habits for the service of mind and will. Such a development rounds out the growth and training needed for public performance.

Personality Growth in Singing

Personality (fr. L. *persona:* mask) presents the outer or behavioral characteristics of expression, while *individuality* indicates the inherent or latent capabilities that are not necessarily apparent to the onlooker. Hence, it may be said that the interpreter is judged largely by his personality and, ideally, the *outer* should always represent or outpicture the *inner,* for that is the function of communicaton.

The most convincing expression comes from the heart of the performer. On the other hand, simulated or artificial expression is merely a mold in which personalities are projected without individual support. Nevertheless, whether the personality is ultimately sincere or synthetic, it grows only through exercise in the art of vocal projection and self-expression.

It is necessary, therefore, that the potential artist free himself from fear and self-consciousness before he can make an impressive showing before an audience. In other words, no one can attain histrionic prominence in theater, opera, or concert unless he has first experienced the fullest and freest self-release in all forms of vocal and bodily expression.

This, then, becomes a teaching problem. How can enthusiasm and self-release be stimulated in a timid or phlegmatic person? How can the pupil be taught to generate an intense interest which is sufficient to promote the outpouring of spirit rather than the superficiality of a planned exterior that lacks depth or dimension? How can he discover those latent possibilities of expression that are all but hidden from view by the frozen or inhibited behavior of a well-mannered but overcautious mentality and its superficial counterpart, the restrained personality? In short, how can he learn to communicate creatively without fear or self-consciousness and in the expansive and inspirational manner that is required for public performance? These are problems that motivate the discussions that follow.

The Use of Dramatic Disciplines

One of the first things the interpreter needs to learn is the control of dramatic forms of expression. Dramatic interpretation rests on the premise that there is some special worth in what is being done or said, that there is a concentration of values beyond everyday needs, and that these unusual values are exciting enough to be conveyed with force and clarity.

This does not imply that mildness of expression is never desirable. Rather, it suggests that mildness, when used, needs to be juxtaposed against other, stronger dramatic elements that help sharpen the contrast between them. Even lyric tonality is capable of expressing drama when it suggests a subdued, but deeply felt mood.

In other words, the excitement, uplift, emotional enthusiasm, and inspiration of the concert stage are, at best, the portrayal of the unusual experience and the intensified feeling or thought. And these demand more than casual utterance. They require the ability to express contrasts, colors, and intense thoughts and feelings, and to portray sharply, through vocal media, their underlying behavioral elements. Therefore, the study of interpretation necessarily encompasses the study of the unusual, the dramatic, the forceful and stronger-than-usual expression of ideas, and, of course, the vivid thinking processes that underlie them. For this reason an artist interpreter needs to make a special study of the use of dramatic disciplines. Not the least of these is the art of declamation. The following practice procedure is recommended:

1. Declamation is the emotional intensification of speech or song. Anything ordinary becomes, in fact, extraordinary when it is intensely felt and uttered or juxtaposed against opposites or given a special meaning and value in life. Declamation is not to be construed merely as exaggerated, bombastic, and sensational utterance. Rather, it is the compact or intensified statement of thought and feeling values made vivid through contrasting elements of personal experience. Declamation, therefore, is an important tool in developing the art of interpretation and should be used as a practice device.

2. The Use of Exaggeration. Exaggeration is also an excellent practice device. It is a personality builder. A complete let-go stirs up creative imagination, arouses dormant energies, and elicits a vigorous outpouring of the singer's thoughts and feelings in voice and action. The inhibited pupil is therefore taught to intensify or *exaggerate* his expression by practicing with declamatory and dramatic song texts.

At first, he reads the text aloud with deeply felt *spoken* exclamations of mood and meaning. With each repetition, he increases the intensity of his reading and gradually learns to project himself vocally *beyond* the dimensions of conversational speech. Thus, he eventually attains a sense of authority and self-realization that is part of his preparatory training.

Both speaking and singing texts may be used for this type of practice. Musical values are temporarily subordinated for the purpose of emphasizing the meaning of words and the feelings that accompany them. Precise diction is also demanded. This practice device will help restore a proper balance between tone and word for singing purposes. In short, *declamation* and *exaggeration* are practice methods that help release the performer from inhibitions and restrained behavior.

3. Overstatement vs. Understatement. Whether the depths of thought and feeling are expressed or implied depends, in large measure, on the type of interpretation to be used. Some song texts lend themselves to overstatement, some to understatement. But even understatement suggests a hidden potential that lies within the meaning of the text. This hidden potential is first brought to light by practicing the same words with exaggerated emphasis. Following this, the subdued expression thereof has more meaning to the performer.

Exaggeration and overstatement are, therefore, valuable as practice devices that pave the way for the subtle nuances of understatement. In other words, the pupil must learn to declaim and exaggerate his song text before he can interpret it musically with proper restraint and nuance. To reiterate, overstatement begets a margin of competence *beyond* the requirements of satisfactory performance, and therefore ensures a feeling of power, authority, and poise in delivering the finished product.

The singer is cautioned, however, that this practice procedure does not call for the ranting, strutting style of the ham actor. Rather, it is a carefully studied use of expressional force, depth, and power. In other words, no one may learn the art of interpretation without first mastering the art of declamation, both in speech and song. This mastery spells self-release, ease of expression, flexibility of voice, and versatility for the performing artist. It is also an excellent personality builder.

4. The Use of Recitative. Musical recitative provides another medium for improving the communicative aspects of singing. *Recitative* is a rhythmical vocal passage in which a singer intones a narrative text in a manner approaching conversational speech. It is usually syllabic in style and it encompasses a rather small tonal range. By means of this quasi-talking style a student can learn to convey a musical text with meaningful intent, as though its message mattered both to the audience and to himself. The type of recitative used for practice will, of course, depend on the aptitude and vocal proficiency of the pupil.

How to Win and Hold an Audience

The Function of Creative Imagination

Imagination is a creative faculty of the mind. It deals with man's power to form mental images that are not actually present to the senses. Inasmuch as there are no limitations of time or space in mental imagery, the powers of creative imagination are practically limitless. Hence, the mind can conjure up a finished performance in every detail, even though the physical body lacks the competence to do so. Furthermore, the art of interpretation would be but a slavish imitation of borrowed styles and models were it not for the creative faculty of the imaginative mind.

In keeping with this concept, it is important that the singer learns to see himself, mentally, from an audience viewpoint. In due time he acquires a *transcursive sense* that hovers over every public appearance he makes and dictates a proper adjustment to the listener's needs during a performance.

In other words, the interpreter must realize that he is enacting for his audience the type of imaginative release which provides the essence of their own musical enjoyment. Listeners do not wish to be made conscious of the rigors of discipline and self-restraint as witnessed in the studied, overcautious behavior of the stilted amateur. Nor do they want a portrayal of overcultivated behavior that bespeaks the conventionality of their own lives. Rather, they desire the fullest and freest abandonment of mind and body and the realization of complete freedom, relaxation, or let-go.

There is nothing more enjoyable than complete freedom in any form, at any place, for freedom is the instinctive and natural behavior of man. All of life may be construed as a reaching toward greater freedom of expression in each individual and, for this reason, life in its purest form is a complete liberation of spirit and a resultant expression of unadulterated joy. The artist performer contributes to this feeling of joyous release in an audience by creating an illusion of spontaneity in his own performance and he thereby creates an empathic response in his listeners.

The Importance of Empathy

According to Webster, *empathy* is defined as the imaginative projection of one's consciousness into another person so as to be able to participate in that person's feelings or ideas. It is a type of self-identification, the kind of selflessness or self-oblivion we experience when we are completely absorbed by any artistic performance. The purpose of all public entertainment is to achieve this empathic listener response.

The Illusion of the First Time

It is, therefore, the responsibility of the artist singer to convey every aspect of freedom in his own performance. Even if he does not feel it in his heart, he must simulate it with such fidelity that the enactment is totally convincing to his listeners. It must create the impression of being unstudied, unrehearsed, and unprepared. In stage parlance, it is called *the illusion of the first time*.

Individual Deviations Exist

Because the voice is human, it is subject to individual characteristics that distinguish one singer from another. The artist, therefore, never imitates the standard that is set by another performer. Rather, he arrives at his own interpretations by first mastering his own vocal instrument and then expressing himself creatively, not mechanically, thereon.

These individual differences distinguish the human from the mechanical product. However, they are not to be sought. They will occur naturally when interpretations are sincere. Furthermore, they are never obtrusive. Some amateurs have a noisy flair for creating sensational effects, much to their detriment and the dismay of their audiences. One should never countenance a deliberate departure from musical and esthetic standards. One should merely surrender himself to the exigencies of normal human behavior which, if minutely analyzed, will reveal these imperceptible deviations in musical expression. They constitute the characteristics of the individual singing voice and all artistic behavior is tempered thereby.

Creating Atmosphere and Mood

Finally, in every piece of music there is a predominant mood that permeates the composition and produces a harmony of effects in interpretation. The same mood probably engendered its creation by the composer. The singer must recapture this mind set and allow it to pervade the rendition of the song, thus creating its esthetic tone or *atmosphere*.

A performer may acquire this insight from either music or text, or both. Then he proceeds to study the characteristic behavior patterns that accompany such moods or feelings. In doing so, he induces appropriate breathing rhythms and bodily responses that effectively outpicture this state of mind, and thus he creates the desired vocal effects for the expression of that mood. This approach is a study device that can be helpful.

Summary and Conclusions

In conclusion, interpretation is something more than faithful technical rendition. The interpreting artist must penetrate the surface features of the music, since the score can only approximately indicate thought and feeling processes that engendered it. A musical score is symbolic, rather than explicit. Therefore, the singer's responsibility is to bring to life the musical intentions of the composer, including all the elements of expression that lie dormant within the printed manuscript. He must ready himself for this responsibility by acquiring a mastery of all his mental, physical, and vocal resources.

Song texts and musical scores are not merely nursery ballads to be memorized and repeated by rote. They are likely to be the products of fine minds and musical geniuses. The songs and scores that the singer is called upon to interpret, as time goes on, will embody and reflect many imaginative and fanciful situations. These include exalted moods, tragic and soul-searing conflicts, dreams of rapturous and inspired love, the turmoil and triumph over every type of situation or problem that might arise out of intensified and dramatic living.

Expression in song, therefore, demands more than technical competence. It requires growth of character, reinforced by a mature understanding that can interpret and communicate the thrilling dramatic, philosophic, and esthetic content of a musical composition to an audience.

The voice is but the servant of the mind in this respect. A singer's performance, therefore, must not be stereotyped. It must remain individual. It must be kept flexible, fluent, and freely responsive. It may be rich and mellow and capable of superb intonation. But it must also have vitality. It may be the flawless archetype of singing virtuosity in every technical sense. But it must also have imaginative release and vividly express the originality and imagery of the creative artist. The resultant balance between these two aspects of training, the mental and the physical, provides a vocal instrument that is indeed an effective medium for the artistic interpretation of song literature.

Individuality is, therefore, the priceless asset of the artist singer, and his performance will ultimately stand or fall by virtue of the uniqueness of his expression. Considerable discretion and skill are required in this process. To remain completely impersonal is to devitalize the song. On the other hand, to exaggerate one's personality is to contaminate or diffuse its message. A proper balance between these two extremes is called for.

To this end, the singer must have at his command a full range of emotional color so that he can properly control the projection of mood in a vocal medium. That is why he studies declamatory and dramatic techniques and he embellishes every performance with the earnestness, intensity, and creative zeal that inevitably produce an empathic response, or rapport, in the listener.

Finally, it is the nature of man to perceive and *absorb* new experiences; to comprehend, evaluate, and *assimilate* what he perceives; and then to *express* what he understands through his own individual behavior. Adequate self-expression is, therefore, in a sense, the fulfillment of growth, and it is a necessary process if the individual is to develop in artistic stature as a singer. Progress in the study of interpretation will thus endow the singer with self-confidence, poise, and a sense of audience control that he needs in his role as a performing artist.

REFERENCES AND NOTES

[Those interested in pursuing the subject of interpretation beyond basic considerations will find the topic expanded in the references listed below.]

Books

1. Dart, Thurston, *The Interpretation of Music*. London: Hutchinson Press, 1954.

2. Greene, Harry Plunket, *Interpretation in Song*, 2d ed. New York: St. Martin's Press, 1956.

3. Lehman, Lotte. *More than Singing*. London: Boosey and Hawkes, 1946.

4. Moore, Gerald. *Singer and Accompanist*. New York: Macmillan Co., 1954.

5. Rich, Martin. *Art Songs and their Interpretation*. Bryn Mawr, Penna.: Theo. Presser Co., 1960.

6. Schiøtz, Aksel. *The Singer and His Art*. New York: Harper and Row, 1970.

7. Copland, Aaron. *Music and Imagination*. Cambridge, Mass.: Harvard University Press, 1952.

8. Burgin, John Carroll. *Teaching Singing*. Metuchen, N.J.: The Scarecrow Press, Inc., 1973, Chap. 10.

Articles

9. Barrett, Clara. "Putting Over a Song." *Etude* (May 1945): 255.

10. Drew, W. S. "How to Become an Artist in Song." *Musical Times* 91 (April 1950): 156.

11. Holst, Harald B. "Interpretation in Singing." *American Music Teacher* 12 (Sept.–Oct. 1962): 14.

12. Kelsey, Franklyn. "The Singer and the Song." *Musical Times* 92 (August 1951): 348–350.

13. Lewando, Olga Wolf. "Dramatizing Song Lyrics." *Music Journal* 17 (September 1959): 24.

14. Newton, George. "On Imaginative Singing." *NATS Bulletin* 7 (Nov.–Dec. 1950): 5.

15. Sayão, Bidu. "Performer—or Artist?" An Interview. *Etude* (December 1953): 12.

XV

The Role of the Performing Artist

It is now apparent that technique, virtuosity, and understanding provide functional supports for any professional singing career. But artistry in singing is more than a synthesis of interrelated technical and psychological components. It is also a final realization and evaluation of these factors as they relate to public performance. Every aspect of previous preparation contributes to this end result.

In this reappraisal, therefore, it will be necessary to review those elements of execution, style, characterization, song study, rehearsal, and repertoire that favorably influence the singer's audience and enhance his artistic stature in the public eye. Meritorious achievement must become natural to the performing artist and he must have a foreknowledge, a certainty of successful outcomes. Lamperti's maxim is explicit: "To know the result before we act is the golden rule of singing."[1]

The Artist's Attitude

A performing artist does not shout his wares. He is not advertising his techniques. Rather, he stands humbly before his Muse and, in all modesty, offers himself for the real pleasure of his listeners. He does not seek or expect honors for himself. He does not claim credit for the song he is singing.

Rather, he endeavors to bring it forth in humble subservience to its own inherent capacity for creating beauty and enjoyment for others. He maintains this posture of simple modesty and humility throughout his performance and never allows his own private feeling to obtrude itself upon the attention of the listener.

Essentially, then, the expression of the performing artist is impersonal. Although his preparation for performance may involve deeply personal interests, his final presentation must be accomplished on an impersonal plane and in an impersonal way. He must be a giant of stability and strength of character who readily adjusts himself to situations that might try his patience and taunt his will. In other words, he must be resilient and must not allow himself to become temperamental or allow his artistic sensitivity to be contaminated with the worldly indulgences of selfish or small-minded people to whom life is merely a matter of bartering for advantage and personal gain. He is a creator, an instrument through which creation flows. His idealism and lofty vision enable him to rise above worldliness. To be otherwise is to betray the immaturity of a novice.

The artist's attitude, of course, is strengthened by *character*. The growth of character is therefore included in the training program for, without it, the entire product of voice teaching could be stunted. It is not within the scope of this treatise to discuss this subject in depth. But its importance is obvious. Such factors as sincerity of purpose, idealism in living, the weighing of personality traits, good and bad, and the worthy use of leisure time might be profitably considered. Indeed, the entire range of spiritual, moral, ethical, and esthetic values in life might pass in review as the training program progresses.

Naturally, character, like voice, cannot be built in a day. A gradual transformation must take place, almost imperceptible to the casual onlooker but nevertheless appreciable to the teacher who serves as master, counselor, mentor, and guide. The pupil will eventually come to realize that character is essentially composed of those *principles* in which he firmly believes.

Stage presence is a quality of self-confidence that evolves with the growth of character and a firm knowledge that what one is doing is rooted in sound principles and is therefore right. The attitude of the artist performer is not apologetic and diffident. Nor is it overbearing, haughty, or arrogant. It bespeaks, rather, a sense of security that is born of the truth of being. It is this firmness in the right that creates personal magnetism. Naturally, an artist singer seeks the ideal of complete technical virtuosity that is obediently responsive to the dictates of an inspired and lofty character. But this type of performance always expresses itself with great simplicity and economy of means.

There is also a tremendous *endurance* factor in any performance. Flawless perfection is to be sustained from beginning to end without a single lapse of energy, interest, enthusiasm, or skill. Thus, the proficient vocal instrument is always instantly obedient to the will of the singer and the will is sustained at its highest peak of competence. This sustained intensity of purpose and self-assurance gives the poise and distinguished bearing to a performer which commands immediate respect and creates a magical effect called *stage presence*.

Creating Unity of Effect

In its finished presentation the various parts of a song are completely concealed in a concept of *wholeness* that prevails in the artist's mind. Although the singer may have encountered many separate problems in study and rehearsal, there should be no evidence of discontinuity in his thinking. Unskilled amateurs often tend to neglect the continuously sustained effect. They seem to sing the song from problem to problem until, with a sigh of relief, it is completed.

The artist singer attains an overview of the entire composition and maintains its integrity at all costs. There is continuity of action, wholeness of conception, and the listener never perceives the part as distinguished from the whole. It is as though the individual threads of an intricate embroidery were lost sight of as one views the total design in a tapestry. Likewise, the bricks of a building cease to be perceptible, as such, when the completed structure rises before us. Nor does one hear a composition with an awareness of notes, phrases, pauses, cadences, transitions, harmonies, melodic design, or any of the numerous technical vocal elements that make up a piece of music, any more than one reads a good novel with a conscious awareness of its wordiness or its grammatical structure. Indeed, all the musical and technical fragments are forgotten in the framework of the entire performance as performed.

Unity of effect is therefore the ultimate goal in a finished performance.[2] But to accomplish this result the singer must build a margin of competence beyond the minimum requirements of performance. That is to say, he must guage his proficiency *beyond* the demands of the most difficult parts of a song and thereby appear at ease therein. With these preliminary attitudes in mind, we may approach practical problems relating to style and characterization in song and operatic literature.

Style in Singing

In its broadest sense, *style* is our way of doing things. Our way of doing is directly related to our way of thinking, to our understanding, to the idiom of our beliefs and to the accepted usage of our time. *Style in singing* may therefore be defined as that use of musical and vocal language or behavior that serves to exhibit the spirit and intention of the composer.[3] This is especially important in the characterization of a song; that is to say, whether its presentation is to be brusque or tender, deliberate or rhapsodic, elegant or ordinary, methodical or careless, taciturn or effusive, and so on.

A dictatorial style might serve for the commander of a platoon of soldiers. A persuasive style would become a lawyer or politician. A pleading style would suggest helplessness or great need, a matter-of-fact style would derive from an attitude of self-sufficiency, and so on.

Style is therefore an all-pervasive manner that contributes to characterization and atmosphere in singing. The utter helplessness and dramatic pathos of Florestan would certainly differ from the passionate jealousy of Don José, the sauciness of Carmen from the gentle but subtly persuasive lovemaking of Delilah. The imperious manner of the Queen of the Night would not befit the young and tender innocence of Gilda. Characterization in the interpretation of any song or aria is therefore greatly influenced by style.

In a historical sense, our way of doing things is also influenced by the times we live in, by the mode of behavior that prevails, by environmental conditions, and by the situation and scene in which we are expressing.

For example, the early *Renaissance* period (1300–1500) was characterized by refinement and reserve; it produced the chorale, motet, and madrigal. The *Baroque* (1550–1750) was a period of innovation with a more ornate complexity of form and considerable improvisation. The opera, cantata, oratorio, passion, and mass were the principal forms evolved.

The period of *Classicism* (1750–1820) is noted for greater precision and strict formality in which the standardized patterns of opera buffa, chamber music and the sonata form appeared.

Romanticism (nineteenth century) may be said to emphasize melodic content, individualism in thought, and personal warmth in behavior. These are characteristics that appear in the styles of the symphonic poem, instrumental solos, overtures, and art songs of that period.

Post-romanticism features the styles of the so-called *modernists* (1890–   ) which are more impressionistic and are inclined to abandon traditional forms. Nonmelodic and atonal music is often featured. In more recent times, there is an even more pronounced and conscious break with the past and an apparent search for still newer forms of expression. These historical influences are all contributory conditioning elements that affect style in singing.[4]

The mood and temperament of a people or nationality will also affect their style of vocal expression. *Italians* are considered to be warm and passionate, effusive and volatile in expression. The *French* often have an aristocratic poise and restraint in their manner. *German* styles are generally more dramatic, declamatory, personal. And so on.

Style is also embodied in the musical composition itself. For it is the composer's style of expression that created it. That is to say, Mozart's music would not, as a rule, be violently declaimed or shouted. Handel and Scarlatti wrote a pure *bel canto* style that is characterized, mainly, by smooth-flowing melody, simplicity of movement, a sequential recurrence of design and occasional florid passages. Bach and Gluck are exponents of ornamentation. Naturally, the composer's intentions and peculiarities should be reflected in the singer's performance if the music is to be artistically recreated.

In his role as performing artist, a singer therefore relates his thinking to the stylistic trends of a given period, as represented by the music. A folksong will differ from an art song. A florid or frivolous expression would not be used in ecclesiastical plainsong. Some pieces of music call for declamatory rendition, others for simple, almost naive expression, still others for straightforward recitative effects, and so on.[5]

A singer's interpretation and style must therefore embody the following three factors: 1) a correct musical understanding and analysis of the composition and the character portrayed therein; 2) an evaluation of the work to be performed in the light of the historical period to which it belongs; and 3) an awareness of the composer's characteristic manner of expression and his aims and purposes or intentions in writing a particular piece of music.

The Development of Song Styles

How modern song styles evolved is a subject for extensive musicological study beyond the scope of this treatise. However, a brief synopsis will provide the artist-to-be with a quick glimpse of this historical development. It will also serve as a useful background to aid him in his study of prevalent styles of singing and the interpretation of vocal repertoire. The contributions of *folksong, fioratura, recitative, art song,* and *ecclesiastic singing* are especially worth noting, since they pervade our present singing literature and strongly influence much of a singer's repertoire.

Folksong. Written folksongs did not appear until the thirteenth or fourteenth centuries, and it is therefore likely that they were at first improvised by the singer and only occasionally accompanied by an instrument. Most folk music probably developed in this way. Even after printed music appeared, individual variations by performers continued inasmuch as the crude notation of that period suggested only an outline of what was to be performed. A singer was therefore permitted, and even expected, to add embellishments and vocal flourishes as often as he wished. Thus, as time passed, a style of ornamented singing known as *fioratura* was born and it was featured in all public performances.[6]

Fioratura and Bel canto. The art of *fioratura* reached its zenith in the *bel canto* style of the seventeenth and eighteenth centuries. It was the secular equivalent of *melismatics* in church music. It was distinguished by beautiful tone, fine legato phrasing, and an expressive cantilena with a flawless vocal technique. It also featured long-flowing phrases and highly elaborated passages which gave the singer ample opportunity to demonstrate sheer brilliance in performance and superlative vocal virtuosity.

Bel canto was a style that flourished in the opera, cantata, and oratorio singing of that period, and, since it required much improvization, the bel canto singer eventually became as much a creative artist as the composer. A mere sketch of the vocal music was written down. Accompaniment was also left to improvizational skill, and the instrumentalist was often guided only by the indications of a figured bass part.[7]

Many exceptional singers were produced in this era. In due time, however, as the art of notation grew, the composer's authority superseded the creative inclinations of the soloist and, by the time of Mozart (1756–1791) nearly all embellishments in vocal scores were authorized and provided by the composer himself.

Recitative. The sixteenth-century recitative style (e.g., Peri, Caccini, Monteverdi, and others) was a concurrent development. Composers of this period evidently held the belief that the singing voice should, when possible, imitate the inflections of speech. In their music they featured *recitativo secco,* a type of *parlante* intonation pattern in which the notes and rhythm followed the verbal accentuation. Scanty accompaniment was used. In due time, however, parlante intonations became more elastic, varied, and rhythmical, and eventually developed into *recitativo accompagnato* or *stromentato* with a full musical background to support the quasi-spoken phrase.

The Art Song. Eventually, melodic outlines developed that were no longer adaptable to parlando style. The increasing use of strophic and stanzaic texts led to the use of rhythmic and musical phrasing and, by the middle of the seventeenth century, melodic phrasing, rather than recitative, began to dominate the song structure. Thus, in a historical sense, the recitative was a transitional link between early plain style and the later art-song and dramatic styles of singing.[8] Early folksong gradually evolved into modern art song as the former became more sophisticated and more complicated; and this eventually developed into the elaborate, ornamented, more personalized, dramatic, and declamatory styles of singing that are now in use.

Ecclesiastical Influences. Unlike secular music, liturgical scores were governed by restrictions laid down by the church fathers as early as the fourth century, and a more formalized style of singing was thus perpetuated in the church. The term *plainsong* was used for the unaccompanied solo chant of the Roman Catholic liturgy. These traditional chants or melodies were later codified by Pope Gregory I (590–604) and became known as *Gregorian Chant*.[9]

Vocal embellishments of church tunes were called *melismas,* and it is therefore probable that melismatic singing in the early church influenced the embellished and ornate style of secular singing from the ninth century onward. The Middle Ages also saw the growth and development of *descant,* polyphonic, and choral singing, and a widespread use of many-voiced part songs in both sacred and secular settings.[10]

Prevalent Styles of Singing

Out of these historical origins we observe the evolution of the principal styles of singing now prevalent in vocal literature. They are called: *plain, ornamented or florid,* and *declamatory.* Early Italians classified them as: *canto spianato, canto fiorito,* and *canto declamato.* A transitional or *recitativo* style also persists to this day, and it is therefore included in this summary.

There are, of course, modern variations and combinations of these four basic styles. Nevertheless, the performing artist must remember that each song has its own distinctive interpretation and that its rendition is strictly influenced by the period in which it was composed.

1. The elements of plain-style singing. Plain style (not to be confused with *plainsong)* is devoid of distracting embellishments. It lacks complexity of design and uses a rather moderate tempo, simplicity of form, a gently flowing melody, a conservative pattern of musical light and shade, and steadiness of voice with distinct and expressive diction. There is also a directness of expression without emotional or dramatic involvement.

The plain style uses dynamic shadings from piano to

forte, and vice versa, messa di voce effects, portamento, rubato, and, now and then, an appogiatura, turn, or trill. It is essentially the *legato* or salon type of singing, a lyrical style in which tonal beauty and evenness of voice are featured. *Cantilena* is the term used to descibe a melodious, smooth-flowing lyric passage that is to be performed in a graceful legato style.

Most folksongs, whether solemn or joyful, are written in plain or legato style, as are liturgical hymns, madrigals, lyric art songs, and some of the German lieder. The plain style is also featured in modern song literature whenever simplicity of mood and lyric tonal beauty are desired. The composer's indications on the notated score and the type of text used will provide the singer with cues for rendition or interpretation.

2. The ornamented style. Ornamentation (fioritura) is the embellishment of a melody by adding extraneous notes to it that do not necessarily belong to the essential harmonies of the piece. Ornaments are used to enhance, emphasize, prolong, and dramatize the melodic effect. They are also used for display purposes, to vary recurring musical thoughts and to sustain an emotional climax or special effect. However, the vocalist must be careful to avoid the cheapening effect of over-elaboration. Embellishments are intended to beautify the melodic line. Therefore, any ornament, if it is not skillfully and gracefully handled, should be omitted.

3. Recitative styles. The art of recitative flourished in early opera and oratorio. It is a style used to facilitate the presentation of a passing incident. When singing *recitativo secco,* the first thought must be given to text, rather than music, since phrasing, accent, and emphasis are those of the spoken words. No attempt is made to render the piece solely for vocal effect. In other words, eloquence, rather than singing, predominates and the interpretation is essentially that of a dramatic dialogue. It is musical speech at its best. *Recitativo accompagnato,* on the other hand, demands the dramatic and declamatory style of modern opera. Accompaniment is fuller and more organized in musical content, and melodic continuity is therefore more evident in its vocal presentation.

The oratorio (and opera) singer must have a command of recitative styles, since this method of speech-in-song is freely utilized by oratorio composers like Bach (1685–1750), Handel (1685–1759), Haydn (1732–1809), Mendelssohn (1809–1847), etc. Recitative reached its zenith in Wagnerian opera and, of course, there is free intermingling of *secco* and *accompagnato* styles in modern score writing, since modern composers have taken liberties with all forms of musical expression.

In whatever form it is used, however, recitative must be thought of as a type of song. It is to be sung and not shouted or barked, and it should always be rendered with artistic finesse, a pure and mellow vocal tone, poetic feeling, and esthetic taste.

4. Singing in declamatory style. In declamatory style, the soloist becomes the actor, although he does not necessarily move about the stage or use gestures, except in opera. In concert, oratorio, and recital performances, his acting is therefore more or less self-contained and purely imaginative.

Declamatory singing may be robust, passionate, and colorful. It is often monosyllabic with little or no vocalization. It may be serious or comic. There are vivid contrasts and striking vocal climaxes. Sighs, strascino, portamento, laughter, and other effects are employed which serve to highlight the vocal expression. Nevertheless, although declamatory singing is dramatic, intense, and vocally demanding, it is strictly rhythmical, an integral part of the musical score, and it is always maintained at the highest level of musicianship and vocal virtuosity. Incisive diction is demanded and there is no letting down of either mood or meaning, even during the brief musical interludes of the accompaniment.

Declamatory styles are now employed in a wide variety of dramatic songs and especially in oratorio and opera. The music and text supply cues to interpretation for song and oratorio. But for operatic singing a definite characterization is called for which demands a special type of training. Every vocal student should, in time, master several typical operatic roles which will help free him from some of the restraints and formalities imposed by an overdose of salon, concert, and recital singing. For this reason, the basic principles of *characterization* or character portrayal should be carefully studied. A gradual preparation for more advanced repertoire is thus achieved.

In summation, *style* may be considered in four general aspects: 1) it is our way of doing things; 2) it is influenced by the times we live in; 3) it is affected by the mood and temperament of a people or nationality; and 4) it is embodied in the musical composition itself. The four styles most prevalent in the singer's art are: a) plain; b) ornamented; c) recitative; and d) declamatory. Each has distinctive characteristics that should be noted and rehearsed by the artist-to-be.

Principles of Characterization

This topic introduces the student to those aspects of training which prepare the performing artist for operatic repertoire. *Characterization* is a way of delineating the attributes of thought, mood, and behavior that are peculiar to a given personality and that distinguish one individual from another. These qualities are depicted by facial expression, body movement, and gesture as well.[11]

Character nuances are both audible and visible and the performer actually impersonates the character he assumes. That is why this form of vocal portraiture is considered the most advanced and most difficult form of singing. It deserves special attention and may be practiced in the vocal studio in dramatic episodes and dialogues and in whole scenes from opera.

The musical idiom of a composer will often suggest the type of person portrayed, whether he be drawling or insistent, emotional, nervous and agitated, or hesitant and apologetic. However, the quality of a singer's voice must also take on appropriate personality changes. The voice may sound amused or bored, proud or timid, cruel or kind, bitter or sweet-mannered, arrogant or humble, care-worn and tired or vivacious and carefree, implacable or conciliatory, silly or subtly shrewd, juvenile, immature and naive, or supercilious and pedantic.

For practice purposes, the student should be able to read or sing any appropriate text in each of these moods, with accompanying voice, facial expression, and gesture. Such moods as surly, doubtful, whining, sunny, insinuating, rasping, fearful, proud, vain, juvenile, simpering, haughty, etc., may also be tried. In short, every dimension of human behavior must be represented by a distinguishable quality of voice and manner as the singer projects himself imaginatively into the character being portrayed. The most common vocal variables in the interpretation of character are pitch, color, intensity, tempo, pause, rhythm, phrasing, nuance, diction, accent, stress, and climax.

Although characterization is called for in varying degrees in many types of song interpretation, it is especially important in operatic repertoire where it appears in its most sustained and intensified forms. It may be profitable to use an experimental operatic role as a practice device, from time to time, since it is a good training ground for characterizations that are applicable in other areas of song study.

Preparing an Operatic Role

Three preliminaries are to be considered in preparing an operatic role. They are *analysis, improvization,* and *pantomime.* This type of preparation should precede the actual memorization of the part so as to eliminate excessive action and assure economy of means. Every character trait must be justified in the interpreter's mind if it is to seem convincing to his audience. Ask yourself such questions as: *who? what? when? where? why? how?*

1. Analyzing the role. The mastery of characterization begins in the armchair. First, read and reread the text or libretto. Conjure up in the mind all the scenes that are depicted as though they were actually being experienced. The dramatic situation is thus carefully studied and visualized until it is thoroughly understood. What is the national and domestic background? Is a dialect called for? What type of education or self-discipline has the character achieved? Are his actions and expressions overt or subtle and implied?

Analysis of a role also raises countless questions regarding locale, occupation, situation, manner, idiosyncracies, physique and posture, type of behavior, action patterns, facial expression, and manner of voice and speech. It is helpful to observe the behavior of other persons in real life who may resemble, in whole or in part, the personality depicted in the role that is being studied. How do they react in similar situations?

Bear in mind, also, that nothing in life "just happens." Everything has its cause and effect. There is a motive underlying every behavior pattern, and the character always *reacts* to an underlying cause. Therefore, the art of acting is really the art of *reacting.* There is nothing mysterious about characterization. The performer's *reactive sense* is brought to bear on each situation and the portrayal that he finally outpictures will inevitably affect his voice, body, facial expression, and gesture.

2. Improvising the role. The student next learns to *improvise* the part he is about to enact. Let him *assume* such a character and invent lines that suit his impersonation. In other words, speak out the improvised part fearlessly and with sincerity as though you were really the individual you are impersonating. Let your imagination take over and create a situation that resembles the one depicted in the text of the score. Act it out with impromptu speech or recitative and movement until you can give a convincing performance. Then return to the original script and apply yourself to details of background and nuances of expression that you may have overlooked.

What about the charcter's background, education, philosophy? Are there any peculiarities of thought? Are there external mannerisms? How about living conditions? Who are his friends? Are there any enemies? Considerations like these provide motivating material for voice, diction, and behavior mannerisms. They also give the performer confidence that his characterization has been soundly prepared, and this engenders validity in rehearsal and performance.

3. The use of pantomime. Finally, an impersonation in *silent* pantomime should be tried. Actions often speak louder than words. Therefore, make your silent behavior in the role confirm what would otherwise be evident from your verbal interpretations, and vice versa. Practice this type of silent pantomime in fragments, or episodes, and then in whole sections of the musical drama, as scored.

In summing up the foregoing discussion of *characterization,* the following twelve rehearsal steps are recommended:

First: read the script or libretto and analyze the composer's intentions.

Second: identify yourself with the character. Try to determine his (or her) age, fundamental nature, position in life, function in the drama, the situation in which he appears, and his relation to other characters.

Third: consider the causes of dramatic conflict. How are the conflicts resolved in the text?

Fourth: predetermine appropriate breathing rhythms, posture, and action patterns that would relate to these factors of emotional conflict and their resolution.

Fifth: try to determine the type of voice in song that can be used to convey the indicated thoughts and feelings. Read through the text, *mentally,* with this analysis in mind.

Sixth: next, paraphrase the spoken text, so that all interpretative effects may be ironed out experimentally by using your own words. It must sound unstudied.

Seventh: develop the use and control of your vocal resources against the musical background of the score. Absorb the tempi and the rhythmic and dynamic effects. Consider vocal range and other technical vocal problems and their mastery. Are you proficient enough vocally and flexible enough musically to meet all the requirements of the score?

Eighth: memorize the text and practice reciting it in spoken form. Eliminate every uncertainty as to sequence of ideas and diction.

Ninth: intone the exact text in recitative style, both with and without musical accompaniment, so as to capture rhythmic timing and other musical elements contained therein.

Tenth: plan the behavior pattern or action response to other characters. Consider the use and value of gestures, facial expression, and other body movements as depicted in the actual score. Also consider the overall visual aspects of behavior such as posture, costume, handling props, and cued-in movements that will correlate with scenic details, entrances and exits, and the location of other characters on the stage.

Eleventh: Consider the four principal kinds of audience interest: *passive, recurring, sustained,* and *climactic.* How are these distributed throughout the score? Determine the value of silence and the method of sustaining the interest even during the pauses and rests. Plan the location of climaxes and places of heightened interest so that these may be related to the intention of the text. Work on the firmness of vocal attack in introducing each new entrance and each new phrase.

Twelfth: final stages of rehearsal call for the projection of the desired character as a synthesis of all the foregoing elements of mental, vocal, and physical behavior. Consider such factors as spontaneity of thought and action (illusion of the first time), intensity of expression, overstatement vs. understatement, literal and implied meanings, variety of effect, and achieving vividness of portraiture by using contrast and climax. Eliminate any monotonous areas of interest by reinforcing your interpretation at these points.

Working for Creative Results

During final phases of rehearsal, the teacher stands by for coaching purposes only and allows the student as much leeway as possible. Thus an experimental version of the desired effect evolves from a creative expression of the performer, rather than from an imitative version arbitrarily imposed by the teacher. This process is slower but more dependable than a hurried and misshapen characterization that is borrowed from some source alien to the performer's own way of thinking. In matters of operatic coaching the teacher becomes a collaborator, not the author of the finished performance. There is nothing more wooden and lifeless than an imitated or stereotyped characterization.

Finally, it may be said that characterization is three-dimensional. It embodies: a) the singer's voice and diction (i.e., the verbal text as sung); b) the physical action; and c) the action of the mind. The last of these is often neglected and deserves special attention.

An artist performer, therefore, relates every action to its underlying thought. Furthermore, he tries to *visualize* every detail of the finished performance, for visualization is the mental act that crystallizes the possibility of bringing an imagined idea into active expression. Mental supports can determine the success or failure of the finished performance. These supports include such factors as concentration, keenness of observation, imaginative power, inspirational thinking, intelligence and selectivity or judgment, insight, and, most of all, *understanding*. All the foregoing aspects of execution, style, and characterization provide a firm foundation for repertoire, recital, and operatic training in the preparation of the performing artist.

REFERENCES AND NOTES

1. William Earl Brown, *Vocal Wisdom;* Maxims of Giovanni Battista Lamperti (New York: Arno Press, 1957), p. 28.

2. Harry Plunket Greene, *Interpretation in Song* (London: Macmillan and Co., Ltd, 1956), pp. 37–103.

3. Weldon Whitlock, *Facets of the Singer's Art* (Champaign, Illinois: Pro Musica Press, 1967) Chap. XX.

4. Paul Henry Lang, *Music in Western Civilization* (New York, N.Y.: W. W. Norton & Co., Inc., 1941) Chap. 20.

5. Greene, *Interpretation in Song,* Part IV.

6. Denis Steven, editor, *A History of Song* (New York: W. W. Norton & Company, Inc., 1960), pp. 15–64.

7. Alec Harman and Wilfred Mellers, *Man and His Music* (New York: Oxford University Press, 1962), Parts I and II.

8. Jack Sacher, editor, *Music A to Z* (New York: Grosset & Dunlap, Inc., 1963), pp. 164–266.

9. Ibid., pp. 248, 258.

10. Sir Malcolm Sargent, editor, *The Outline of Music* (New York: Arco Publishing Co., Inc., 1962), Chap. 3.

11. Richard De Young, *The Singer's Art* (Chicago: De Paul University Press, 1958), pp. 142–152.

12. Quaintance Eaton, *Opera Production* (Minneapolis: University of Minnesota Press, 1961).

XVI

Song Study, Repertoire, and Recital

A performer's approach to song analysis is somewhat different from that of an audience. The listener may react esthetically to all the details of performance but is not necessarily made conscious of these details. His listening enjoyment is a *whole* response, not a part-by-part synthesis of separated musical experiences. On the other hand, the completed structure of a song must be analyzed in detail to be thoroughly understood and adequately expressed by the performer. In this preparatory procedure, no element of analysis is slighted. The untrained ear perceives only basic rhythms and surface manifestations of pitch and melodic movement. But to the trained ear of the artist singer, listening comprehension is a product of multidimensional musical perception.

A singer therefore examines all the melodic and musical elements in each composition that he studies, and he prepares and practices an extensive and varied repertoire so that he is able to gain a wide experience in all the significant aspects of interpretation previously described. The following survey provides direction finders in this process of analytical inquiry.[1]

The Language of Music

Music is not static. It is a transitory phenomenon, a tonal language based primarily on the movement and interplay of four acoustical variables: *pitch, dynamics, quality,* and *duration. Pitch* contributes such factors as tonal relations, intervals, melody, and harmony. *Dynamics* creates audibility, intensity, volume, projection, and nuance. *Quality* or *timbre* is basically an esthetic interblending of pitch and intensity components in the production and projection of musical sound. *Duration* produces timing and note values, variations in tempo, pause, and rhythmic factors. All these combine in varying proportions and degrees to build up the internal and external *melodic, harmonic,* and *rhythmic* structure of a piece of music. Its final form is determined by the concept of wholeness that unifies its interrelated parts.[2] The singer's approach to song analysis is based on a clear perception of all these fundamentals.

Melodic Factors

Melody is defined as a symmetrically outlined succession of notes or tones in a given key relationship and built on a rhythmic structure. In melody, as in harmony, the ear deals in consonances and dissonances, in reposeful, regular, and syncopated rhythms, in placid moods and dramatic climaxes. The closer the tones in a melody are, the more dissonant its listening effect is likely to be. Wider intervals allow room for the imaginative recognition of underlying harmonic values. We also find it natural that a note should be longer on the strong beat than on the weak beat and that consonant intervals should occur on strong beats.

A crescendo is usually associated with an ascending melodic phrase. Similarly, the chord tone usually suggests rest and balance; the passing tone suggests activity, movement, and unrest. Hence, there is a subtle, almost imperceptible seeking of the ear (and mind) to reach points of balance or repose in the motion of a melody. The singer's expression must hinge upon this sense of balance in the interplay and movement of melodic and rhythmic forces in the song he is singing.[3] The following analytical procedures are therefore recommended:

First: find out which melodic notes are chord tones and

sing them separately in a rhythmic sequence as whole notes, mentally associating them with their appropriate chordal or harmonic accompaniments.

Second: repeat the first step while *mentally* adding the intervening notes that lie between the melodic chord tones. Think of these intervening notes as though they were clustered appogiatura, with each cluster belonging to the next chord tone. Thus, the ear will learn to recognize chord tones as pivotal points in a melody.

Third: determine the location of strong rhythmic beats in the structure of the song, then ascertain the relation of each chord tone to one of these strong beats. This awakens an awareness of *tonal repose* as opposed to *tonal movement*.

Thus we acquire a basic melodic syntax upon which to build a musical interpretation. The ear seeks out important points in each melody and matches them with relevant harmonic or rhythmic details. Where there is exact correspondence between the melodic note and its harmonic base, we have a sense of relative contentment or repose. A cadence, semicadence, or phrase length results. Breath renewal may be expedient at such points. Where they do not correspond, that is, when a melodic note is figuratively off-base, a feeling of unrest prevails, and uninterrupted continuity of expression is mandatory. This alternating upsurge and recession of strong and weak tonalities contributes to our feeling of melodic movement and our grasp of rhythmic values in singing. The postponed or delayed resolution of chords also adds to the feeling of restlessness in melodic music.

Harmonic Factors

Harmonically regarded, a song is a progression of musical consonances and dissonances, a moving series of related and concordant tonalities that are bound together in formal rhythmic design. The singer's well-developed ear perceives melody as a surface contact with these underlying harmonic structures.[4]

By way of analogy, it may be said that any tone in a melody represents a moving point that generates a one-dimensional line. A chord or transient harmony suggests a two-dimensional plane in musical thinking. Then, as harmonies move rhythmically they generate a three-dimensional tonal magnitude that takes on "solid" form in the ultimate expression of the entire composition.

Thus, the progression of harmonic tonalities builds the solid structure of music that underlies and embodies all the individual tones of a melody. In other words, tones and melodies are to be thought of as punctate and linear or surface manifestations of an underlying organic structure.

Rhythmic Factors

All the foregoing elements of intonation, melodic movement, harmonic structure, and organic form are bound together by a rhythmic pattern that governs the movement of music through intervals of time. It is this movement that creates factors of duration, pause, timing, and rhythm in a composition. Rhythmic thinking, therefore, concerns itself with such elements as the ebb and flow of mood and dynamics, passivity and rest as opposed to accentuation and climax, turbulence followed by repose, and so on. More of this later.

The art of interpretation obviously requires a thoroughgoing analysis of vocal literature that comprises every aspect of preparation described in the preceding chapters and culminates in the actual performance of the public recital program. To this end, a review of the different song forms now in use is mandatory. The artist thus develops a versatility and breadth of understanding that is commensurate with the varied demands of concert and operatic performance.

Variety and Scope of Repertoire

The singer's art employs a medium of vocal expression that is essentially built on the musical setting for a poetic or dramatic text. This includes such types as *folksong, ballad, art song, lied* (chanson), *recitative, aria, arioso, scena, song cycle,* and at least four forms of *opera.* All are lyric or dramatic types of the secular song material now in use.

In addition to these, a singer must familiarize himself with the more prevalent forms of religious vocal music that are heard in church, choir, or concert performance. These include the *hymn, sacred solo, anthem, cantata, oratorio, mass,* and *passion.*

There are, of course, many variations of these standard patterns but each has a distinctive and basic musical and textual design which should be familiar to the student. A brief description of each type is therefore given.

1. *Folksong* is so called because it represents the characteristic expressions and popular feelings of a people. Therefore, folk music is distinctly moody and typical of the idiomatic expression that prevails in a given ethnic communicty. Geographic, climatic, political, and linguistic factors are to be considered in the interpretation of the folksong. The strophic form is typical, in which the same music is repeated for each succeeding stanza or verse.

2. *Ballad* is a simple, popular, romantic song set in narrative verse and having the same melody for each stanza. Its strophic or stanzaic style is an elaboration of the folksong.

3. *Art song* is a skillfully contrived and more pictorial song in which text, melody, and music are suitably blended to create a unified effect and each factor contributes equally to the overall musical impact and mood. It may be narrative, dramatic, lyrical, tragic, florid, atmospheric, or humorous. But in any form the art song is *through-composed,* that is, the text as a whole is set to music in a continuously flowing rather than stanzaic or repeated pattern.

4. *Lied* is an elaborate romantic German art song. The *chanson* is the French equivalent.

5. *Recitative* is a type of vocal solo in which the words are delivered in more or less declamatory or quasi-spoken

style, with or without a full accompaniment.

6. *Aria* is an artistically constructed and usually dramatic song vehicle consisting of several parts, with instrumental accompaniment. It is somewhat extended or amplified in thematic and dramatic content and usually exploits the virtuosity of the soloist. It may be part of a larger work, such as an opera, oratorio, mass, or cantata, and then it is often preceded by recitative.

7. *Arioso* is a rather melodious vocal solo or aria that is delivered in the style of a narrative or recitation.

8. *Scena* is an elaborated aria or operatic fragment embodying several sequential episodes such as an accompanied recitative, various contrasting melodic passages, and a dramatic aria.

9. *Song cycle* is a grouping of several songs under one distinctive title, often with a continuity of theme or mood. Sometimes the cycle of songs is based on the poems of a single author; sometimes a number of poets are represented. They are, for the most part, intimate mood pictures or dramatic scenes, but they may have a larger scope. The composer no doubt grouped his songs because he preferred their being sung in a unified sequence.

10. *Opera,* in a broad sense, is a picturesque theatrical or stage representation of a drama that is sung with elaborate costumes, scenery, and action. Recitative or spoken dialogue may be used to separate the related dramatic and musical episodes. These consist of arias, recitatives, dialogues, choruses, duets, dances, overtures, and other musical interludes. The four most common forms of operatic presentation are *comic opera, grand opera, music drama,* and *operetta.*

11. *Comic opera* (opera buffa), as distinguished from *grand opera,* has a simple plot with spoken and more-or-less-whimsical or humerous dialogues between the musical numbers.

12. *Grand opera* has a more elaborate dramatic plot whose entire text is set to music. Its story and action are more or less episodic, and the story develops slowly, as a rule, since

the major interest is centered on the musical rendition of its component parts.

13. *Music drama* is an opera in which the music throughout is determined by its dramatic appropriateness. It is continuous music and not episodic in treatment; nor is it interrupted by arias, duets, and other opportunities for vocal display by the singers, as in grand opera.

14. *Operetta* is a light opera or musical play with a rather slight and cheerful plot. It may include an overture, songs, interludes, spoken dialogues, and dances.

15. *Hymn* is a simple song of praise and glorification for solo and chorus, usually with a biblical text.

16. *Sacred solo* is an art song, aria, or scena based on a religious text.

17. *Anthem* is a song of praise and glorification for solo and chorus, usually with a biblical text.

18. *Cantata* is an extended dramatic story, either sacred or secular, that is set to music for orchestra. It consists of vocal solos, recitatives, choruses, and musical interludes.

19. *Oratorio* is a more extensive work for chorus and solo voices with orchestra. It is constructed like an opera but performed without action, costumes, or scenery. It has a religious and devotional text, and it is generally in narrative form.

20. *Mass* is a musical religious service for soloists and chorus, with orchestra, organ, or other instrumental accompaniment, consisting of several distinctive episodes or parts. These are usually the *Kyrie, Gloria, Credo, Sanctus,* and *Agnus Dei;* but the musical mass may include subdivisions, extensions, or variations of these five principal parts.

21. *Passion* is an oratorio-like dramatic and musical setting to the biblical narration of events that directly pertain to the martyrdom and suffering of Christ, with spiritual commentaries.

The student is again reminded that analytical song study involves a consideration of many musical elements, the knowledge of which is the basis of good musicianship. A potential artist examines all of them carefully and, to this end, a varied repertoire should be studied, including folk music, art song, religious, dramatic, and operatic styles.

Representative titles are suggested in the pages that follow, to guide the singer in the selection of a suitable and progressive study program. Printed editions of this literature can be found listed in published bibliographical texts which also list the names of publishers, grade of difficulty, voice classification, and range available for each selection.[5] Both teacher and pupil should become familiar with the composers whose works are listed therein and their many different song styles. Excellent translations of favorite classics are also available.[6]

Of course, there are many excellent art songs of American, British, French, German, Scandinavian, Russian, and other nationalities that have not been listed here. Not included, also, are the numerous contemporary styles that now appear in twentieth-century song idiom. Some of the newer forms derive from so-called *atonal, expressionistic, polytonal, polymetric, twelve-tone,* and *whole-tone* music, and comprise such modern media as *neo-Baroque, neo-classic, neo-mystic, neo-primitive, neo-romantic,* and others. The more advanced vocal artist may wish to investigate modern song forms for their possibilities in repertoire building.[7]

Song Materials for Practice and Study

The following lists, totalling more than 500 titles, cover a wide variety of song forms. They are intended to provide a sampling of the types of practice material needed in building a varied vocal repertoire. The selections here listed include many favorites of the recital and concert stage which contain voice-building materials for the student singer. Art songs embodying certain special technical problems have also been classified.

The materials are grouped for beginners, intermediate, and more advanced students, and include typical lieder of Beethoven, Schubert, Schumann, Brahms, Wolf, Strauss, and others, as well as popular sacred solos, operatic arias, and other vocal gems that will challenge the artistic and interpretative abilities of the potential recitalist and concert performer.

It is not intended that this vocal music will meet all instructional needs but, rather, that it will point the way to the type of material that may be used to meet these problems.

The titles hereafter suggested are obtainable, for the most part, in either high, medium, or low voice, although some are sacred solos, arias, and specialty numbers that are best assigned to the voice classification for which they were originally intended. Musical, technical, and esthetic considerations demand that compositions for male and female voices should not, as a rule, be interchanged, except when they are used for problem analysis and studio practice. A teacher will, of course, have to use his own discretion in adapting the list to individual needs. Nevertheless, a variety of song materials should be used for practice and study, since a mixed repertoire will promote well-balanced and wholesome growth, as well as interpretative skill, personality development, versatility, and musicianship.

I. Typical Songs for Beginners

These selections may be used during the first year of study. They avoid extremes and for the most part are adaptable to the range and tessitura of the average pupil's voice, i.e., high, medium, and low, male or female. Most of these songs are in English.

Alberti	God's Plan
Arne	Where the Bee Sucks
Barber	Daisies
Barnett	The Dreams of the Sea
Bassett	The Icicle
Bishop	Love Has Eyes
Brahms	The Little Sandman
Britten	The Ash Grove

Buzzi-Peccia	Under the Greenwood Tree
Carew	Spring Comes Laughing
Chadwick	He Loves Me
Charles	Clouds
Charles	When I Have Sung My Songs
Clokey	The Rose
Coates	Bird Songs at Eventide
Cox	To a Hilltop
Curran	Rain
Deis	Come Down to Kew
Dobson	Cargoes
Edwards	By the Bend of the River
Edwards	Into the Night
Edmunds	Jesus, Jesus, Rest Your Head
Farley	I Am the Still Rain
Foote	I'm Wearin' Awa'
Franck	Panis Angelicus *(Messe Solonelle)*
Franz	Widmung (Dedication)
Ganz	A Memory
Gatty	Bendemeer's Stream
Giordani	Caro Mio Ben
Guion	Prayer
Hadley	Evening Song
Hadley	My True Love
Handel	Where E'er You Walk
Homer	Sheep and Lambs
Ireland	Down by the Sally Gardens
Ireland	Sea Fever
Jacobs-Bond	In a Meadow
La Forge	Supplication
MacDowell	Long Ago
MacDowell	Thy Beaming Eyes
MacFayden	Home
Mana-Zucca	Michava
Manning	In the Luxembourg Gardens
Massenet	Ouvre Tes Yeux Bleu (Open Thy Blue Eyes)
Mendelssohn	On Wings of Song
Moore	Children's Song
Moss	The Floral Dance
Mozart	Cradle Song
Mozart	Voi Che Sapete *(Le Nozze di Figaro)*

Needham	Four Ducks on a Pond
Nevin	O That We Two Were Maying
Niles	I Wonder As I Wander
O'Hara	Two Little Stars
Old English	When Love Is Kind
Pergolesi	If Thou Lov'st Me
Quilter	O Mistress Mine
Cadman	O Mistress Mine
Sanderson	Green Pastures
Schubert	Cradle Song
Schubert	Hedge Roses
Schumann	The Lotus Flower
Schumann	Thou Art Like a Flower
Speaks	The Night Has a Thousand Eyes
Spross	Sunrise and Sunset
Stanford	My Love's an Arbutus
Veracini	Yarmouth Fair
Watts	Blue Are Her Eyes
Williams	Linda Lea
Wilson	Mary of Allendale
Young	The Sleepy House

II. Problem Songs for Intermediate and Second Year Study

1. Breath Control and Sostenuto

Brahms	Wiegenlied
Cimara	Fiocca la Neve
Fauré	Après un Rêve
Godard	Berceuse *(Jocelyn)*
Grieg	A Swan
Griffes	In a Myrtle Shade
Handel	Ah, Mio Cor
Hahn	L'Heure Exquise
Kramer	Swans
Liszt	Die Lorelei
Martini	Plaisir d'Amour
Massenet	Elégie

Schubert	Hark, Hark, the Lark
Schubert	Ave Maria
Schumann	Dein Angesicht
Schumann	Die Lotosblume
Schumann	Im Wunderschönen Monat Mai
Stradella	Pietà, Signore
Tosti	La Serenata
Wolf	In Einem Garten
Wolf	Verborgenheit

2. *Intonation Problems*

Beethoven	In questa tomba
Charles	Clouds
Dvorák	Songs My Mother Taught Me
Fauré	Clair de Lune
Franz	Widmung
Grieg	Autumn Storm
Griffes	By a Lonely Forest Pathway
Handel	He Shall Feed His Flock *(Messiah)*
Handel	Ombra mai fu *(Xerxes)*
Quilter	Go Lovely Rose
Rimsky-Korsakoff	In the Silent Woods
Rimsky-Korsakoff	Hymn to the Sun
Sadero	In mezzo al mar
Schubert	Der Lindenbaum
Strauss, R.	Nachtgang

3. *Cantabile and Legato*

Beethoven	Adelaide
Brahms	Die Mainacht
Brahms	Sapphische Ode
Debussy	Romance
Gluck	Che faro senza Euridice *(Orfeo)*
Mozart	O Isis und Isiris *(Magic Flute)*
Rachmaninoff	In the Silence of the Night
Rubenstein	Es blinkt der Thau
Schubert	An die Musik
Schubert	An Sylvia

Schubert	Der Neugierige
Schubert	Frühlingsglaube
Schubert	Geheimes
Schumann	Der Nüssbaum
Schumann	Die Lotosblume
Tchaikowsky	Nur wer die Sehnsucht Kennt
Thomas	Connais-tu le pays? *(Mignon)*

4. Staccato Problems

Arne	Polly Willis
Cadman	Welcome, Sweet Wind
Delibes	Bonjour, Suzon
Grieg	Solvejg's Lied
Haydn	My Mother Bids Me Bind My Hair
Mozart	Das Veilchen
Massenet	Première danse
Puccini	Si mi chiamano Mimi (*La Bohème*)
Schumann	Volkslied
Schubert	Der Jüngling an der Quelle
Thomas	Je suis Titania *(Mignon)*
Watts	The Little Shepherd's Song

5. Diction Problems (*vowels and consonants*)

Brahms	Meine Liebe ist Grün
Beethoven	In questa tomba
Caldara	Come raggio di sol
Carissimi	A morire
Debussy	Mandoline
Durante	Vergin, tutta amor
Durante	Danza, danza, fanciulla gentile
Foster	Jeannie with the Light Brown Hair
Ireland	Sea Fever
Jensen	Frühlingsnacht
La Forge	Sleep Song
Mozart	Il mio tesoro (*Don Giovanni*)
Purcell	Passing By
Old English	Drink to Me Only with Thine Eyes
Quilter	Love's Philosophy

Rachmaninoff	Floods of Spring
Schubert	Ungeduld
Scarlatti	Se Florindo è fedele
Scott, Cyril	Tell Me Not of a Lovely Lass
Schumann	Frühlingsnacht
Schumann	Die beiden Grenadiere
Schumann	Ich grolle nicht
Speaks	Sylvia
Tschaikowsky	Warum?
Verdi	La donna è mobile *(Rigoletto)*

6. *Voice Quality and Phrasing*

Böhm	Still wie die Nacht
Brahms	Der Schmied
Brahms	Volkslied
Bridge	Isobel
Franck	La Procession
Gluck	Divinités du Styx *(Alceste)*
Handel	Care Selve *(Atalanta)*
La Forge	How Much I Love You
Liszt	Die Lorelei
Ponchielli	Cielo e mar *(La Gioconda)*
Schubert	Ave Maria
Wolf	Das verlassene Mägdlein

7. *Dynamics and Nuance*

Charpentier	Depuis le jour *(Louise)*
Clarke	The Blind Ploughman
La Forge	Hills
Leroux	Le Nil
Scarlatti	O cessate di piagarmi
Schubert	Du bist die Ruh
Secchi	Love Me or Not
Strauss, R.	Die Nacht
Verdi	Celeste Aida *(Aida)*
Wagner	Elizabeth's Prayer *(Tannhäuser)*
Watts	Wings of Night

8. Rhythmic Problems

Arensky	On Wings of Dream
Curran	Nocturne
Debussy	Les Cloches
D'Indy	Lied Maritime
Handel	Where'er You Walk *(Semele)*
Leoncavallo	Mattinata
Mozart	Porgi amor *(Le Nozzi di Figaro)*
Olds	Nocturne
Paisiello	Chi vuol la Zingarella
Rachmaninoff	Lilacs
Ravel	Tout gai! *(Cinq melodies populaires)*
Scarlatti	La Violette
Schumann	Intermezzo *(Liederkreis)*
Strauss, R.	Allerseelen
Strauss, R.	Morgen
Weaver	Moon Marketing

III. Problem Songs for More Advanced Study[8]

1. Melodic Skips and Intervals

Beethoven	Die Ehre Gottes aus der Natur
Brahms	An die Vielchen
Brahms	Saphische Ode
Franz	Die blauen Frühlingsaugen
Grieg	Ich liebe dich
La Forge	To a Messenger
Mozart	Deh vieni non tardar *(Le Nozze di Figaro)*
Saint-Saëns	Amour viens aider *(Samson et Dalila)*
Schubert	Die junge Nonne
Schubert	Ständchen
Stradella	Pietà, Signore
Strickland	My Lover Is a Fisherman
Wagner	Ho-jo-to-ho! *(Die Walküre)*
Wagner	Dich theure Halle *(Tannhaüser)*
Wagner	Prize Song *(Die Meistersinger)*
Wolf	Er ist's
Wolf-Ferrari	Angiolo delicato

2. Scales and Runs

Beethoven	Mit einem gemalten band
Bizet	Habanera *(Carmen)*
Bizet	Seguidilla *(Carmen)*
Debussy	La Mort des amants
Farley	The Night Wind
Fauré	Mandoline
Franz	Das Macht das dunkelgrüne Laub
Franz	Im Herbst
Gounod	Au Printemps
Hageman	At the Well
Pergolesi	Tre giorni son che Nina
Respighi	Nebbie
Rimsky-Korsakoff	Song of India *(Sadko)*
Schubert	Die Forelle
Thomas	Sonnet d'amour
Watts	The Poet Sings

3. Agility and Fluency

Acqua	Villanelle
Chopin	The Maiden's Wish
Grieg	Solvejg's Lied
Handel	Rejoice Greatly *(Messiah)*
Handel	Why Do the Nations *(Messiah)*
Loewe	Canzonetta
Massenet	Gavotte *(Manon)*
Mozart	Alleluja *(Exsultate, jubilate)*
Purcell	Nymphs and Shepherds *(The Libertine)*
Rossini	Una voce poco fa *(Il Barbiere di Siviglia)*
Scarlatti	Già il sole dal Gange
Schubert	Die Post
Schubert	Liebesbotschaft
Schuman	Aufträge
Strauss, R.	Ständchen

4. Ornamentation and Fioritura

Bishop	Lo, Here the Gentle Lark
Bizet	Air de Leila *(Les Pêcheurs de Perles)*

Bizet	Pastorale
Grieg	The Princess
Handel	But Who May Abide the Day of His Coming *(Messiah)*
Haydn	With Verdure Clad *(The Creation)*
Lotti	Pur dicesti
Mozart	Deh vieni non tardar *(Le Nozze di Figaro)*
Schubert	Im Abendrot
Schubert	Litanei
Schumann	Waldesgespräch
Verdi	Caro nome *(Rigoletto)*

5. Dramatic Expression and Interpretation

Brahms	Ständchen
Ferrari	Le Miroir
Griffes	Lament of Ian the Proud
MacDowell	The Sea
Puccini	Un bel di vedremo *(Madame Butterfly)*
Schubert	Am Meer
Schubert	Der Doppelgänger
Schubert	Der Tod und das Mädchen
Schubert	Erlkönig
Schubert	Rastlose Liebe
Schumann	Die beiden Grenadiere
Sibelius	The Tryst
Strauss, R.	Ständchen
Watts	Wild Tears

IV. Sacred Solos for Advanced Study[9]

(The vocal range is indicated by the letters S, A, T, B.)

Bach	Agnus Dei (A) *(Mass in B Minor)*
Bach	Ah! My Soul (T) *(St. John Passion)*
Bach	Benedictus (T) *(Mass in B Minor)*
Bach	Die Schaumenden Wellen (T) *(Cantata No. 81)*
Bach	Doch Weichet ihr Tollen (B) *(Cantata No. 8)*
Bach	Es ist vollbracht (A) *(St. John Passion)*

Bach	Et in Spiritum Sanctum (B) *(Mass in B Minor)*
Bach	I Follow Thee Also (S) *(St. John Passion)*
Bach	Jauchzet, Jauchzet Gott (S) *(Cantata No. 51)*
Bach	Laudamus Te (S) *(Mass in B Minor)*
Bach	Prepare Thyself, Zion (A) *(Christmas Oratorio)*
Handel	Behold, Darkness Shall Cover (B) *(Messiah)*
Handel	Every Valley Shall Be Exalted (T) *(Messiah)*
Handel	Father of Heaven (A) *(Judas Maccabeus)*
Handel	He Was Despised (A) *(Messiah)*
Handel	Honor and Arms (B) (Samson)
Handel	I Feel the Deity Within (B) *(Judas Maccabeus)*
Handel	I Know That My Redeemer Liveth (S) *(Messiah)*
Handel	The People That Walk in Darkness (B) (*Messiah*)
Handel	The Trumpet Shall Sound (B) *(Messiah)*
Handel	Why Do the Nations (B) *(Messiah)*
Haydn	From Out the Fold (B) *(The Seasons)*
Haydn	In Native Worth (T) *(The Creation)*
Haydn	O How Pleasing to the Senses (S) *(The Seasons)*
Haydn	Rolling and Foaming Billows (B) *(The Creation)*
Haydn	With Verdure Clad (S) *(The Creation)*
Mendelssohn	Be Thou Faithful Unto Death (T) *(St. Paul)*
Mendelssohn	But the Lord Is Mindful of His Own (A) *(St. Paul)*
Mendelssohn	Hear Ye, Israel (S) *(Elijah)*
Mendelssohn	If With All Your Hearts (T) *(Elijah)*
Mendelssohn	Is Not His Word Like a Fire (B) *(Elijah)*
Mendelssohn	It Is Enough (B) *(Elijah)*
Mendelssohn	Jerusalem, Jerusalem (S) *(St. Paul)*
Mendelssohn	Lord, God of Abraham (B) *(Elijah)*
Mendelssohn	O God Have Mercy (B) *(St. Paul)*
Mendelssohn	O Rest In the Lord (A) *(Elijah)*
Mendelssohn	Woe Unto Them (A) *(Elijah)*
Mozart	Agnus Dei (S) *(Coronation Mass)*
Mozart	Confutatis Maledictis (B) *(Requiem)*
Mozart	Et Incarnatus Est (S) *(Mass in C Minor)*
Rossini	Cujus Animam (T) *(Stabat Mater)*
Rossini	Fac ut Portem (A) *(Stabat Mater)*

Rossini	Inflammatus (S) *(Stabat Mater)*
Stainer	King Ever Glorious (T) *(Crucifixion)*
Sullivan	Love Not the World (A) *(The Prodigal Son)*
Verdi	Ingemisco (T) *Requiem)*
Verdi	Libera Me (S) *(Requiem)*
Verdi	Lacrymosa dies illa! (T) *(Requiem)*

V. Song Cycles for Advanced Study

Barber	Hermit Songs
Beckwith	Five Lyrics of the T'ang Dynasty
Beethoven	An die ferne Geliebte
Berger	Villanescos
Berlioz	La Nuit d'Eté
Brahms	Romanzen aus Magelone
Brahms	Vier ernste Gesänge
Brahms	Zigeunerlieder
Britten	Les Illuminations
Britten	Winter Words
Carpenter	Gitanjali
Chanler	The Children
Chausson	Poème de l'Amour et de la Mer
Debussy	Chansons de Bilitis
Debussy	Fêtes Galantes
Debussy	Proses Lyriques
DeFalla	Seven Spanish Songs
Diamond	The Midnight Meditation
Fauré	La Bonne Chanson
Fauré	L'Horizon Chimérique
Finzi	Before and After Summer
Henze	Fünf Neopolitanische Lieder
Hindemith	Marienleben
Lees	Cyprian Songs
Malapiero	Quatro Sonetti del Burchiello
Milhaud	Trois Chansons de Troubador
Mussorgsky	The Nursery
Mussorgsky	Without Sunlight
Nordoff	The Story of Sweeney
Pizzetti	Tre Canti Greci

Poulenc	Chansons Galliardes
Poulenc	Chansons Villageoises
Prokofieff	Children's Songs
Ravel	Histoires Naturelles
Ravel	Don Quichotte a Dulcinée
Ravel	Five Greek Songs
Respighi	Cinque Canti all'Antica
Rorem	Hearing
Schubert	Die schöne Mullerin
Schubert	Die Winterreise
Schumann	Dichterliebe
Schumann	Frauenliebe und Leben
Sowerby	The Edge of Dreams
Thompson	La Belle en Dormant
Weisgall	Soldier Songs

VI. Operatic Arias for Advanced Study[10]

1. Soprano (coloratura)

Bellini	Ah! non credea mirarti (*La Sonnambula*)
Bellini	Qui la voce (*I Puritani*)
Bellini	Vien, diletto e in ciel (*I Puritani*)
Delibes	Ou va la jeune Indoue (*Lakmé*)
Donizetti	Mad scene (*Lucia di Lammermoor*)
Donizetti	Regnava nel silenzio (*Lucia di Lammermoor*)
Flotow	The Last Rose of Summer (*Martha*)
Meyerbeer	Ombra leggiera (*Dinorah*)
Mozart	Der Hölle Rache (*Die Zauberflöte*)
Rossini	Una voce poco fa (*Barber of Seville*)
Thomas	Je suis Titania (*Mignon*)
Verdi	Ah! fors'è lui (*La Traviata*)
Verdi	Caro Nome (*Rigoletto*)

2. Soprano (lyric)

Bizet	Je dis que rien ne m'épouvante (*Carmen*)
Boito	L'altra Notte (*Mefistofele*)
Charpentier	Depuis le jour (*Louise*)

Herbert	I List the Trill in Golden Throat *(Natoma)*
Gounod	Air des bijoux *(Faust)*
Gounod	Je veux vivre *(Romeo et Juliette)*
Mascagni	Voi lo sapete *(Cavalleria Rusticana)*
Massenet	Il est doux, il est bon *(Hérodiade)*
Mozart	Ach, ich fuhl's *(Die Zauberflöte)*
Mozart	Batti, batti *(Don Giovani)*
Mozart	Deh vieni, non tardar *(Le Nozze di Figaro)*
Mozart	Dove sono *(Le Nozze di Figaro)*
Mozart	L'amero *(Il Re Pastore)*
Mozart	Vedrai carino *(Don Giovanni)*
Mozart	Mi tradi quell' alma ingrata *(Don Giovanni)*
Puccini	Donde lieta uscì *(La Bohème)*
Puccini	Mi chiamano Mimi *(La Bohème)*
Puccini	Vissi d'arte *(Tosca)*
Verdi	Ave Maria *(Otello)*
Wagner	Einsam in trüben Tagen (Elsa's Dream) *(Lohengrin)*

3. *Soprano (lirico-spinto)*

Bellini	Casta diva *(Norma)*
Debussy	Air de Lia *(L'Enfant Prodigue)*
Leoncavallo	Stridono lassù *(Pagliacci)*
Massenet	Dis-moi que je suis belle *(Thais)*
Mozart	Come scoglio *(Cosi fan tutte)*
Mozart	Porgi amor *(Le Nozze di Figaro)*
Puccini	Quando m'en vo' *(La Bohème)*
Puccini	Sola, perduta abbandonata *(Manon Lescaut)*
Verdi	O patria mia *(Aida)*
Verdi	Ritorna vincitor *(Aida)*
Wagner	Euch Lüften, die mein Klagen *(Lohengrin)*
Weber	Wie Nahte mir der Schlummer *(Der Freischütz)*

4. *Soprano (dramatic)*

Boito	L'altra notte in fondo al mare *(Mefistofele)*
Giordano	La mamma morta *(Andrea Chenier)*
Gluck	Divinités du Styx *(Alceste)*
Mozart	Non mi dir *(Don Giovanni)*
Mozart	Or sai, che l'onore *(Don Giovanni)*

Ponchielli	Suicidio *(La Gioconda)*
Saint-Saëns	Mon coeur s'ouvre à ta voix *(Samson et Dalila)*
Verdi	D'amor sull'ali rosee *(Il Trovatore)*
Verdi	Pace, pace, mio Dio *(La Forza del Destino)*
Wagner	Dich, teure Halle *(Tannhäuser)*
Wagner	Allmächt'ge Jungfrau *(Tannhäuser)*
Weber	Ozen du Ungeheur! *(Oberon)*

5. *Mezzo-soprano*

Bizet	Habanera *(Carmen)*
Bizet	Seguidilla *(Carmen)*
Donizetti	O mio Fernando *(La Favorita)*
Gluck	Che faró senza Euridice *(Orfeo ed Euridice)*
Gounod	Faites-lui mes aveux *(Faust)*
Massenet	Les lettres *(Werther)*
Meyerbeer	Ah! mon fils *(Le Prophète)*
Meyerbeer	Nobles seigneurs, salut! *(Les Huguenots)*
Mozart	Non so più *(Le Nozze di Figaro)*
Mozart	Non piu di fiori *(La Clemenza di Tito)*
Mozart	Voi che sapete *(Le Nozze di Figaro)*
Ponchielli	Stella del marinar! *(La Gioconda)*
Rossini	In si barbara? *(Semiramide)*
Rossini	Une vote poco fa *(Il Barbiere di Siviglia)*
Saint-Saëns	Amour, viens aider *(Samson et Dalila)*
Saint-Saëns	Printemps qui commence *(Samson et Dalila)*
Thomas	Connais tu le pays *(Mignon)*
Verdi	O don fatale *(Don Carlos)*
Wagner	Geliebter, komm! *(Tannhäuser)*

6. *Contralto*

Bizet	Je crois entendre encore *(Les Pêcheurs de Perles)*
Bizet	En vain pour éviter *(Carmen)*
Boito	Padre Nostro *(Nerone)*
Gounod	O ma lyre immortelle *(Sapho)*
Handel	Verdi Prati *(Alcina)*
Massenet	Qui m'aurait dit la place *(Werther)*
Ponchielli	Voce di donna *(La Gioconda)*
Saint-Saëns	Mon coeur s'ouvre à ta voix *(Samson et Dalila)*

Tschaikowsky	Pauline's aria *(Pique Dame)*
Verdi	Redel 'abisso affretati *(Un Ballo in Maschera)*
Verdi	Stride la vampa *(Il Trovatore)*
Wagner	Weiche Wotan, weiche *(Das Rheingold)*

7. Tenor (lyric)

Bizet	Air de la Fleur *(Carmen)*
Donizetti	Spirito gentil *(La Favorita)*
Donizetti	Una furtiva lagrima *(L'Elisir d'Amore)*
Flotow	Ach, so fromm (M'appari) *(Martha)*
Godard	Berceuse *(Jocelyn)*
Gounod	A! Lève-toi, soleil *(Roméo et Juliette)*
Gounod	Salut! demeure chaste et pure *(Faust)*
Leoncavallo	O Columbina *(I Pagliacci)*
Mascagni	Siciliana *(Cavalleria Rusticana)*
Massenet	En fermant les yeux (La Rêve) *(Manon)*
Meyerbeer	Plus blanche que la blanche hermine *(Les Huguenots)*
Mozart	Dalla sua pace *(Don Giovanni)*
Mozart	Il mio tesoro *(Don Giovanni)*
Rossini	Ecco ridente *(Il Barbiere di Siviglia)*
Rossini	Se il mio Nome *(Il Barbiere di Siviglia)*
Thomas	Elle ne croyait pas *(Mignon)*
Verdi	Ouesta e Quella *(Rigoletto)*

8. Tenor (lirico-spinto)

Giordano	Amor ti vieta *(Fedora)*
Giordano	Un di al Pazzuro spazio *(Andrea Chenier)*
Massenet	Ah! fuyez douce image *(Manon)*
Puccini	Che gelida manina *(La Bohème)*
Puccini	E lucevan le stelle *(Tosca)*
Weber	Durch die Wälder *(Der Freischütz)*

9. Tenor (dramatic)

Berlioz	Nature immense *(La Damnation de Faust)*
Giordano	Come un bel di di Maggio *(Andrea Chenier)*

Halévy	Rachel, quand du Seigneur *(La Juive)*
Leoncavallo	O mio Piccolo tavolo *(Zaza)*
Leoncavallo	Vesti la giubba *(I Pagliacci)*
Ponchielli	Cielo e mar *(La Gioconda)*
Puccini	Non piangere Liù! *(Turnandot)*
Puccini	E lucevan le stelle *(La Tosca)*
Verdi	Ora e per sempre addio *(Otello)*
Wagner	In fernem Land *(Lohengrin)*
Wagner	Morgenlicht leuchtend *(Die Meistersinger)*

10. Baritone Arias

Bizet	Toreador's Song *(Carmen)*
Donizetti	Bella siccome un angelo *(Don Pasquale)*
Donizetti	Vien Leonora *(La Favorita)*
Giordano	Nemico della patria? *(Andrea Chenier)*
Gluck	De noirs pressentiments *(Iphigenie En Tauride)*
Gounod	Avant de quiter ces lieux *(Faust)*
Leoncavallo	Si puo? (prologue—*Pagliacci)*
Massanet	Salome *(Hérodiade)*
Massanet	Vision fugitive *(Hérodiade)*
Mozart	Deh, vieni alla finestra *(Don Giovanni)*
Mozart	Non piu andrai *(Le Nozze di Figaro)*
Offenbach	Scintille diamant *(Les Contes d'Hoffman)*
Rossini	Largo al factotum *(Il Barbiere di Siviglia)*
Verdi	Cortegiani *(Rigoletto)*
Verdi	Credo *(Otello)*
Verdi	Di Provenza il mar *(La Traviata)*
Verdi	Eri tu *(Un Ballo in Maschera)*
Verdi	È sogno? O realtà? *(Falstaff)*
Verdi	Il balen del suo sorriso *(Il Trovatore)*
Verdi	Pari siamo! *(Rigoletto)*
Wagner	Blick ich umher *(Tannhäuser)*
Wagner	O du mein holder Abenstern *(Tannhäuser)*

11. Bass Baritone

Bizet	Cancion del Toreador *(Carmen)*
Donizetti	A tanto amor *(La Favorita)*
Gounod	Le veau d'or *(Faust)*

Mozart	Aprite un po quegli occhi *(Le Nozze di Figaro)*
Rossini	A un dottore *(Il Barbiere di Siviglia)*
Rossini	La Calumnia *(Il Barbiere di Siviglia)*
Verdi	Ella giammai m'amo *(Don Carlos)*
Verdi	O tu, Palermo *(I Vespri Siciliani)*
Verdi	Infelice! e tu credevi *(Ernani)*
Wagner	Leb' wohl, du kühnes, herrliches Kind *(Die Walküre)*

12. Bass Arias

Délibes	Lakmé, ton doux regards se voile *(Lakmé)*
Donizetti	Udite! udite! o rustici *(L'Elisir d'Amore)*
Gounod	Sérénade *(Faust)*
Gounod	Sous les pieds d'une femme *(La Reine de Saba)*
Halévy	Si la rigeur *(La Juive)*
Mozart	La vendetta *(Le Nozze di Figaro)*
Mozart	In diesen heil'gen Hallen *(Die Zauberflöte)*
Mozart	Madamina! Il catalogo è questo *(Don Giovanni)*
Puccini	Vecchia zimarra *(La Bohème)*
Verdi	Dormirò sol *(Don Carlo)*
Verdi	Il lacerato spirito *(Simon Boccanegra)*
Wagner	Mein Herr und Gott, nun ruf' ich dich *(Lohengrin)*

Preparing a Song Recital

The song recital is a program of vocal music presented by an artist-pupil for public performance. It is carefully planned, and it offers a coherent and well-balanced sequence of songs, arias, and other vocal compositions in finished professional style. Such a program may be likened to the preparation of a full meal. It starts with an appetizer, develops into heavy eating, and winds up with some light refreshment. The balance and variety of courses to be served are determined by the interest and appetite of the recipient. The more eager the audience, therefore, the heavier the food. Make the choice of materials fresh-tasting and satisfying in every detail and do not attempt to put over an unsavory dish. It may spoil the entire meal. A musical menu must be planned with freshness, variety, skillful rendition, excellent quality, and service.

A well-balanced recital program should, therefore, be both interesting and musically palatable from start to finish with a pleasing variety in the sequence of numbers. This will prevent monotony and fatigue to performer and listener alike. The singer must stay within his vocal range to assure comfortable expression. He should avoid any foreign language songs that have clumsy translations. They are difficult to sing. He must also be sure to master foreign diction before attempting to sing it. And above all, he should memorize thoroughly.

The average song recital may last from about an hour to an hour and a half, which would include the short rest intervals between numbers and a ten-to-fifteen-minute intermission. The program is divided into two main parts, as a rule, and each part roughly comprises three ten-to-fifteen-minute units, six units in all. Each unit may include two or more songs, depending on length, such as a group of German lieder; traditional folksongs; French, early English, early Italian, or American songs; or a single long number. The more advanced singer will wish to include a song cycle, an operatic aria, or a selection from oratorio.[11]

Although there is no set rule for program building, it is preferable to arrange items in chronological order, i.e., classic, romantic, modern. A program may be unified by topical headings announcing each group of songs, such as folksongs, spirituals, martial songs, songs of faith, excerpts from opera, etc. An indiscriminate assortment of mixed types of music should be avoided.

Part One may open with a group of songs that are slow, melodious, and interesting (e.g., Handel, Bach, or Purcell). Two or three such songs are desirable, rather than a longer dramatic work, because an audience is often restless at the start of a program and late-comers may intrude and destroy the mood of a longer work. However, since first impressions count, the opening numbers should be chosen with great care and executed with flawless artistry and finesse. From then on, the most important works on the program may be featured, such as an operatic aria, a dramatic or declamatory song, or a song cycle.[12]

A historical or chronological sequence of composers is traditional but not mandatory. It is best not to mix languages in any single recital group, and the performer should try to avoid too much moderato singing at one time. In other words, tempo, mood, and sequence of keys should be varied from song to song to avoid monotony. The climax of Part One may be an operatic aria which is introduced by recitative and it may be followed by a short rhythmical or humerous item.

The *Intermission* usually marks the halfway point or slightly past the halfway mark, so that the heavier portion will have been completed by the time intermission arrives. More than one intermission is inadvisable, since this tends to dispel interest and creates too many distractions. Nor should intermissions be overlong, so as not to dissolve audience rapport which the first half created.

Part Two would parallel Part One in general framework, but it would feature simplicity of style, rhythmic ease, and pleasant contours to provide relief from emotional and dramatic pieces that may have preceded it in Part One. Open the second half with any number that focuses attention after the intermission.

In general, start each half of the program with a light mood and moderate tempo. Then build to an emotional and dramatic climax and end with a refreshing change of pace that leaves the audience in good humor. A devotional song, a lively folksong, a rhythmical, humorous, brilliant character number will serve as a fitting conclusion to the program. Contemporary songs, either American or British, of contrasting mood always make an interesting finale. Encores, if used, should be short, brilliant, and few in number. They should blend well with the concluding part of the program. Choose a varied sequence from the following styles: dramatic, declamatory, narrative, atmospheric, characterization, lyrical, florid, strongly rhythmical, humorous, folk, introspective, reminiscent, devotional, supernatural, dialect, brilliant, tragic, etc.

Clumsy "stunt" numbers are inadvisable, especially if

there is any uncertainty as to outcomes. A well-seasoned performer prefers not to gamble with the tolerance of listeners but provides them with a pleasant variety of savory, stimulating, and satisfying musical fare. Too many long or elaborate numbers wear on an audience. Too much frivolity fails to penetrate. There must be balance, proportion, and variety. In other words, materials should be so arranged that there is a gradual development toward serious, climactic, or tragic moods which, after reaching a peak, resolve into lighter, pleasanter atmosphere.

Final Briefing

Bear in mind that you are communicating intimately with each individual in your audience and do not perform as though you were on display. Realize that you are in command of the performance and assume the authority to be so, even if you feel otherwise. You must create the illusion of effortless ease in everything you do. Don't strive—*let* yourself sing. Feel good about it, as though you enjoyed it immensely, for you will impart your own enjoyment to your audience in like measure.

Make your entrances and exits with self-assurance and walk with good posture and graceful gait. A woman always precedes a man in entering or leaving the stage. Carry nothing with you, and memorize your text and music to perfection so that there is never a moment of mental faltering throughout the performance. Do not become self-critical. If errors occur, let them pass. There is no room for retrospection until it is all over.

Dress should be dignified and in good taste to provide a neutral background for musical presentation. The audience is primarily interested in hearing, not in seeing. Finally, be sure to acknowledge applause graciously and gratefully with equal measure of appreciation for your accompanist who will share the applause with you. Bow several times with reserve and dignity.

The accompaniment should never drown out the voice of

the singer. This, all too often, is a cause of failure in an artist's recital. In the finished performance there is always a proper blending of vocal line against a harmonic background. To effect this balanced relationship, a vocalist must acquire his own musical stature and his performance must not lean too heavily on accompaniment. Even if the latter should falter or stop, the singer must be able to go on alone and not sound as though he depended on the supporting instrument for cues or tonalities.

In other words, a vocalist's ear should be self-reliant and a singer must be able to sustain his own melodic line fearlessly and independently. Only then will the accompanist be able to blend his performance with the soloist's and the finished effect will be artistically satisfying. Of course, to achieve this result much rehearsal is necessary.[13]

Don't attempt to imitate the performance of others. No two artists interpret alike. Therefore, any obvious resemblance to the style of another is a form of imitation that disparages artistry and belittles the effect.

Watch the physical and acoustical dimensions of the recital or concert hall, since that will affect the distinctness of your diction and the dynamic nuances of expression. It is also desirable to rehearse in front of a few invited friends who will simulate audience response and thereby lessen the possibility of stage fright.

Pay strict attention to text at all times. In good song writing, the word inspires the melody and this brings the song to life. Therefore, unless words are intelligible and distinctly understood by the audience, the song is likely to lose much of its meaning. Remember, also, that a singer holds his audience because there is direct communication between them. Therefore, *talk* to your audience with your voice throughout a performance. *Tell* them something in every word and note you sing, and never let go of that concept until you have finished. Becoming audience-minded is an essential factor in rounding out a rehearsal schedule for concert or recital. To this end, technical proficiency must gradually be deemphasized in favor of the projection of personality traits that bespeak artistry and musicianship in a convincing manner. Mediocrity rises to excellence under such treatment.

REFERENCES AND NOTES

1. Ira Schroeder, *Listener's Handbook* (Ames, Iowa: Iowa State University Press, 1966).

2. James L. Mursell, *The Psychology of Music* (New York: W. W. Norton, 1937), Chap. 3.

3. Hermann L. F. Helmholtz, *On the Sensations of Tone*, 2nd edition, tr. and rev. A. J. Ellis (New York: Dover Publications, Inc., 1954), pp. 252, 289, 368.

4. John Redfield, *Music, a Science and an Art* (New York: Tudor Publishing Co., 1935), p. 93.

5. Berton Coffin, *Singer's Repertoire*, 2nd edition (New York: Scarecrow Press, Inc., 1962), 5 vols.

6. Berton Coffin, Werner Singer, and Pierre De Lattre, *Word by Word Translations of Songs and Arias* (New York: Scarecrow Press, Inc., 1966).

7. David Ewen, *Complete Book of 20th Century Music*, rev. ed. (Englewood Cliffs, N.J.: Prentice-Hall, Inc., 1959).

8. See also: Van A. Christy and Carl Zytowski, editors, *Classic Period Songs* (Dubuque, Iowa: Wm. C. Brown Company, 1968); Giusepe Verdi, *Composizion da Camera* (New York: G. Ricordi & Co., 1967).

9. See also: Max Spicker, *Anthology of Sacred Songs*, 4 vols., Sop., Alt., Ten., Bass (New York: G. Schirmer, Inc.); *Oratorio Songs*, Sop. only (Bryn Mawr, Pa.: John Church Co., Theo. Presser); *52 Sacred Songs* (New York: G. Schirmer, Inc., 1939).

10. See also: Weldon Whitlock, *Master Lessons on Fifty Opera Arias* (Champaign, Illinois: Pro Musica Press, 1967); *The Prima Donna's Album of 42 Opera Aria* (New York: G. Schirmer, Inc., 1956).

11. John W. Peirce, *The Art of Program Making* (New York: G. Schirmer, Inc., 1951).

12. Weldon Whitlock, *Facets of the Singer's Art* (Champaign, Illinois: Pro Musica Press, 1967), Chap. 9.

13. Kurt Herbert Adler, *The Art of Accompanying and Coaching* (Minneapolis: University of Minnesota Press, 1965), Chap. 10.

XVII

Hints and Helps for the Artist Student

Special vocal problems that relate to actual performance are gathered here in a unified alphabetical sequence. Although some of these subjects have been previously discussed, they are now applied mainly to the preparation of repertoire. Such refreshers and reminders include twenty-seven topics that range from *bravura* to *warming up*. Together they provide a practical resumé of hints and helps that enhance a singer's performance and lead him to the level of virtuosity required for audience presentation. Obviously, the art of interpretation requires a thorough-going analysis of vocal literature that comprises every aspect of preparation described in the preceding chapters and culminates in the actual performance of the public recital program.

Bravura is a term that calls for dexterity and boldness of execution. It is a challenge to the vocalist to summon forth his best artistry. It is as though the spotlight were turned on him and the composer said, "Now, show what you can do!" A bravura passage is therefore not to be hurried over, but, rather, performed with poise and flawless timing and a display of consummate artistry.

Breathing. Each thought takes its own breath in singing.

Sometimes a tiny sip of air suffices; sometimes a quick gulp; sometimes a gasp for dramatic vehemence. But, as in speaking, the intake of air is always appropriate to the meaning, duration, intensity, and feeling value of the ensuing phrase.

Never breathe in the middle of a word, nor between words that are intimately united by grammatical sense. When the melodic phrase is overlong, sections of phrases provide possible breath points. Sometimes a half-breath is used to tide the performer over until the next convenient breath point appears. The breathing action is always skillfully concealed so that the audience ignores it. Either nose or mouth may be used. Never breathe while singing a portamento. Breathe *after* the portamento.

Study the breathing habits of prominent singers. You will find they rarely seem to breathe at all, so clever are they in suiting technique to the meaning of each phrase unit. Breath retention and breath budgeting become distinguishing traits of the artist singer (see *phrasing*).

Cadenza is an ornamental vocal flourish of indefinite form occurring at any important point in an aria, usually at a cadence. There is a momentary suspension of musical meaning while the singer is given an opportunity to exhibit his technical skill and vocal dexterity. In earlier compositions, singers could take liberties, since embellishments were not always indicated. More modern scores print out every cadenza and little is therefore left to improvizational skill. Obviously, only a finished artist would attempt a cadenza in public performance.

Clef. In addition to the *treble or G clef* and the *bass or F clef* commonly seen in piano scores, a *C clef* is used movably to denote the location of *middle C* on the musical staff. It consists of a large florid sign printed so that whatever line it grips is *middle C*. The C clefs most commonly used in song and operatic scores are the *soprano clef* (with middle C on the first line), the *alto clef* (middle C on the third line) and the *tenor clef* (middle C on the fourth line). A singer should be familiar with soprano or tenor clefs and he should be able to read at sight from either of them, in addition to the conventional treble and bass clefs.

Coloratura (fioritura) is the term that indicates florid ornamentation. This includes rapid scale passages, runs, trills, arpeggi, and similar ornate effects that demand vocal virtuosity. A coloratura soprano has special aptitude in this direction. Naturally, her voice must be light, quick, and flexible, and able to leap about in a sparkling manner. High range, great agility, and consistent purity of tone are called for. Coloratura passages must be finely etched, never slurred or slighted, each tone having a definite pitch, duration, and volume, and contributing to a definite musical pattern. A sensitive ear and consummate musicianship are requisites for coloratura singing.

Diction. English can be as singable as any other language. When it is not, the trouble usually lies with the singer, not the language. For clear, intelligible English diction the tongue must be flexible, nimble, and able to move independently. Minimize all jaw movement. Economy of effort is mandatory. *Short – light – independent* is the rule for lingual mobility.

Short-tongue action may be practiced by using twin syllables *(ta-ta, da-da, na-na, la-la, ra-ra),* slowly at first, then at different speeds. In all these sounds the tongue is slightly retracted and the tongue tip lightly contacts the alveolar or gum ridge. The *s* sound likewise demands a slightly shortened tongue, using the alveolar orbit described above. *S* should be a subdued and fleeting sound, never a noisy hiss (review chapter fourteen on "Diction").

Filar-di-voce (L. *filum,* a thread) is a type of portamento. The voice is carried across intervals with smoothness and the softest possible tone, literally drawing the voice out to a fine thread, without crescendo or diminuendo, while moving from one note to another. This type of slurring should have a clear, musical quality in spite of its delicate texture. Artists may also use it in rapid legato singing to avoid the staccato separation of large or small intervals. *Filar-di-voce* should be practiced lightly for all intervals until it is mastered. It is scarcely audible when well executed (see *legato*).

Dynamics, or variations in vocal intensity, should not be confused with *accent,* which relates to the beat of music. A performing singer must be careful: a) not to make crescendos and diminuendos too soon; b) not to make prominent dynamic contrasts where they are not indicated or implied; c) to choose the proper degree and gradation of loudness for each dynamic level indicated; d) to subordinate accompaniments, when necessary, so that vocal nuances are not drowned out; e) to recognize that vocal range, type of composition, type of accompaniment, and size and acoustics of the room all affect the use and control of vocal dynamics.

Grace Notes are musical ornaments. Those most frequently encountered in singing are: a) *appoggiatura;* b) *mordent;* c) *turn;* and d) *trill*. Since each is included in vocal literature, it will be helpful to discuss them from the singer's point of view:

a. **Appoggiatura** may be single or double, ascending or descending. It may be a discordant note. It is usually sung diatonically above its principal note, unless chromatically altered. It usually falls on the strong beat or on the long syllables of words, but it takes a bit of time value away from the note it precedes. When two identical notes end a phrase and are followed by a rest, the *first* note always takes the accent and must therefore be turned into an appoggiatura (e.g., Mozart).

b. The **mordent** (single or double) lies immediately above and alternates several times with its principal. It derives its value from the note it embellishes and is never started before the beat on which it occurs. Thus, it creates the effect of a passing shake, or trill, between identical tones.

c. The first note of a **turn** is placed diatonically above the principle note and the third note a minor second below it (unless chromatic alterations are indicated). It, too, borrows its note value from the duration of the note which it embellishes.

d. The **trill** is formed by a rapid alternation of a melodic tone with an auxiliary tone lying immediately above it in the scale. The upper tone is always attacked first, as though it were an appoggiatura, and the trill always ends on the principal note by using a turn, half turn, or some other appropriate ornament to round out its closure.

Whatever its form, an ornament is never sung carelessly. It should not be slurred and it must be distinct from the note it precedes and leans on. It requires a firm attack and demands definite artistic treatment, whether it be appoggiatura, mordent, turn, or trill (see *trill*).

Humming. Before each performance, a head hum should be practiced aloud to establish basic resonance in the singing voice. With lips *lightly* closed, swell the hum very gradually, until optimal sonority is attained with *minimum* effort. Then gradually open the jaws and try vowel sounds without lessening the sonority achieved in the hum. Always mentally associate the humming tone with an "ng." This induces a slight retraction and arched elevation of the back of the tongue, a device that also promotes the resonance of the voice (e.g., *hung-ah, ng-ah, ngah, ngah,* (ng)*ah,* (ng)*ah,* etc. Also review the discussion on *humming* in chapter twelve).

Laughter. The use of *laughter* in song texts is not uncommon. It is generated in the region of the diaphragm and it should never be throaty. Study yourself in moments of unrestrained laughter when it occurs naturally. Thus, you will capture the bounce-like breath attack that characterizes a hearty belly laugh. This technique is also employed, in a modified way, in singing *martellato*. Laughter in song must always be rhythmically and musically perfect.

The belly laugh may also be used as a voice projection

exercise. Try laughing up and down the scale. Then laugh (martellato fashion) through every note in the song you are singing. It will induce great vocal freedom. Good tone production is always close to laughter.

Legato. Unlike consonants, vowels always convey tonality. In legato, therefore, except for minute interruptions caused by nonvocal consonants *(p, t, k, f, s,* etc.), never break the continuity of vowel sounds in the text of a song. A continuous ribbon of tone is thus generated for each melodic phrase. Also give special attention to unaccented syllables lest they be hurried over. Each syllable contains a vowel sound which contributes its share to the melodic line and no vowel is therefore unimportant.

In dramatic singing, consonants may require special attention and ways must be found for making them more prominent, especially when the words of the text need emphasis. For practice purposes, separate each phonetic element in the word with equal time allotment to each sound (e.g., *take* = *t-a-k; build* = *b-i-l-d;* etc.). With the use of this attention-arresting device, the singer's ear becomes sensitized to phonetic values and slurring tendencies disappear. A slow-motion rendition of any text is also helpful.

In legato singing, all notes are joined by a fine, continuous tonal thread. They are not detached by the complete cessation of sound, as in staccato. However, there is an infinitesimal letting-go of the stretching action of the vocal cords between tones, just enough to slacken the pitch adjustment for an imperceptible instant of time, without halting phonation. The singer's ear unconsciously governs this process. Thus, instead of dragging or sliding the voice up and down in portamento fashion, each legato note is individually but firmly attacked on its own true pitch. Breath support is continuously maintained throughout. In the final phases of legato practice, mentally transfer to the next note while sounding the preceding note.

In all legato singing, the final consonant of a word or syllable belongs to the vowel that follows it, not to the vowel preceding it. Thus, from first to last, you create the illusion that your tone never stops.

Martellato is a type of staccato used for dramatic effect. An independent attack with expiratory emphasis is required for each note. The tone must be terminated as abruptly as it starts to avoid slurring. The chest must be high to prevent fitful breathing. An abdominal-diaphragmatic attack is used, accompanied by a shaking of the lower ribs. The action resembles that of laughter *(hah-hah-hah-hah)* directed from the midriff in a bouncing manner. The lower torso shakes. The upper chest wall is motionless and there is no sound of breath, only tone.

Memorizing. A vocalist may memorize a piece of music in two ways: a) *visually,* by silently recalling the mental image of the printed page and, thus, in a sense, reading from the visualized mental picture of the score; 2) *audibly,* by recalling the tonal counterpart of the score, as *heard*. Both types are used.

Memorization is a laborious, time-consuming, and patience-testing process. But its rewards are immeasurable. Memorization also means strengthening the power of concentration and acquiring a strong sense of accuracy and precision. Self-confidence is the result.

Messa di voce is a useful practice device for controlling dynamics in singing. It is a gradual crescendo to full power, followed immediately by a diminuendo almost to the vanishing point, all on the same note and on a single breath. Because of its unusual length *messa di voce* can exhaust the lungs. Hence, when practicing, it must be preceded and followed by full inspiration. Care must be exercised not to force or push the breath or hurry the crescendo. Quite the contrary, breath is to be restrained for reasons of economy. Concentrate on tonal values and uniform texture of the voice throughout.

When the apex of the crescendo is reached, prolong the climax for a moment before commencing the decrease. When starting the diminuendo the lessening action should be slow at first, then, toward the end, faster until it terminates in a soft *mezza voce*. The usual fault is to hurry the diminution of sound. Careful budgeting of time and breath are called for.

Messa di voce may be practiced in two parts: first < then >. Be careful not to run out of breath, stay on pitch, and avoid a falsetto effect at either end. Always hold the breath for a moment after the tone ends, so as to prevent an explosive or gasping finish.

Mezza voce means vocal expression at half-power. Its peculiar nonresonant quality is caused by the pulsation of a smaller mass of vibratory material at the glottis and a diminution of the area in which voice is resonated. The firmness of laryngeal contact against the spine is also lessened so that the tone is deprived of its sonority. It is as though a tuning fork were touched to soft wood rather than hard wood or metal. Some of its vibrations are dampened thereby. The entire musculature of the vocal tract is less firm than for full voice, though it is not lax or inert.

To practice *mezza voce*, attack each tone as if falsetto were desired but use firmness in the attack. Thus, the ear will decree a light voice but the firmness of attack will produce a definite adjustment of the vocal mechanism for vocal utterance. The result will be *mezza voce*. To test a *mezza voce*, gradually swell the tone. If it does not break or bleat it is a well-established half-voice, not a falsetto tone.

Phrasing. Each singing phrase has a *beginning, climax,* and *ending*. The *beginning* is not to be a sudden dynamic thrust of tone. Nevertheless, a firm attack is needed. In declamatory singing and recitative, modifications to suit mood, music, and meaning are permissable.

The *climax* of a phrase is the *point d'appui* toward which all tones appear to lead and from which a recession is felt. This may be a pitch summit or a dramatic highpoint. Usually the climax occurs on a single note which is sounded a little stronger than its predecessor or a trifle longer (rubato) than its indicated duration so that its prominence will be assured.

As a rule, the *ending* of a phrase calls for a slight diminuendo without loss of tonality or resonance. When ending a phrase, do not explode the breath but retain it until *after* all sound has ceased. Practice each phrase unit in slow motion, until correct action is memorized.

Portamento is the connection of two tones of a wide interval by means of a continuous glide through all its intervening tones. It may rise or fall in pitch, resembling the inflection of the speaking voice. Portamento may be practiced by imitating the moaning of the wind (up or down). The portamento is strictly uniform in quality and volume and is never hurried. It is most impressive when used in the *strascino* or dragging effect of the voice to express tragedy.

Repeated notes. When they occur in rapid succession, repeated notes should be regarded as the fracturing of a single sustained note. Each of the repeated notes is to be of equal duration, equal intensity, and on the same pitch as its predecessor, with a continuity of musical thought and tonal imagery that will unify the entire repeated series.

Rubato. *Tempo rubato* (stolen time) in singing refers to the lengthening of a note by borrowing time from the note which follows it (sometimes from that which precedes it). This prolongation is temporary, of course, and very slight, and is never sufficient to make a recognizable change in the basic meter. In other words, the rhythm of the melody is not to be distorted. A rule for the beginner is: *if in doubt, keep strict timing throughout.* Tempo rubato may be used impressively where there is an emotional climax or melodic peak in expression.

Scales, arpeggios, and runs deserve special comment. They may be used as gynmastics, vocalizes, or voice-freeing exercises. But they sometimes occur in song literature, often as embellishments sung on a single vowel. The artist-pupil must be ready for them. The importance of matching each note in the scale for uniformity of quality and resonance is obvious. Hence, the scale or figured passage should be sung slowly, at first, while steadily maintaining the quality, intensity, and pitch of each vowel in the series. All syllabic vowels may be worked thus, and at all speeds and dynamics, legato and staccato, for voice-building exercises.

Scales should be practiced in major, minor, whole-tone, and chromatic modes, without accompaniment. An occasional touch on the keyboard would suffice to test for pitch accuracy. To avoid tension in reaching for high notes, think *descent* while ascending the scale. Never break the breath during a scale passage in a song or aria.

Arpeggios are harp-like sequences of chord tones. They often define a harmonic structure and they must therefore be practiced with precision and accuracy.

Runs are a rapid series of tones, usually in the scale, occurring on one syllable. A run may also be a short, distinct, rapidly ascending sequence of trills.

Song cycle. A song cycle may depict a dramatic characterization. Because of its extended nature, the interpretation of a song cycle is challenging to the resourcefulness, versatility, and endurance of an artist. Monotony must be avoided at all costs. On the other hand, overelaboration will cheapen the effect. The singer must saturate his mind with the predominant mood and maintain his characterization to the very end.

Staccato is the crisp, detached, or nonlegato execution of a note, or series of notes, all on the same breath. Each tone is cut short and separated from its neighbor by a minute but audible gap of silence. To produce a true staccato, it is necessary to end each note as abruptly as it was begun. But do not relax the breath after a staccato tone. Keep the chest high and stationary. Use the abdominal-diaphragmatic attack predominantly, as in the martellato or in laughing, and avoid making audible breath sounds. For practice purposes, try the staccato on every pitch in the vocal range and on every vowel, at first with medium dynamics, then in pianissimo, and finally in full voice.

Sustained tones are often found in vocal literature. They are used in advanced vocal technique. To learn to sustain a prolonged note on a uniform dynamic level, practice at first as if it were a series of minutely interrupted staccato notes, each one of equal duration, force, and pitch. Scan each subdivision for equal pitch, intensity, quality, resonance, and support.

In due time, the perfected segments of staccato tone become blended into a continuous whole and the sustained tone then maintains flawless uniformity throughout its entire duration. Always use a clean-cut ending, exactly on pitch. After the sustaining technique has been mastered, *messa di voce* may be attempted.

Timing is the duration of notes (e.g., *whole note, half note, quarter note, eighth,* etc.). It is considered the mainspring of artistic musical expression. Therefore, firmness and precision of *time* are essential in every accompanied performance. A singer should understand the varied nomenclature of timing and the seven basic terms associated therewith, i.e., *beat, accent, bar, measure, tempo, meter,* and *rhythm*.

a. **Beat** is the basic unit of time used for musical measurement.

b. **Accent** is the special emphasis or strength of a note in relation to those immediately preceding it.

c. **Bar** is a vertical line across the staff, dividing it into equal measures of time.

d. **Measure** is the group of beats occurring between two adjacent bars. *(Bar* and *measure* are often used synonymously.)

e. **Tempo** is the rate of movement of a piece of music (e.g., *moderato, allegro, adagio, presto,* etc.).

f. **Meter** is the division of music into measures (or bars). It is indicated by a time signature (e.g., 2/4, 3/4, 6/8, 4/4, etc.).

g. **Rhythm** is the prevailing pattern, combination, or grouping of notes and rests and their time values (e.g., *quarter notes only, dotted-quarter followed by an eighth, quarter followed by two eighths, eighth-quarter-eighth*, etc.). The term *rhythm* may also be used to suggest the division of a piece of music into motives, figures, subsections, sections, and other groupings like *three-measure rhythm, five-measure rhythm,* etc. This melodic ebb and flow is marked by the regular recurrence of such distinguishing features as cadence, phrasing, dynamic climax, and symmetrical design. In any case, rhythm strictly depends on the duration, accent, and grouping of time values. *Polka, march, mazurka,* and other rhythms are thus developed from the relative groupings of notes, accents, and rests.

Only when a decided rhythmic accent is called for (e.g., *march rhythm*) is it necessary to stress the first beat of each measure. Otherwise, one should keep strict time, mentally, but ignore bar lines and concentrate on phrasing to achieve broader melodic unity.

Modifications of time are also important. These may be indicated by such terms as *rallentando, accelerando, ad libitum, tempo rubato, syncopation,* etc. The artist singer must familiarize himself with all of them.

Trill. Although it appears more often in music for soprano, the acquisition of a good trill is considered an index of freedom and flexibility in any well-placed voice and should therefore be mastered by all singers. The trill is often taught by imitation but it may be cultivated by preparatory exercises. Four stages of practice are suggested:

a. Sing any two notes, a major second apart, using the vowel "ah." Repeat these two notes slowly in legato *couplets*. Accent the *upper* note of each couplet as you repeat the sequence in a slow, *even* tempo. A comfortable pitch level is best.

b. Next, start with and accent the *lower* of each couplet as you repeat them in a slow, legato sequence.

c. Next, slowly sing the same *two* diatonic notes in a sequence of *triplets*. However, start with the *upper* note and accent every *fourth* note. This will create an alternating accent which first falls on the *upper* note, then on the *lower* note of each succeeding triplet. Repeat often.

    d. Now, *gradually* increase the tempo of this triplet exercise until maximum speed is attained. When oscillations reach a frequency that is beyond conscious control, the ultimate reliance is on the ear. The pitch interval between trilled notes is always accurately maintained as a semitone or full major second. Avoid the tendency to sound flat on the higher note and always attack the lower note on the pitch indicated.

    Once it is established, practice the trill on all vowels, at all pitch levels, at all degrees of loudness, and at all speeds. Be careful, in a song, not to take a separate breath for the trill, since it is part of the phrase in which it appears. A trill is usually ended with an ornamental turn.

    A bird-like trill can also be produced by allowing the slackened extrinsic musculature of the larynx to fluctuate freely during phonation. Thus, the entire larynx will oscillate minutely. This vertical movement of the entire larynx will disturb the pitch level being sounded; and this variation of pitch will be just enough to produce a trill-like effect within the interval of a semitone. Listening to a good vocal model is also helpful.

    Finally, *trill* is not to be confused with *tremolo*. Trill is an intentional vocal embellishment. Tremolo is a wobbling, uneven pitch, often the result of carelessness or faulty phonation. The vocal trill is always a precise alternation of two distinct pitches in the interval of an exact semitone or major second.

    Warming Up. A preliminary warming up or tune-up of the voice may be used just before any singing lesson or any strenuous vocal performance. The following procedure lasts from five to ten minutes and is used before rigorous singing is attempted. Use a standing position, if possible:

    a. Check posture. Raise, then lower the arms to restore the optimal high-chest position needed for singing.

    b. Practice slow, deep breathing for a minute or two. With each inspiration, feel the sidewise expansion of the lower rib cage but keep the upper chest stationary. With slow expiration, use a restrained compression of the lateral chest wall with an accompanying gradual *inward* and upward abdominal lift.

c. Now repeat exercise (b) while using a soft humming sound. Try to sustain the hum on each breath as long as possible, perhaps thirty or forty seconds for each hum.

d. Yawn silently, then audibly, several times.

e. Roll the head slowly, if necessary, to relax neck muscles. The under-chin area should always be relaxed and flaccid to the touch, especially during intonation.

f. Alternately hunch or roll each shoulder, roll the head slowly, flex and twist the torso, etc., to release abnormal tensions throughout the body.

g. Now, use the "ng" head hum exercise, as previously described, to limber up the posterior lingual muscles (e.g., *ngah, ngah, ngah, m-mah, m-mah, m-mah,* etc.).

h. Loudly hum a few simple, slowly *descending* triads while using maximum head resonance; then try any five-tone sequence as if sighing or moaning down the scale. Start in the middle range of the voice, on any vowel. Attack the *initial* note of each descending sequence one pitch higher than the initial note of the preceding sequence.

i. Now, with full resonance, sing a slow *ascending* scale on "ah," without breaks, while thinking *descent.*

j. Work with wider intervals and arpeggi in the same way, first descending, then ascending. Alternate robust hummed tones and open vowels to test for uniformity of resonance (e.g., *m-m-m-e-e-e, m-m-m-e-e-e, m-m-m-a-a-a, m-m-m-a-a-a, m-m-m-o-o-o, m-m-m-o-o-o,* etc.).

k. Sing a simple, melodious song that lies well within the range of the voice. Continuity is more important than precision in a preliminary exercise of this kind.

l. Silent or mental practice is sometimes used as a salutary forerunner of audible vocal exercise. Correct neural controls will be stimulated by silent or mental exercise. Likewise, *mild* calisthenics are sometimes effective for improving circulation in a sluggish or inert body.

m. After the warming-up period, assume a joyous attitude, laugh heartily several times, yawn loudly, and swallow once or twice to relax vocal muscles. Clear the throat with a rapidly repeated *very light* staccato glottal cough. Then hum again in a *crescendo* for several seconds to establish a sense of optimal resonance. You are now ready for vocal performance.

In conclusion, a singer must breathe *life* into his song during a performance, whatever its form or structure may be. His interpretation uses attitude, tone coloring, and appropriate diction to express character, mood, and meaning. The song must be kept alive with the artist's creativity and personal understanding. It is not a stereotyped or orthodox pattern of words and tones. Rather, it is vitalized and renewed from moment to moment with the singer's own imagination and understanding and it imparts to the listener a feeling of living interest in a perpetual atmosphere of communication that stimulates audience response.

No amount of intellectual insight or technical virtuosity can compensate for the wooden and lifeless expression of an otherwise mechanically perfect performance; and the study of repertoire would be fruitless without the competence to give mood and meaning to the music performed. All the foregoing discussions serve to suggest and describe the varied approach that is needed to master the singer's art. With understanding, infinite patience and perseverence, teacher and pupil are guided along paths of study and practice that lead to mastery and ultimate success. The urge to excel provides motivation and incentive. Knowledge and practice provide method and means. Idealism, esthetic taste, and a step-by-step sense of accomplishment provide the ambition to succeed.

REFERENCES AND NOTES

The following references provide additional vocalizes, exercises, and helpful suggestions for student singers.

1. Brodnitz, Friedrich S. *Keep Your Voice Healthy.* New York: Harper and Brothers, 1953.

2. Franca, Ida. "Adventure of the Trill." *Etude* (June 1951).

3. ———. "The Vocalist's ABC's—Breathing, Sound Attack, Sound Detachment." *American Music Teacher* (Nov.–Dec., 1951).

4. Fuchs, Viktor. *The Art of Singing and Voice Technique.* New York: London House and Maxwell, 1964.

5. Kelsey, Franklyn. *The Foundations of Singing.* London: Williams and Norgate, 1950.

6. Lawson, James Terry. *Full-Throated Ease.* Vancouver, B.C.: Western Music Co., 1955.

7. Lehmann, Lilli. *How to Sing.* 7th ed. New York: Macmillan Co., 1962.

8. Mallett, Lloyd. *50 Exercises for the Young Singer.* New York: Belwin-Mills Publ. Co., 1962.

9. Mancini, Giambattista. *Practical Reflections on Figured Singing.* Champaign, Ill.: Pro Musica Press, 1967.

10. Meano, Carlo. *The Human Voice in Speech and Song.* Springfield, Ill.: Charles C. Thomas, Pub., 1967.

11. Moses, Paul J. "Pathology and Therapy of the Singing Voice." *Archives of Otolaryngology* 69 (1959): 577–582.

12. Randegger, Alberto. *Singing.* New York: H. W. Gray Reprint, 1951.

13. Rothmüller, M. "Evaluating Vocal Performance." *Music Journal* 18 (March, 1960): 50.

14. Shakespeare, William. *Plain Words on Singing.* London: Putnam, 1938.

15. Witherspoon, Herbert. *Thirty-six Lessons in Singing for Teachers and Students.* Chicago: Miessner Institute of Music, 1930.

XVIII

Summation of Guiding Principles

This final chapter is designed to serve as a philosophical summation. It consists, largely, of pointed paragraphs that are the endpapers of a long-range inquiry into the nature of the singer's art, and it includes a recapitulation of guiding principles.

The development of skill in the *teaching* of singing has been consistently emphasized in this text in the belief that the successful practice of the singer's art really begins with the adequate training of its teachers. This approach embraces at least three levels of preparation: 1) background theory in physiology, psychology, and acoustics; 2) technical training in intonation, diction, and musicianship; 3) problems of interpretation, song analysis, and repertoire for public performance. A firm grasp of pedagogical theory and practice includes all these areas of study in a program of preparation that equips both teacher and student with the foundations of his art.

Singing Is an Inspired Art

What is singing? It is the perfect blending of music and text in vocal expression. It contains the poetic richness of language, the color and quality of human feeling, and the intangible beauty of tone and harmony. In essence, it is a sublime form of communication, a type of expression in the abstract, covering the fullness of thoughts and feelings that are often too rich for ordinary conversational utterance. A good song composer utilizes only the best materials, since it is a tonal medium that combines fine music with exceptional language.

The singer's vocal powers must therefore encompass the sublime tonal media of music, as well as the inspirational poetics of linguistic expression. The two are blended into a unity that touches the mind and spirit of the listener. A singer's voice and diction must supply depth and intensity for the coloration of every mood, however subtle it may be, and much study is needed to acccomplish this result.

Nevertheless, much of the vocal response in singing is necessarily spontaneous and unrehearsed. Why? Because the art of singing demands more than the tangible components of a study program, however important they may appear to be. The *spirit* which the finished performer infuses into his art is equally important in determining a successful outcome. It is the quality of life that he generates spontaneously, without preparation or restraint, whenever he opens his mouth to sing.

According to Webster, *inspiration* (from L. *spirare:* to breathe) is an invisible force compelling creation or expression. It implies a miraculous enlightening of the mind and a mysterious infusion of power that qualifies men to receive and communicate the truth of being. It also denotes an awakening or quickening of the creative impulse as manifested in high artistic achievement.

In other words, inspiration is the channel through which man expresses his spiritual nature without reliance on external stimulus or aid. It enables him to solve problems that would otherwise seem impossible to him. Hence, it raises him above the mechanisms of mere imitation and physical manipulation into the realm of creativity and originality. When a singer is truly relaxed in performance, he becomes more receptive to inspiration and he also behaves more genuinely like himself.

In a sense, therefore, *inspiration* means, literally, bringing life into expression. That is also what singing consists of. It brings life substance (including breath) into audible expression. The breathing function is all-important as a means of supplying sustenance to the body. But it also performs the same function for the singing voice.

The way a person breathes is important in many ways. It is strongly related to the way he thinks and feels and, of course, vocal expression is influenced thereby. When thoughts are free, breathing is regular and rhythmical. When there is even the slightest mental restraint, nervousness, or emotional tension, breathing rhythms are disturbed. Thus, each mood induces its characteristic breathing rhythm, and this, in turn, produces expressive and colorful vocal changes in the interpretation of song. It may be said, therefore, that the pupil's singing voice is likely to become distorted, pinched, gutteral, or strained whenever his breathing is disturbed by mechanical controls and chronic worries or fears. This psychophysical factor also provides a clue to the therapeutic value of good singing instruction.

The Therapeutic Value of Song

Children love to sing. All people, when aroused to enthusiasm, find it easy to burst into song. On the other hand, one who is afflicted with worries or fears, who suffers from inferiority complexes, from habits of introspection and self-criticism, from thoughts of despair, anger, and other restraints, finds it difficult, if not impossible, to sing. An indifferent or matter-of-fact view of life rarely engenders a singing response.

Singing is therefore considered one of the enjoyable activities of self-expression. Song provides exhilaration and a quickening of spirit that frees the mind from the cares of everyday living. Singing also promotes the natural activity of the breathing and vocal organs to a marked degree. Good singers, as a rule, have good lungs because they learn to breathe deeply and regularly at all times.

Because of its salutary effects, therefore, singing may be recommended as one of the best forms of exercise. Any musically minded young person may be well-advised to take singing lessons, or to join a good singing society, choir, or chorus if he can. Besides being enjoyable, artistic singing will help the speaking voice, correct breathing deficiencies, sharpen concentration and hearing acuity, and build a well-balanced personality and physique.

The Importance of Text

Singing also uses words in a special way that features artistic economy in expression. The poet is an artist of verbal economy. His words are descriptive and colorful and each word is charged with intense thought and feeling value. Therefore, the words of a song text must be stressed for meaning rather than meter. A good poem, like a good song, is one in which the metrical rhythm corresponds to the spontaneous speaking rhythm that engenders it. The rise and fall of vocal inflections are thus directly related to variations in thought and feeling contained within each verse of an appropriate song text. This relationship of words to melodic inflection should be imparted to the pupil. His understanding thereof will improve his ability to communicate melodic ideas.

Speech a Predominant Influence

Singing and speaking are closely related. The early development of a wholesome speaking voice may very well lay the foundation for the cultivation of a beautiful singing voice. The singer's art is, in a sense, a sublimation of speech values, and the teacher of singing might well begin by prescribing some simple speaking exercises that will enhance the pupil's voice for everyday use. The carry-over will accrue to the benefit of his singing voice.

From this standpoint, however melodious it may be, a good song can be ruined by poor diction. Therefore, a singer must learn to convey all the esthetic qualities of vocal expression in his interpretation without sacrificing the verbal message of the text. He sings a text as he would tell it. This thought is basic to artistic performance.

Importance of Ear Training

A vital problem in teaching singing is to create right hearing concepts that will adequately monitor the output of a responsive vocal instrument. It is also apparent that the voice of singing is not merely a technical phenomenon, a behavior pattern to be analyzed and consciously controlled. It is a physiological response to thinking and feeling. Exercise materials must therefore be appraised on two levels: those that deal with mental or psychological causes and those that deal with physiological effects. The former are more or less unconscious, the latter can be more deliberate. Both are habit-forming.

Therefore, whenever a singer studies his own vocal action analytically he loses the spontaneity thereof and synthetic action is substituted. The final product of self-analysis no longer reflects a natural response. The true preparation for the singing tone is, in large measure, a *mental* preparation, anticipation being its governing factor.

In other words, the sound wave that leaves the singer's lips will reflect the mental as well as the physical conditions that created it. Clean-cut tonal concepts are therefore important. If this faculty of imagery is lacking, a pupil can never become an artist. He must always know exactly what a vocal passage sounds like *before* he sings it. The importance of ear training in voice-building is therefore apparent.

How to Improve the Teaching Situation

There is no doubt that the act of phonation is governed by nerve impulses that originate in the desire to *express* something. Therefore, in vocal pedagogy, we consider the mental climate and intensity of the desire to express as part of the act of singing. Is vocal production accompanied by fear, timidity, nervousness, self-consciousness, self-analysis, or restraint? Is the singer's attitude bold, daring, enthusiastic, spontaneous, free? Naturally, the organs of breathing, phonation, and voice projection will react differently under conditions of restraint or freedom.

The fact that phonation is itself an inborn function, not acquired, indicates its inherent spontaneity, and it is therefore important that our studio techniques impose no self-analytical limitations upon an otherwise spontaneous vocal response. Basically, when phonation is motivated by the sincere desire to communicate, all interrelated musculatures leap into action *unconsciously* to bring about desired results. To make this reaction possible a teacher must work to remove any and all limitations of action that might be caused by previously acquired bad habits. However, these new habit-forming procedures can work only if we are certain that we are training correct habits in the right sequence.

But are we? Do we know what parts of a rather involved vocal musculature will produce right results in a proper sequence to guarantee an artistic singing tone? Do we know whether mouth, tongue, lips, palate, uvula, jaw, pharynx, glottis, when supported by chest, diaphragm, air pressure, posture, etc., are simultaneously controllable through *voluntary* habit-forming procedures? Obviously, much careful observation and research are necessary to guarantee dependable and predictable teaching results. Mechanistic controls and exercises must be approached with great caution lest the pupil's vocal growth be irreparably stunted or impaired.

The principle of *freedom* seems to pervade all voice teaching, especially when such teaching relates to the muscles and organs of singing. We need to remember that, primarily, tone is generated by thinking; pitch is controlled by hearing; projection or volume is influenced by seeing and hearing values; quality is the reflection of deep-felt emotional states that affect breathing rhythms and influence the actuators and resonators of voice.

Furthermore, extrinsic vocal mechanisms are unmistakably

attached to the tonal generator and all parts are affected by the muscular tonus of the body which, in turn, directly relates to emotional states in the individual. Thus, feeling pervades all expressional and behavioral responses and the products of phonation are influenced accordingly.

To produce a single singing tone, a vocalist engages approximately 130 working parts of his body. With incredible synchrony and speed these complex elements coordinate to produce the act of tone production. The teacher of singing must be aware of this inherent complexity of the vocal mechanism, of the entire human organism, of the interdependence of its innumerable parts, of the relevance of psychological controls in voice training, of the importance of good posture throughout the singing act, of the value of reposeful attitudes and freedom from anxiety, of the need for poise and balance throughout the organism. *Freedom* is a condition that does not imply inertia or limpness, but muscular tonicity and equilibrium or, in other words, readiness to perform.

Much of the singing teacher's work, therefore, resolves itself into the diagnosis of a pupil's faults. The analysis of sought-for skills follows in terms of appropriate teaching methods to be used. Finally comes the programming of instructional procedures both in ear training and voice training, so simple and specific that the pupil can understand each step, apply himself to it and achieve success therein. Setting up the conscious goals of every lesson and evaluating results in terms of these goals becomes a formula for successful teaching.

Each studio session should, therefore, have a definite purpose and it should fulfill that purpose. Progress is thus made up of tiny achievements, each of which is equally important to the end in view. If any lesson is not learned or any intermediate achievement not realized, that lesson may be repeated and continued in varying form until mastered. Sometimes a too-difficult assignment may be laid aside temporarily and other important matters pursued so as to relieve the tedium of prolonged effort on a fruitless task.

In short, instruction in voice training should never be

generalized at the expense of the pupil. Specificity in everything is the sine qua non of successful vocal teaching—no vague spots, no unsupported theories, every point demonstrable and explainable. Such an ideal is attainable by any teacher who is willing to equip himself with specific knowledge of the singing art and the ability to apply and demonstrate that knowledge in every practical teaching situation.

The teacher is also admonished to instruct his pupil positively by *what to do,* whenever possible, not negatively by *don'ts.* Forbidding admonitions inhibit vocal response. Voice training should be a freeing, not a freezing process. The pupil must be taught the art of self-release, i.e., the difference between *letting* and *striving.* The former promotes spontaneity; the latter begets cautious, conscious control which is inimical to correct functioning of vocal reflexes.

Measuring Progress

In the actual singing of songs, problems may be isolated for separate treatment and appropriate exercises then devised for remedying them. Such exercises will have the definite purpose of solving a specific problem of immediate importance and value to the pupil. They will not be routine drills of abstract dimensions whose application is a vague and general promise of things to come. Thus, a pupil avoids the endless hours of practicing with a meaningless routine of vocalizes and a feeling of aimless drifting toward unknown objectives, while his thirst for artistic expression remains unsatisfied.

Artistic expression is not an untouchable product that is beyond reach of a younger student. Art is a process of actual living, an everyday experience, a continuous growth through the refinement and correct use of one's esthetic and technical resources.

Simple lessons beget simple problems. Solving them results in a series of simple achievements. As the saying goes, a journey of a thousand miles begins with but a single step; and this formula applies over and over again until the destination is reached. Thus, at any point, a pupil can look over the road traveled and realize the progress he has made.

Such retrospective appraisals encourage his going on for they also represent milestones in the evolution of the finished product. Returning to the song that was originally attempted and then laid aside because of the problem encountered, he can now demonstrate his onward course by a newer performance in which the original problem no longer exists. Hence, progress has been made. Achievement testing of this nature spells effective instruction and strongly motivated learning.

By reviewing the life of any great artist, a pupil can glimpse the perserverence, energy, patience, devotion, and ability that were necessary for success in that career. And it is safe to assume that every artistic success is a history of innumerable problems solved and obstacles overcome.

Growth Through Correct Use

It must also be made clear that artistic singing is largely a product of the culture of mind and ear and that the physical parts of the body must ultimately be made responsive to the singer's will. For this reason, an important part of a teacher's work is directed toward developing a condition of freedom in the vocal tract, freedom to respond readily and sensitively to the dictates of the pupil's mind and ear. When this balance is reached, musical growth is possible through the correct use of exercises, songs, and arias. This development is directed along paths that are musically enjoyable and esthetically rewarding to the pupil. Artistic expression truly begins when this preparatory regimen of mental and physical growth through exercise and correct use has developed to the point of habit formation.

Concluding Remarks

In concluding this treatise, we are reminded of Emerson's advice: "The law is the basis of the human mind. Nothing can bring success but the triumph of principle." *Principle,* of course, is the fundamental law which governs the expression of life in any form. It is therefore the foundation of truth that we discern when we investigate the nature of things.

In the last analysis, our methods of training the singing voice are many and varied. But our success in teaching is a direct result of understanding and applying correct principles. The inexorable laws of nature always work in our behalf when we observe them. But when we ignore them they play havoc with our misdirected intentions. Obey a law and it becomes your servant; disobey it and it becomes your master. A teaching methodology must therefore adhere to principle, but it must also be flexible and adaptable to individual needs.

There are many known methods of teaching voice. Their name is legion. Each teacher has his favorites and swears by them. But, be they ever-so-successful, they are never self-administering. They require interpretation and direction by someone who understands them. Therefore, the test of any teaching device is its useful results; and these are determined by the patience, skill, and watchful guidance with which instruction is administered, as well as by the intelligent comprehension of a willing pupil.

So it may be said that methods of teaching are not invented; they are evolved. They derive from a planned procedure and are appraised in terms of predictable outcomes. But they must always be tested out in practice. Furthermore, they are never inflexibly applied to all alike. They must be constantly adjusted and modified to suit each pupil's needs. Any method may work wonders for one teacher and fail completely for another. Obviously, a method is a working tool. It must be skillfully handled to produce results.

A good teacher of singing is a musician, an educator, a psychologist. He tries to develop good singers, not just good voices. Therefore, songs that are used for exercise material, repertoire, and practice are chosen because they stimulate creative as well as technical abilities of the pupil. The right kind of music will always help educate the singer's voice.

All the foregoing pedagogical principles are presented as reminders and refreshers. They are foundational truths that need to be reaffirmed from time to time, since they constitute the teacher's professional faith, his credo. A good teacher plans his work, then works his plan, but his knowledge of principle gives him a confident expectation of successful outcomes.

Finally, teaching spells energy, drive, infinite patience, and unflagging interest in a pupil's welfare. It includes a sane and levelheaded outlook on the future, a wholesome philosophy of life, a healthy physique with stamina and endurance that will not readily succumb to the nervous tensions generated by fatigue. There is also a resolute determination to acquit oneself creditably in every situation.

Knowledge and understanding, emotional stability, and unselfish devotion to the welfare of others are keynotes of the teaching profession. Financial rewards may seem important in life but they are secondary to a dedicated teacher, and one should not attempt a life of teaching if one is not willing to sacrifice self, time, and money for the ideal.

Hence, the love of teaching for its own sake emerges as an essential qualification of the successful vocal pedagogue. In singing, as in medicine, law, and other worthy professions, the attitude of service for its own sake is the spirit that nourishes professional growth and the progress and advancement of the singing world. It is worth repeating, therefore, that the preparation of successful singers really begins with the training of competent and successful teachers. This precept lies at the very foundation of the singer's art.

Index

Abdominal muscles, 53, 55, 56
Accompaniment, 313-14
Acoustical factors, 126-47, 151, 221-22
Alto classifications, 226
Art, defined, 3-6, 9
Art song, 275
Artistry, 28, 258, 268-69, 340
Atmosphere, creating, 264
Attack, defined, 183
    exercises for, 184-87
Audience control, 262, 283, 314

Baritone, *See* Bass
Bass classifications, 228
Battistini, Mattia, 224
Beginners, advice to, 28-29, 61
Beginner's voice, 206-16
Bel canto, 274
Bernoulli principle, 45, 54, 90
Bone conduction, 106, 151
Brandt, Marianne, 224
Bravura, 316
Breath
    capacity, 42
    control. *See* exercises
    economy, 56-58
    renewal, 58
    retention, 33, 46, 57, 59
    support, 46, 55, 59, 62, 63, 192-94
Breathing
    action described, 50-63
    coordination in, 38
    correctives, 63-65, 213
    emotional influences, 334
    for phonation, 45, 53-56, 86, 100
    methods discussed, 32-39, 45-47, 50-56, 60-63, 86, 100, 136, 316
    muscles reviewed, 69, 70, 123
    physiology of, 37, 42
    principles, 32

Breathiness, cause and cure, 213
Buccal cavity. *See* Mouth

Cadenza, 317
Callas, Maria, 224
Calvé, Emma, 224
Campanini, Italo, 225
Cantilena defined, 277
Caruso, Enrico, 225
Character defined, 269
Characterization, study of, 279-84
Chest
    action, 39, 51-53, 55, 60
    resonance. *See* Fremitus
Classifying the voice, 30, 206, 217-19, 225-28
Clavicular breathing, 52
Clefs for singers, 317
Coloratura, 318
Concentration, 15, 25
Concept, defined, 13
Conditioned reflex, defined, 122
Consonants, described, 236-40
Contralto. *See* Alto
Coordination, importance of, 38, 45, 120
Corrective exercise discussed, 2, 28-31,

252, 340
Coup-de-glotte, 47
Covering, 190
Crescendo. *See* Messa di voce

Declamation discussed, 260, 278
Diagnostic procedures, 183-99, 209-16, 338
Diaphragm described, 41, 52-53, 55, 63, 123
Diction for singers, 230, 236-45, 250-53, 314, 318
Diphthong defined, 244
Dramatic disciplines, 259-61
Duration factors. *See* Messa di voce
Dynamics. *See* Intensity

Ear training, 89, 149, 184, 242, 336
Economy of effort, 23, 46
Empathy defined, 263
English
 consonants described, 236-40
 vowels described, 240-45
Epiglottis, 84, 99
Equilibrium, in vocal action, 94, 106, 107, 120
Esophagus described, 44, 110
Exaggeration, use of, 260
Exercise, value of, 2, 340
Exercises
 breath control, 56-58, 61, 63-69, 185, 192-97, 213
 diction. *See* Diction
 dynamics, 194-204
 ear training, 155-61
 glottal, 185-86
 head-hum, 197-99, 320
 intonation, 199-204
 laughter, 61, 65, 320
 legato, 321
 melodic, 188
 messa di voce, 58, 195, 322
 mezza voce, 323
 pitch control, 186-92
 posture, 34-38
 quality and resonance, 197-99
 speech-song approach, 187-89, 233-36
 staccato, 65, 325

 tonal attack, 183-86
 vocal trill, 327-28
 vowel rotation, 242-45
 warming-up, 328-30
 whispering, 194
Expression defined, 256, 265
External mechanisms of larynx, 105
Extrinsic muscles. *See* Muscles

Falsetto, 191
False vocal cords, 85-86
Fauces, 119
Fear, overcoming, 24, 259
Filar-di-voce, 318
Fioritura, 274, 277, 318
Focus, vocal, 131
Folk song, 274
Foreign language, 245-47, 249-51
Formant, vowel 144, 241
Freeing the voice, 19-20, 22, 30, 262-63, 337-39
Fremitus, vocal, 144, 200
Fremstad, Olive, 224
Fundamentals of voice training, 1

Glottal action, 53-56, 77-79, 82-83, 87-91, 94-103, 106, 135-40
Glottal exercises, 183-86
Glottis, controlling muscles, 96, 101-3
Grace notes in singing, 319-20
Gregorian chant, 276
Growth, formula for, 266
Guiding principles reviewed, 332

Habits discussed, 11, 15-18, 28-29, 337, 340
Head-hum exercises. *See* Exercises
Head resonance, 144
Health related to voice, 26, 75, 122
Hearing
 functional loss, 154
 mental, 152, 158
 physical, 151-52, 162
 related to voice, 89, 126
Hints and helps for performance, 316-30
Humming. *See* Head-hum

Imagination, function of, 262
Imitation, use of, 5-6

Improvization, vocal, 171-72, 281
Individual differences, 5, 264
Individuality in singing, 266
Inspiration discussed, 332-34
Intensity, vocal, 127, 140-42, 145, 194-204, 319
Interpretation for singers, 255-57, 264-66, 289, 330
Intonation
　exercises. *See* Exercises
　problems discussed, 183-204
Intrinsic muscles. *See* Muscles

Joy in singing, 20-22, 263

Larynx
　action of. *See* Glottal action
　female, 137
　internal mechanisms, 94-103
　juvenile, 138
　male, 138
　muscles of. *See* Muscles
　non-vocal functions, 47
　position of, in singing, 43, 94, 120
　size of, 222
　structure and function, 74, 79-87, 91, 94-103, 105, 338
Language mastery. *See* Foreign language
Laughter
　as exercise, 21, 26, 61, 64
　in song, 320
Legato singing, 321
Lehmann, Lilli, 224
Lingual muscles. *See* Tongue
Loudness, *See* Intensity
Lungs, described, 41-42

Male-female vocal differences, 222
Malibran, Maria, 224
Martellato, 322
Matzenauer, Margaret, 224
Mechanistic controls, 337
Melodic exercises, 188
Memorization, 322
Mental
　control of voice, 8, 11-31
　imagery. *See* Ear training
Messa di voce, 58, 192, 195, 322, 326
Mezza voce, 323

Moods, creating, 264
Mouth discussed, 118, 123
Muscles
　abdominal, 53, 55, 56, 124
　extrinsic laryngeal, 105-17, 123
　intrinsic laryngeal, 79, 82, 86, 94-103, 123
　jaw, 108, 109, 123
　lingual, 100, 112-14, 123
　lip and facial, 123
　palatal, 114, 123
　pharyngeal, 118, 123
　properties of, 76-79
　respiratory, 69-72, 123
　thyroarytenoid, 86
Musical terms listed, 174-77
Musicianship for singers, 163, 165, 170-71, 181

Natural voice, 16-17
Neurological factors, 46, 57, 87, 88-89, 120-22, 203
Nordica, Lillian, 224

Off-pitch singing, cause and cure, 213
Opera,
　arias listed, 305-10
　defined, 291
Operatic
　repertoire, 178-81
　training, 280-84
Oral cavity. *See* Mouth
Originality discussed, 263, 265-66
Ornamentation. *See* Fioritura
Overtones discussed, 128, 137

Palatal muscles, 114, 123
Pantomime, use of, 282-83
Passagio, 190
Patti, Adelina, 224
Pedagogy, language of, 6
Performance in public, 268, 310-15
Personality in singing, 19, 258-59
Pharynx described, 118-19, 123
Phonation
　mechanisms of, 75, 78, 85-87, 95-103, 337
　related to breathing, 45, 53-63, 87, 100

345

theories of, 88-91
Phonetic chart, comparative, 249-50
Phonetics as a teaching tool, 247-50
Phrasing in song, 323
Physiology defined, 37
Pitch
　defined, 127-28
　range classifications, 216-17, 225-28
Pitch control
　discussed, 135-40, 145
　exercises, 186-92, 201
Plainsong, 275-76
Portamento, 324
Posture
　exercise, 35
　for singing, 34-37, 54, 60-63
Practice methods discussed, 30
Principles defined, 7, 340-42
Problems, vocal, 315-30
Program building, 310-13
Progress, measuring, 339-40
Psychological principles, 11-15, 28
Public performance, 268, 310-15

Quality
　improving vocal, 75, 143-46, 197-99, 214, 221
　musical, defined, 128-29

Recital, preparing a, 310-14
Recitative discussed, 262, 275, 277
Reflex action defined, 122
Registers, vocal, 189-92
Rehearsal techniques, 280-84, 314
Relaxation
　defined, 22-23
　fallacy, 202-3
Repeated notes in singing, 324
Repertoire
　scope of, 289-93
　materials for, 293-310
　operatic, 178-81
Resonance. *See* Quality
　acoustical factors, 131-34, 137, 144-46
de Reszke, Jean 224
Rhythm. *See* Timing
Rib action described, 51-52
Rubato tempo, 324

Sacred solos, 302-4
Sandhi effect, 238, 240
Scale, musical, defined, 128
Scales, practicing, 324-25
Schumann-Heink, Ernestine, 224
Science, defined, 4, 9
Score reading practice, 168-70
Self-expression in singing, 18-20, 334, 336-37
Self-study materials reviewed, 172-77
Sight-reading methods, 166-71
Silent practice, 189
Sing-as-you-speak approach, 187-89, 233-36
Singers, unusual, 224-25
Singing
　acoustical elements, 134-46
　an art and a science, 9
　communication in, 18
　defined, 129, 332-33
　on the breath, 46, 57
　personality, 19
　self-expression in, 18-20
　therapeutic value of, 334
Solfeggio, 167
Song analysis, 286-93
Song and speech compared, 230-32, 251
　cycle, 291, 304-5, 325
　forms, defined, 290-93
　literature, studying, 177-78
　materials listed, 293-310
　recital. *See* Recital
　study, discussed, 286-89, 292-93
Songs
　for advanced study, 300-2
　for beginners, 294-96
　intermediate grade, 296-300
Soprano range, categories of, 225-27
Sound, defined and discussed, 126-31
Speech habits, effects of, 26-27, 335
Speech-song differences, 230-32
Speech-song approach, 187-89, 233-36, 260-61
Spine
　related to breathing, 39-40, 51-52, 61
　related to larynx, 106-7
Spinto voices, 224-27
Stability of vocal organs. *See* Equilibrium
Staccato exercises, 65, 325

Stage
    deportment, 313-15
    fright, 24-25, 121, 314
    presence, 270
Style in singing, 271-73, 276-79
Success defined, 25
Sustained tones. *See* Messa di voce
Sutherland, Joan, 224
Swallowing, action of, 44-45

Teaching
    objectives, 12, 27-31, 208-11
    requirements, 3-5, 6, 8-10, 332, 336-42
Technique, defined, 9
Temperament and timbre, 217-19
Tenor range, categories of, 227
Tessitura, 219-20
Text, importance of 257, 335
Thyroarytenoid muscles. *See* Muscles
Timbre, vocal. *See* Quality
Timing and rhythm discussed, 326
Tone, characteristics of, 126-31
Tongue
    independence of, 318
    muscles of, 100, 112-14, 123
Trachea described, 44, 111
Trill, practice methods, 320, 327-38

Unity of effect, creating, 270-71
Unusual voices, 224-25
Uvula, action of, 117

Vibrato, vocal, 78
Vital capacity, 43
Vocal action
    theories of, 88-91
    attack, defined, 183
    cords, 85-86
    improvization, 171-72, 281-82
    nerves, 78, 87, 88
    organs, structure & function 74-91
    problems reviewed, 316-30
    registers. *See* Registers
    training objectives, 9, 208, 210-11
Voice
    acoustical elements, 134-46, 221-22
    classifications, 30, 206-28
    mental controls, 8, 11-31
    natural, defined, 16-17
Voices, unusual, 234-35
Volume, vocal. *See* Intensity
Vowel
    formant, 241
    rotation exercises, 242-45
Vowels
    English, described, 240-45
    function in singing, 240-42

Warming-up procedures, 328-30
Weak voice, cause and cure, 214-16, 221-22
Whispering exercise, 194
Whole response in singing, 19